Semiotics in
the United States

Advances in Semiotics
General Editor, Thomas A. Sebeok

Semiotics in the United States

THOMAS A. SEBEOK

INDIANA UNIVERSITY PRESS
Bloomington & Indianapolis

This paper used in this publication meets the minimum requirements of American National Standard for Information Sciences—Permanence of Paper for Printed Library Materials, ANSI Z39.48-1984.

∞ ™

Manufactured in the United States of America

Library of Congress Cataloging-in-Publication Data

Sebeok, Thomas Albert, date.
    Semiotics in the United States / Thomas A. Sebeok.
       p.   cm. — (Advances in semiotics)
    Includes bibliographical references and index.
    ISBN 0-253-35134-0 (cloth)
    1. Semiotics—United States. I. Title. II. Series.
    P99.37.U5S44   1991
    302.2—dc20   90-25040

1 2 3 4 5 95 94 93 92 91

CONTENTS

Semiotics in
the United States

I.

Solitary, singing in the West, I strike up for a
New World.

—Walt Whitman, "Starting
from Paumanok," *Leaves of Grass*

Semioticians are, at least in regard to this deficiency, in full agree-
ment: that no comprehensive (let alone "complete") treatise—
or even a handy compendium—dealing with the history of semiotics as yet exists. Moreover, as Eco has emphasized (forthcoming), no such monumental achievement can nowadays even be
contemplated by any single would-be author.

At the most, some of us are ready to contribute bits and pieces
in the expectation that such scraps of *bricolage*, or recoding, may
eventually be gathered up into a reasonably integrated collective
mythic record (cf. Bouissac 1976b). It is well to remember that
Lévi-Strauss's *bricoleur* himself practices applied semiotics, for,
as his originator said, the *bricoleur* works with signs, hallowed
in tradition. These signs "resemble images in being concrete
entities but they resemble concepts in their powers of reference,"
and these "images and concepts play the part," in the Saussurean mode, "of the signifying and signified respectively" (1966:
18).

There is as yet no universal consensus among us as to *what*
mosaic fragments will be pertinent to such an envisaged synthesis, or precisely how the parts, once identified, ought to be
combined, for "the decision as to what to put in each place also
depends on the possibility of a different element there instead,
so that each choice which is made will involve a complete re-
organization of the structure, which will never be the same as
one vaguely imagined, nor as some other which might have been
preferred to it" (ibid. 19).

Definitions of semiotics are plenteous: some thrive, but all are

1

misleading. For semiotics is not *about* something, unless you want to say that it is about *semiosis*, which does not help much. Semiotics *is* something, something by means of which we can conjure reality from illusion by the use of signs—some of these means will, I hope, become a good deal clearer by the end of my story.

Signs do, of course, have several *functions*: we can say that one of these is *signification*. However, Peirce wrote in 1908 to Lady Welby, this "is only *one* of the *two* chief functions of signs"; it is, namely, the one which is limited to the study of the relations of signs to their interpretants. To which he added: "But I am satisfied that in the present state of the subject, there is but one General science of the nature of Signs." As Rey noticed in his sharp-eyed and fecund consideration of this issue, "Criteria for relevance are . . . linked to the perspective, or 'theoretical style' of each text; then to its objects; and finally to its method" (1984:92). For Peirce, signs in relation to their objects have to do with another function: "the *Truth* of Signs" (CP 8.378). Semiotics must also be concerned with *communication*, which, according to Morris, when restricted to signs is "the arousing of common significata by the production of signs" (1971:360).

In my view, the midmost target of semiotics is indeed, as Rey so persuasively argued, *epistemology*, understood in the broad sense of the cognitive constitution of living entities, comprehending the physiological and psychological make-up of each in their interaction. In semiotics, we must in any case think of ourselves as both working within a tradition that changes over time and trying to grasp things as they "really are."

The currently fashionable tag *cognitive science*, nowadays routinely involving computers, and said to be a movement, or "a perspective rather than a discipline" (Hunt 1989:603f.), seems to me, at best, a stylistic and methodological variant for *semiotics* (cf. Yates, forthcoming, p. 3). At worst, it is a historically untutored and—dare I use so pejorative a word—pretentious relabeling of an ancient multidisciplinary enterprise, said by Hunt (1989:603f.) to attempt to "unify views of thought developed by studies in psychology, linguistics, anthropology, philosophy, computer science, and in the neurosciences," focally concerned with mediating structures, viz., signs, intervening between stimuli and responses, i.e., between objects and interpretants (see particularly Parmentier's treatment of this issue in Mertz and Parmentier 1985, Ch. 2 and passim).

Both endeavors are concerned with internal representation or mental models (Eco, Santambrogio, and Violi 1988) or the "recognition of abstract symbol structures" (Hunt 1989:625). Nesher (1990:44, 1), in particular, has demonstrated that that "mechanism of the Cognitive process is the central issue of Peirce's semiotics," and that it is "a natural conclusion of [his] pragmaticist philosophy." Thus semiotics is not simply a theory of signs, including a philosophy of language, "but also . . . a philosophy of cognition and mind." The schema theory, developed by Arbib and Hesse to account for cognition, and their theory of symbolism, which they call "the *semiological* view" (1986:162), are therefore eminently and explicitly compatible with Peircean semiotic and some of its recent elaborations (as Daddesio [1989] has also strongly emphasized).

The cooperative goal of both semioticians and cognitive scientists, particularly those experimenting with artificial neural networks, is to reach an understanding of the basic mechanisms of thought, especially human reasoning, image schemata, learning, perception and "preconceptual" structures, motor control, development, emotion, and, of course, language. Up to now, computer models have been hardly more than high-tech simulations of the banal, with probably uninformed guessing about how the brain might work. In the decades ahead, brain physiology will doubtless be used to modify the semiotic models and perhaps enable us to make more robust specific predictions. At this time, however, studies of the interaction between semiotic model and biological reality are still in their infancy.

The centrality of the representation relation is a fundamentally semiotic undertaking. Ouellet, in introducing *Semiotica* 1989 (pp. 1f.; see also this multi-authored special issue *passim*), devoted entirely to matters of this sort, affirms:

Cognition is no less than a kind of *semiosis*, as Peirce would say, involving different types of representations, having the property of "thirdness" needed to explain any representational process as "a sign stand(ing) *for* something *to* the idea which it produces or modifies"—"that for which it stands (being) called its *object*; that which it conveys, its *meaning*; and the idea to which it gives rise,

4 Thomas A. Sebeok

its interpretant." So the "language of thought" is "spoken" with signs—even if they are tacit—and the goal of AI research is, precisely, to make explicit those "semiotic" mechanisms of mind by means of an overt symbolic language, artificially constructed in close linkage with natural symbolism . . . in such a way that their processing by a machine would be analogous to their mental processing by a human being.

Minsky (1986:57), for example, answers the question, How do we ever understand anything? thus:

> Almost always, I think, by using one or another kind of analogy— that is, by representing each new thing as though it resembles something we already know. Whenever a new thing's internal workings are too strange or complicated to deal with directly, we represent whatever parts of it we can in terms of more familiar signs. This way, we make each novelty seem similar to some more ordinary thing. It really is a great discovery, the use of signals, symbols, words, and names. They let our minds transform the strange into the commonplace.

This salient affinity is also quite clear from reading recent books by such linguists or philosophers as Grace (1987), Johnson (1987), Lakoff (1987), Lakoff and Johnson (1980), and Langacker (1987). And, as the psychologist Johnson-Laird recently noted (1988:28), it is a tenet of cognitive science that perceptions, ideas, images, beliefs, hypotheses, thoughts, and memories are "mental representations or *symbols* of one sort or another. There is a huge literature on signs, symbols and signals," he adds, but he stops short of saying that these, and the like, constitute the operational primes of the age-old "doctrine of signs." On the one hand, Santambrogio and Violi (Eco, Santambrogio, and Violi 1988:19) rightly stress "the many points which the two traditions have in common and reveal numerous points of convergence between the European semiotic tradition . . . and a large sector of the research being carried out in language within the cognitive field," and that such points of convergence "are far from coincidental," while correctly naming Eco as a prominent European locus for such conflux. On the other hand, they exhibit their seeming inexperience with American semiotics when they add: "Semiotics is essentially a European discipline" (cf. also Jorna

1991). I hope, among other things, to show in what follows that in this respect, their reading is far from accurate.

A unified theory of human cognition, and of cognition throughout the animal world generally (cf. Grace 1989:360), is our ultimate shared ambition: a long-range aspiration of semiotics is therefore to bridge the yawning gulf between, and to synthesize a wealth of particulars being daily uncovered by neuroscience about, the chemistry and biology of neurons with the maximally viable and compatible theory available. The details of the biology of the artificial must be mapped onto the biology of the "real" cells that compose the brain. As a shorter-range goal— to be achieved in the next decades, perhaps—it should be possible to build a computer to simulate by means of electronic "neurons" some events in the brain of a honeybee, a social creature with a remarkably sophisticated semiosic endowment.

The burden of this particular account is to depict in rough-hewn fashion the story of semiotics in this country, past and present, and perhaps to cautiously extrapolate from the known to the unknown. I intend to stay clear of a rigid chronology here, relying instead on the quasi-cinematic principle of flashbacks and flashforwards of experience, transporting my readership as and where appropriate within the confines of my own tenaciously associative memory. So the following narrative will on occasion proceed by rapid projection, fixed as if by strobe lighting, of discrete snapshots of persons, ideas, and incidents—and maybe dreams as well—onto the reader's mental screen. Excessive engagement with history can be stultifying, but some measure of it is imperative.

The boundaries of the United States are of course far less impermeable than most. Jakobson and a throng of other academics, myself not exempted, were trained, more or less, in other conventions and worked for a varying number of years in foreign parts. The sources of U.S. semiotics are thus many, while its potency radiates all over the world. The ongoing dialectic between the local and the global must constantly be borne in mind lest this story turn into distasteful fiction. The expression "Anglo-Saxon Semioticians," on occasion set off against "Structuralist Semioticians" (Harland 1987:4), at other times against "Continental Semioticians" (Parret 1984:220), is a bogus opposition, bordering on racism, to which Jakobson's cosmopolitan career stands not alone in giving the lie.

My inclination is to assign to the "great elders," as Barthes
(1988:6) referred to them—such canonical protagonists as Peirce,
Morris, and Jakobson, the first and third of whom have inspired
reams of nervous exegetic literature—walk-on parts when called
upon, and to place center-stage instead their precursors, con-
temporaries, epigones, acolytes, and scores of other competent
artisans. In short, instead of starring Hamlet, I want, like Tom
Stoppard, rather for once to feature Rosencrantz and Guilden-
stern.

As for the temporal dimensions of my harlequin braid, these
enfold but a moment in history. Of forty thousand antecedent
generations of humans, less than one one-thousandth—about
a century and a half —produced the actors in this domestic saga.
The first one hundred years or so of this period are already a
matter of more or less detailed, if nonetheless controversial, record. As to the most recent third, I remain, if not an altogether
innocent bystander, at least one living witness.

Any inquiry of this sort must of course yield a highly eccentric,
not to say idiosyncratic, narrative—or even a quirky one. Quirki-
ness and prejudice are valuable, I think, if only because they
counteract clichés. Each of the two previous attempts to limn
semiotics in the United States—by Wendy Steiner (1978) and
Roberta Kevelson (1986)—bears its peculiar subjective mark.
Their respective accounts don't merely differ the one from the
other as much in conception and perspective as in style and
execution, but the latter chose to entirely ignore the earlier.
Those two pieces might be regarded as balancing each other out
to a degree but, even when combined, as complementary to this
third, perhaps more irreverent report. About the objectivity of
the views here put forth, let there be no misapprehension; they
inevitably relate to the context from which they issue.

The evident fact that both of these previous assessments were
written by women who are themselves productive in the field
underlines a fact worth pointing out, if parenthetically: that prior
to the late 1960s, the entire global—including American—semiotics enterprise was shockingly barren of female participation.
Victoria Lady Welby, Peirce's epistolary partner and the "mother
of significs," in Duneaves, and Ethel M. Albert, a cultural anthropologist by training who became a pioneer teacher of semiotics in Evanston (as discussed further below, partly on
information provided through the courtesy of Bonnie E. Litow-

itz, one of her students), were, each in her way, quite exceptional figures.

Steiner's and Kevelson's articles, too, are bereft of female figures. This baleful situation has radically changed, however, and continues to improve in several important ways. For one thing, the presidents of the Semiotic Society of America since it was founded in 1976 have included professors of the stature of Irmengard Rauch, Naomi Baron, Bennetta Jules-Rosette, Linda Waugh, and Nancy Armstrong. (While women now populate much of our semiotic prospect, the virtually total absence of black faces from and contributions to meetings and publications, here as well as in the Old World, remains odious.)

Although Peirce served as Steiner's pillar of departure and, not surprisingly, continued as Kevelson's uncontested hero, my own biases demand an earlier start. The prominence which American thinkers gave to the conception of signs, symbols and emblems, representations, counterparts, and the way these concepts are either analyzed or used, especially in their connection with action and practice, and with political discourse and institutions, is currently being studied by the Toronto philosopher David Savan. Savan (in a personal communication dated November 20, 1988) wrote:

> I showed (to my own satisfaction) that from Jonathan Edwards on through Emerson, Judge Stallo, Johnson, Chauncey Wright, et alii, there was a strong concern with signs, evidence and evidences, representation and representatives, and the connection of all this with action. So that Peirce's semiotic is not a creatio ex nihilo but can be seen as the culmination of 120 years of development, a historic peak sloping down on its hither side, rather gently through James and Royce and Lewis and Morris, and now rising again.

Savan is now preparing for a future volume of our WEB what will surely be an eye-opening study of the native roots of Peircean semiotics, but it should be mentioned that the comparison with Edwards was earlier noted by Conkin (1976:193):

> Peirce had the ambition and many of the intellectual attributes of Jonathan Edwards. In New England, he was Edwards' first real successor, the first to reason so exactly, to probe so deeply, to

8 Thomas A. Sebeok

seek such a complete, all-embracing system of philosophy. Like Edwards, [Peirce] sought a vast, architectonic structure, encompassing all knowledge, perfectly unifying religion and science, and explaining everything, past and future.

I propose to begin my present chronicle with the little-known Frederick A. Rauch. Shea Zellweger (cf. 1990), a psychologist at Mount Union College with an abiding interest in Peirce's notations for logic and in man-sign engineering, called my attention to A. A. Roback's *History of American Psychology*, where he discusses the work of Rauch, an immigrant from Germany. Roback characterized Rauch as one of the "most remarkable pioneers" in American psychology (1952:55). Rauch was also the organizer and became the first president (1836) of Marshall College in Lancaster, Pennsylvania.

Rauch's first book in English appeared in 1840 (2nd ed., 1841), titled *Psychology; or A View of the Human Soul: Including Anthropology*. Roback (1952:57) further refers to Rauch as "a pioneer in semantics, or at least semeiotics, which is more general," and cites in support of this assertion several passages, which are indeed remarkable and worth quoting here at some length, especially considering the obscurity of the source. In a section he subtitles "Semeiotic Imagination," Rauch (1840:225–27) writes:

The term *semeiotic* is not found in the English language. It is of Greek origin from the word *semeia*, sign. With this explanation we may be permitted to use it here. Every thing in nature upon which man may impress his will, must suffer itself to be used by him as a sign. Even rivers may become the signs of boundaries. Yet the more susceptible a thing is of receiving a mark from the hands of man, the better it is qualified for a sign. Thus, the staff in the hand of Agamemnon, "which sent forth no leaves, and retained no life, after the knife cut it from its trunk and peeled and smoothed it," is the sign of power; so the hickory pole with its flags is a sign, intelligible to all the citizens of the union. The signs of semeiotic imagination are contained either in space or in time, either in rest or in motion, and may be thus classified: Signs in *space* may have different forms, yet they are not to be valued by their forms, but by what they indicate. The cockade, the flag which indicates a nation's ideas of its liberty, and which though at rest themselves may cause the greatest commotions, as the flag when unfurled and waving in the air; are of more importance than the most showy sign before a tavern. The signs that are only in space are innumerable; those that I make in a book while reading it, in my walks, and those made by private individuals in their gardens or houses, used by companies on their seals, by nations in the uniform of their soldiers, &c. At first these signs had a meaning in themselves, but this meaning was gradually lost, and semeiotic imagination used them for whatever purpose it pleased.

When, on the other hand, a sign is something which exists only in *time*, it must always be in motion. The numerous signs that belong to the art expressing thoughts by the motions of the body [are alluded to earlier in Rauch's book]. Other signs are: rockets discharged in the air; the waving of a handkerchief; the hoisting of a flag, &c. These are all of them for the eye, and must be noticed at the very moment, when they are in motion. Imagination is more rich, however, in the signs it produces for the ear. Sounds become signals. Clapping the hands may indicate applause, hissing, disapprobation. The same sounds may affect us in the most different ways, and these different effects depend wholly on the meaning we attach to them. In Germany, where in former times every occurrence of the day was brought into connection with religion, it was announced by the same bell that summoned worshippers to the house of God on Sabbaths and holy days. The bell accompanied the life of an individual from his cradle to his grave; and it was also the tongue to announce the grand divisions of the day. All these things the bell proclaimed by the same sound, and yet how different were the feelings excited in us when its rich sounds fell upon the ear at Easter, from those called forth by the same bell on Good Friday, on the Sabbath, or early in the morning when it announced the rising of the sun! Again, the chimes of a bell, that reach us from the summit of a hill covered with forests, where silence reigns and nothing is seen but a solitary chapel—how sweetly are we affected by them! Poets like Uhland, Schiller and others, have made these chimes the themes of some of their finest poems.

Next in rank are organical sounds, or such as are produced by the organs of man; hence sounds of instruments, the trumpet, flute, &c. The sounds of the trumpet govern the motions of a body of cavalry, those of the flute for the expression of love. Whistling is likewise a signal, but a signal of uncertain character. The watch-man in pursuit of a thief makes use of it, and so does the thief.

Finally, articulate sounds must serve as signs. But what sounds are *articulate*? Those produced by *articulos*, by the tongue, teeth, and lips; those therefore that are formed by all of them. The

sounds of animals differ from those of instruments; the latter are
based in the vibrations of bodies, the former rests in the voice.
The superiority of the latter may be seen even in the external
form. Musical instruments are either long, as the flute, the horn,
the clarinet, or voluminous as the drum, &c; but the throat of the
animal producing the voice, unites both length and depth. Yet
while the voice of the animal is superior to the sounds of instruments, the voice of man is superior to that of animals; for it is
capable of producing the *word*. The Latins have one root for voice
and word, *vox—vocabulum*. The word contains more than a mere
sign—a sign for light indicates only light as visible to the eye. The
word *light* contains all that natural philosophers know about it.
Hence with articulate sounds as words, we approach a higher
sphere of the mind, and as conceptions are connected with each
other by the power of our self-consciousness, so are words as the
signs of thought, and in this union they form *language*.

Rauch's observations on language (ibid. 227–44)—which, he
says, "is either that of *signs* or that of *words*" (ibid. 228) —follow
these passages. Roback (1952:59) remarks of them that they "are
strikingly modern, and hold some value even today," and indeed
this may be so, but they are too lengthy to rehearse here. Further
as to the "imagination," on which Rauch also lengthily dwells,
he reflects: "It is at first *symbolical*, then it becomes *emblematic*,
and finally *semeiotical*" (1840:224).

But what do these triadic terms and distinctions mean? It is
difficult to escape the conclusion that the distinctions (though
not the nomenclature) uncannily correspond, at least in some
important respects, to the Peircean tripartition icon/index/sym-
bol, as borne out by Rauch's explication and examples (ibid. 224–
25), which for this reason are again worth repeating in full:

It is symbolical, when the object by which it represents a thought,
and the thought itself are *homogeneous*. Darkness *cannot be* the
symbol of light; but "when a genius with an inverted torch is
placed as a monument upon a grave, it is symbolical. For there a
life has been extinguished, a light an eye, beneath that monument
the dead lies without life, without light—the light of torch and
the light of life are homogeneous." On the other hand, the pro-
ductions of imagination are *emblematical* when the form and contents become inadequate to each other, or are heterogeneous. The
feeling of thirst and a glass of beer on a tavern sign have nothing
homogeneous; the sign is therefore, not the *symbol* of thirst, but its

emblem. Yet there is still a relation between them; or if a relation no longer exists, the imagination works *semeiotically.* Here the form intended to represent certain contents, does not in the least resemble them; it therefore represents something entirely different from *itself*; the imagination determines that a thing independent of its fitness shall signify or indicate a certain thing, though it bears not the slightest relation to the thing signified. Two triangles, for instance, put into each other, are in many countries used as signs before beer-houses; there is certainly no relation between two triangles and beer. If the things used as symbols and emblems continue to have an existence, whether we place contents in them or not, the sign loses all importance when the thought signified is drawn from it, or when it is no longer used significantly. Many signs which we daily make can be understood by no one except ourselves; the boy, for instance, breaks down a few branches near where he has discovered a bird's nest; this is to him an indicative sign, but not to us, hence we can attach no importance to these broken branches.

Rauch's short lifespan lay embedded in the much longer one of Alexander Bryan Johnson, that "homespun genius on the American frontier," in Read's precisely apt phrase (1973:192). This wealthy Utica, New York (though English-born), banker and lawyer became, years *avant la lettre Peircienne*, America's other early thinker about fundamental semiotic, comprehending linguistic, matters. In a highly critical essay on Johnson's method and conclusions, Max Black nevertheless characterized him as "an original and vigorous thinker dealing with extremely important matters with characteristic independence and determination" (in Todd and Blackwood 1969:49). This inscription on his gravestone neatly sums up how Johnson perceived himself: "The author of many books: / A lawyer by education: / A banker during active life: / A student of philosophy always." His philosophical intention and manner, despite his unsophisticated, crude empiricism, seem uncannily and particularly reminiscent of Wittgenstein's subjective, aphoristic style in the *Tractatus* (1921–22) (cf. Drake, in Todd and Blackwood 1969:8).

When I coined the expression "neglected figures in the history of semiotic inquiry" (in Sebeok 1988a:187, in reference to Jakob von Uexküll), I had not anticipated that I would be starting a mini-trend pursued in repeated section headings at annual meetings of the Semiotic Society of America, variously aimed at re-

12

locating those already housed elsewhere or relabeling others
identified as "cryptosemioticians" (ibid. 9, 259; Rey 1984:92).
But if anyone qualifies under this rubric, it is surely Johnson,
ignored in his lifetime yet at least twice before rediscovered: first
in 1947 (Johnson 1947; see also Rynin 1967 and Drake in Todd
and Blackwood 1969), and next at a conference held in 1967,
aimed (with little success) at durably rehabilitating him (see Todd
and Blackwood 1969). That conference was attended by Black,
who, as I already mentioned, offered a critical appraisal of Johnson's language theories in modern perspective (ibid. 49–66), and
by K. T. Fann, himself the author of the first serviceable monograph on Peirce's theory of abduction (1970; see also his 1990
essay on Johnson as a semiotician). It is odd that Johnson became
so obscure, considering that he was generally well appreciated
by his contemporary critics, with perhaps the notable exception
of President John Quincy Adams, who was his wife's uncle, and
one of the first to point out serious defects, which Johnson later
troubled to remedy, in his philosophy of language.

There is no question that Johnson was well aware of, indeed
indebted to, Locke's sanctified passage that comes at the end of
his 1690 Essay (Book IV, Ch. XXI), later adopted by Peirce (5.488)
as well, about the "doctrine of the essential nature and fundamental rarieties of possible semiosis" (1947:15). Johnson, in fact,
deemed his own work to be exactly that new and other "sort of
logic and critic" Locke only dreamed of, adding, however, in
typically wry fashion: "What a painful but too late dawning of
light, must this have been!"

This is not the place to reevaluate Johnson's always subtle,
always fascinating, if surely sometimes flawed, reflections upon
"the relation" (as he phrased the topic in the subtitle of his
Treatise) "which words bear to things," on the philosophy of
language, especially semantics, and a host of other perennial
semiotic conundrums. These cogitations were well and critically
appraised by Rynin, who believed him to have been a thinker
of the highest rank (exalted at length in Johnson 1947:305–430,
concisely in Rynin 1967; see also Todd and Blackwood 1969 passim).

Here, I would point to this one of Johnson's extraordinarily
prophetic, fecund, far-reaching, and to me most congenially link-
ing insights: "My lectures," he proclaimed before the Utica Ly-
ceum in 1825, "will endeavour to subordinate language to

nature, to make nature the expositor of words, instead of making words the expositors of nature. If I succeed, the success will ultimately accomplish a great revolution in every branch of learning" (1947:40).

His pivotal apprehension was, in brief, that language cannot explain the world, but that the world explains language. The opening sentence of his first numbered paragraph read: "Man exists in a world of his own creation." This can perhaps best be compared with Wittgenstein's first unforgettable numbered sentence: "The world is everything that is the case" (Johnson 1947:29). (This view was remolded a century or so later by Niels Bohr in his famous maxim "We are suspended in language in such a way that we cannot say what is up and what is down. The word 'reality' is also a word, a word which we must learn to use correctly," quoted, inter alia, in French and Kennedy 1985:302; see also below.)

It should be noted that by *nature*—precisely as Uexküll did by the German word *Natur* (cf. Sebeok 1986a:73)—Johnson plainly meant "reality as it appears to us in objects apprehended" (Rynin 1967:287). We can infer that he saw that this reality, which he decomposed into three irreducible categories, was composed of signs and sign-processes (see also Cassirer 1944:23). Johnson's grouping of existences into verbal vs. "unverbal" (presumably his coinage) and the further division of the latter into three fundamental types—sensations, emotions, and intellections—has further ramifications that bear on several seemingly obscure predicaments of the modern doctrine of signs. His divagations about the "unverbal"—he seems to attach little value to "verbal" thinking—the basis for which he locates in what he calls the human "organism," have a Kantian ring to them, but this indebtedness is nowhere made explicit.

Johnson's deliberations about the meaning of "natural signs," which are not a part of language, and his assault on the human tendency to linguistically interpret the information of our senses are, although in some ways deficient (for instance, his distinction between words and sentences was, in retrospect, grossly inadequate), riveting in their overall implications:

> That the significancy of a man's language is limited to his sensible experience would be readily admitted, were we not embarrassed with one difficulty. Bonfire names a sight, and melody a sound.

If these words possessed no other signification, we should immediately understand that the import of bonfire must ever be
unknown to the blind, and the import of melody to the deaf. But
these words, and nearly all others, possess a further signification:
they name words also. This is an important distinction, and till
you understand it, you will be liable to delusion. (Johnson
1947:149–50)

The fascination of Americans with native Indian use of natural
signs—while hunting, tracking, following trails "in an instant,
in shadowy wood or treacherous clearing," in brief, requiring a
"minute examination of the real, however trivial, to uncover the
traces of events which the observer cannot directly experience"—replays on this continent a much earlier, Mesopotamian
experience (dating from at least 3,000 years B.C.), so elegantly
put on view by Ginzburg. Ginzburg emphasizes the "deciphering" and "reading" of such signs by successive generations of
hunters.

This idea—that "the gesture which is the oldest, perhaps, of
the intellectual history of the human race: the hunter crouched
in the mud, examining a quarry's tracks"—Ginzburg tells us (in
Eco and Sebeok 1983:88–91 and passim), flows, in turn, over
thousands of years, into the image of "the book of nature." This
rich and powerful conception, "the book of nature" —traced in
detail, down to the genetic code, by Blumenberg 1986 [1981],
reconsidered by Calvino (1985), and extended by Jones (1989) to
Husserl, Heidegger, and Cézanne—which underlies the still-
deeper notion of indexicality (Sebeok 1985:133; 1991a), and especially the metonymies of symptomatology (Sebeok 1986a, Ch.
4), constitutes the ruling paradigm of all the "natural" sciences
since Galileo (for biology, see Kergosien 1985). Thus, in his *Il
saggiatore*, Galileo famously, if somewhat poetically, formulated
the matter: philosophy—we might just as well say semiotics—

is written in this grand book, the universe, which stands continually open to our gaze. But the book cannot be understood
unless one first learns to comprehend the language and read the
letters in which it is composed . . . [for] without which it is hu-
manly impossible to understand a single word of it; without these,
one wanders about in a dark labyrinth. (1957 [1623]:237–38)

Or, as the Hungarian itinerant mathematician Paul Erdös once put it (Johnson 1990:45), a good mathematical proof is one that comes "straight from the book"; the deity "has a transfinite book of theorems in which the best proofs are written. And if he is well intentioned, he gives us the book for a moment."

In American fiction, the sequence of novels in the Leather-stocking saga, James Fenimore Cooper's romantic depictions of life in the American wilderness, substantiates the mythic space of the Indian world, with the minutiae of displacement through the wilderness landscape. Thus the party in the region of Hawk-eye's second westward journey

> must follow a trail, and in Cooper this means total dependence on immediate perception. As Leatherstocking instructs the others in the art of pathfinding, he urges deliberateness and sensitivity: "Softly, softly, . . . we now know our work, but the beauty of the trail must not be deformed." . . . A delicacy associated with the feminine object of the journey is required: "Touch the leaves lightly, or you'll disconsart [sic] the formation. That! that is the print of a foot . . . [of] the dark hair's [Cora's]." . . . In their pursuit of the sisters, these pathfinders must "read" nature. Rather than simply move through the landscape, they must move within it, follow its streams, inspect its grass and trees; nor did he cross a rivulet, without attentively considering the quantity, the velocity, and the color of its waters.

Eventually, the interpretation of the trail becomes too difficult even for the frontiersman Leatherstocking, who is not himself a "noble savage" but one who only shares in the savage ways. At this point, only Uncas, son of Chingachgook and the last of the Mohicans, is able to "read a language that would prove too much for the wisest [of white men]." Uncas's second "discovery of a footprint" is crucial: "It makes it possible for Hawkeye to say confidently, 'I can now read the whole of it' " (Peck 1977:122–24). So also Peirce, in a memorable illustration of what a clue entails, recalls that the footprint Robinson Crusoe found in the sand "was an Index to him of some creature" (Sebeok 1985:133).

The romantic interest in secret codes, in the hidden meanings of small objects and events, indeed cryptology, was compellingly glamorized by Edgar Allan Poe, especially in his prize-winning story "The Gold Bug" (1843; see Kahn 1967:783–93). Savan, reasonably enough, thought that Peirce had read this story; it would

certainly so appear from his use (in CP 5.275–76, dated 1868) of
the decoding of a cipher, or the deciphering of a code, to illustrate
both abduction ("hypothesis") and induction, and to bring out
the difference between them. "If you compare this passage in
Peirce with LeGrand's explanation toward the end of The Gold
Bug," says Savan, "I think you will be struck, as I was, with the
close relation between the two." Barring Poe's and Peirce's reliance on a common source, the philosopher must have been
thinking of the teller of tales. Fisch, in his introduction to Sebeok
and Umiker-Sebeok 1980 (p. 10), quotes from the *American Law
Review* (July 1870) concerning the Sylvia Ann Howland will investigation by Peirce and his father, Benjamin, where it was said,
"Hereafter, the curious studies of Poe will be thought the pal-
triest imitations."

It was also no accident that Peirce (6.460) used Poe's remark,
to the effect that "those problems that at first blush appear utterly
insoluble receive, in that very circumstance . . . their smoothly
fitting keys," as his prime example to reinforce his notion of
Play of Musement (cf. Sebeok 1981b). Incidentally, the first to
have juxtaposed Cooper's noble savage hunter with Poe's Dupin
and with Sherlock Holmes seems to have been the Canadian
would-be guru Marshall McLuhan (1946), who on occasion fancied himself as a sort of sleuth figure and once even permitted
himself to be photographed in a Sherlock Holmes outfit.

John Wilkins, in 1641, in the first English book on the subject,
Mercury: Or the Secret and Swift Messenger, was already using the
term *semaeologia* for the secrecy of signs (1984:8). Cryptology,
"the science of secret communications," is clearly that branch of
semiotics—in its origins, akin to divination—which utilizes
codes with a restricted distribution (Kahn 1986:154f).

The first American grand master of the realm of the "unverbal," Garrick Mallery, happened, like Johnson, to be a jurist
(admitted to the bar in Philadelphia in 1853), who thereafter
made an illustrious career as a gallant soldier, until disability
from wounds received in the war caused his retirement from the
army in 1879. In the course of his six years of service in the
Signal Service Bureau (created in 1870), while on duty at Fort
Rice, he in 1876 became engrossed by the pictography and sign
language of the (Siouan) Dakota Indians. His work led to his
being ordered the next year to report to Major John Wesley Pow-

ell, the influential American geologist and ethnologist, in whose company he conducted fieldwork in the Rocky Mountains. Upon his retirement from the army, he joined the Bureau of Ethnology under Powell's directorship and proceeded to produce a sequence of substantial and still peerless works based on assiduous collections of original data on, supported by impressive comparative and philosophical ruminations about, sign language among North American Indians (see, e.g., Mallery 1972 and Umiker-Sebeok and Sebeok 1978:1–437).

While Johnson's work was semiotic in every respect excepting terminological, Mallery, whom Mounin dubbed "a born semiologist" (1985:73), was a semiotician *au pied de la lettre*. He employed the technical noun—note its spelling (Sebeok 1985:51–52)—and the adjective both freely and with astonishing accuracy and versatility. (Incidentally, Mallery also cites and discusses Dalgarno's *sematology* [1972:25–26].)

He characterized, for example in 1880, his own writings as *native semiotics* (Umiker-Sebeok and Sebeok 1978:8). In the same monograph (ibid. 43), and again in 1881 (1972:74), he told of the white deaf-mutes' *semiotic code*, and of signs in succession as exhibiting a *semiotic syntax* (ibid. 150). Then we find this sentence: "Men, in groping for a mode of communication with each other, and using the same general methods, have been under many varying conditions and circumstances which have determined differently many conceptions and their *semiotic execution*, but there have also been many of both which were similar" (1972:74; italics mine). And he spoke of the precise mode of *semiotic expression* of the several tribes (ibid. 88).

Mounin wondered "if Mallery had read Peirce . . . or if Peirce had read Mallery" (1985:74)—and so must we all. Charles Morris's oft-cited 1946 dictum, according to which "Peirce was the heir of the whole historical philosophical analysis of signs" (1971:337), turns out to have been exaggerated, for we have no reason to suspect that Peirce was acquainted with the writings of, among others, John Poinsot (cf. Deely, in Poinsot 1985:492, n. 132) or, incredibly, those of Johnson, who died when Peirce was twenty-eight. By then, Peirce had already published more than what is now encompassed in the initial tome of his chronological writings (1982, covering 1857–66). Mallery, furthermore, is never mentioned by him, or vice versa, although Max H. Fisch and we are convinced that the two must at least have known *of* each other, and may well have intermingled socially (for grounds, see Umiker-Sebeok and Sebeok 1978:xxxii, n. 6).

Mallery's thinking is permeated throughout, beyond his nomenclature, with a fine semiotic sensibility, but the sources of both are still shrouded in mystery. Since the twenty-four parts of William Dwight Whitney's *The Century Dictionary*, for which we know Peirce wrote numerous entries, and where the very form *semiotics* is well attested, began appearing only in 1889 (see Whitney 1891, Part 19, p. 5486), I can but hazard a guess— subject to refutation if eventual research in military history fails to bear this out—as to Mallery's use of *semiotics*: that in the course of his protracted service in the Signal Service Bureau, he may have become inured to the use of this term in a military context (the French word *sémiotique* comparably denoted in the nineteenth century the "Art de faire manoeuvrer les troupes en leur indiquant les mouvement par signes" [Sebeok 1985:54, n. 2]).

"Semiotics," Bailey (1978:68f.) justly maintained, "is neither as revolutionary nor as continuous as various ones of its proponents sometimes argue," adducing Whitney. "Within the framework of semiotics, in which human language is but a special case of a sign system, Whitney's contributions are both interesting as history and instructive as a guide to further research." Whitney (1867:103) himself saw the study of language as only one manifestation of a "sign-making faculty," but, although he always remained a student of the former, he was aware of the larger context, as when he cited the architecture of medieval cathedrals as a sign-system. Bailey concludes (1978:79) that, although "Whitney's contribution to the rise of semiotics is mainly indirect," he was nevertheless an American counterpart, as it were, of Saussure, and a "pioneer in treating signs as arbitrary and conventional and in seeing that no semiotic fact can be described outside the system of which it is a part."

The recorded usages of *semiotics* in America make for a far more complicated story than has hitherto been traced—note that Rauch used the noun and adjective *semeiotic*, as well as the forms *semeiotical* and *semeiotically*, in the 1840s—but this can only be hinted at here. Thus this very form is listed in the U.S. printing of *The Imperial Dictionary of the English Language*, with Def. 1 reading: "The doctrine or science of signs; the language of signs," followed by Def. 2: "In *pathol.* that branch which teaches how to judge of all the symptoms in the human body, whether healthy or diseased; symptomatology; semeiology" (Ogilvie 1883:IV:27). The listing then recurs, almost verbatim, under the lemma *semiotics, semeiotics* in *The Century Dictionary* (Whitney 1891:19:5486). In Peirce's marked copy of the 1889 edition (duplicated afterwards by several Peirce scholars), the item is marked in green, which may have meant (according to a personal communication from Christian Kloesel, present director of the Peirce Edition Project) "that Peirce simply recommended that the *Imperial* definitions be included in the *CD*." At the least, it is clear that the -*ics* form was already in use when Peirce worked on his contributions for the *CD*, but we don't know how widely, and we still don't know where Mallery picked up the term or why Peirce, or so it would appear, never employed it himself (at least in his identified writings).

Of course, Mallery's knowledge of the history of "the systematic use of gesture speech" (1972:23–35) from antiquity to his own times, including its uses by orators and actors, was also enviable, and he could easily have absorbed ideas and vocabulary through his extensive readings that ran from quotations of the Stoic Chrysippus to Canon De Jorio's encyclopedic 1832 treatise about inferences based on Neapolitan gestures to reconstruct those of the ancients (Magli 1986).

Mention of De Jorio brings us forward directly to David Efron, another pioneer "contributor to the now rapidly growing field of research into facial expressions and body movement in social interaction" (Paul Ekman, Preface to Efron 1972:7). Efron, who was born in Argentina but lived in New York City, wrote his exemplary book comparing groups of immigrant Italians and Jews in the United States—of which Davis rightly pointed out that the "wealth of information presented in text, drawings, and notation has yet to be developed with the vision and breadth that [he] displays here" (1972:59)—at Columbia University, where he conducted his fieldwork under the direction of Franz Boas. His focal topic was their nonverbal behavior in conversational settings. The question to which he sought the answer, empirically, by a judicious mixture of qualitative and quantitative methods, was: "Are gestures culturally determined?" He found that, on the one hand, the assimilated Eastern Jews and the assimilated Southern Italians in New York City appear to differ greatly from their respective traditional groups, but, on the other

20 Thomas A. Sebeok

hand, they appear to resemble each other. Hence, his provisional conclusion was affirmative, or at any rate it ratified that this form of human behavior is not determined by biological descent.

Efron later gave evidence of his allegiance, if intermittent, to semiotic methods and goals, for he was an active participant in the 1974 Congress of the International Association for Semiotic Studies, where he vigorously and profitably debated my plenary lecture and gave a clever (but to me wholly unconvincing) paper of his own, making the strong though vacuous claim that telepathy not merely exists but is "of a semiotic character" (Efron 1979:221, n.; 1102–1108).

If Efron, who drew on Old World sources with erudition, including especially De Jorio's book (although misspelling his name), knew the works of Mallery (easily familiar to other students of Boas, such as Kroeber), he never cites them. His own subsequent influence, however, was, if not always explicitly credited, pervasive in specialized corners of semiotic endeavor, rechristened at times by such names as "nonverbal communication" (Ruesch and Kees 1956; Kendon 1986), "proxemics" (Hall 1968), "nonverbal behavior" (Ekman and Friesen 1969:63), "kinesics" (Birdwhistell 1970), "body language" (Scheflen 1972), "body movement" (Davis 1972; Davis and Skupien 1982), "motor signs" (Jakobson 1972), gesture or gesticulation, and several other such tags (Sebeok 1985:159–62).

These semiotic specialties have hugely proliferated and ramified, under the aforementioned and similar labels, since the 1950s. Martha Davis, formerly the president of the Institute for Nonverbal Communication Research and editor of the magazine *Kinesis: News and Views of Nonverbal Communication*, was also an indefatigable chronicler of this vast literature, who published two successive, handy annotated bibliographies of the subject (1972 and 1982). The *Journal of Nonverbal Behavior* (previously titled *Environmental Psychology and Nonverbal Behavior*) has also existed since 1976.

Of the aforementioned, Hall (e.g., 1968), Ekman (1987), and Birdwhistell (1970) were among the many who took part in the 1962 conference, reported in Sebeok et al. 1972 under the premonitory title *Approaches to Semiotics*, in the course of which American semiotics was "organized"—at any rate, according to the informed judgment of an observer from afar, Alain Rey

(1984:92) in the sense that it acquired its "institutional existence." Ten years after that meeting, Ruesch published his own massive book, with the reverberatory title *Semiotic Approaches to Human Relations* (1972). (Ten years earlier, Ruesch had already discussed, if succinctly, "the field of semiosis" [1961:453], and he returned to it again as late as 1975:78.)

But what were the true attainments and consequences of that 1962 conference? One unanticipated outcome was the distinctive, perhaps singularly blended, contour acquired by semiotics in this country over the two ensuing decades. I chose to group the conference around five thematic areas: cultural anthropology, education, linguistics, psychiatry, and psychology. Many prominent participants were, as a matter of course, invited to represent each of these disciplines mentioned, but others were included who, in my view (not necesarily conceded by them, or only halfheartedly), never chose to proclaim themselves "semioticians."

An arresting case in point was that of Erving Goffman, who at times liked to designate himself a "sociologist" (e.g., in Sebeok et al. 1972:139), but who often relished his preferred role as an "outsider" (e.g., ibid. 232). Goffman and I together once amicably organized and ran an international conference, in total concord on the venue (Amsterdam), the participants, and topics to be discussed (Sherzer 1971). Yet we could not agree on the title. I wanted this title to reflect the identifying trademark, "Semiotics." After all, it was aspects of that which we were in the Netherlands to discuss. Goffman, who years before had published what I considered his most insightful contribution to semiotics, *Stigma* (1963; but see MacCannell 1983:23–29), and who later cheerfully offered his "Footing" to be first published in *Semiotica* (1979), kept insisting that he didn't wish his work pinned down by that term, indeed by any one term. Hence we compromised on the *ad hoc* weasel phrase "Interaction Ethology," which scarcely anyone, save a participant or two in that conference (e.g., Drew and Wootton 1988:91), has used before or since (although "interaction order" does appear in the subtitle of this collection of essays on Goffman [ibid.]).

This is all particularly ironic in view of the immediate circumstance which brought about the now all but universal use of *semiotics*, resuscitated in the context of the 1962 conference.

22   Thomas A. Sebeok

Everyone remembers Margaret Mead's declaration that *semiotics* is "the one word, in one form or other, that has been used by people who are arguing from quite different positions," though few recall the contextual occasion for her remark. In fact, the paragraph in question started out: "We have been challenged by Dr. Goffman to say what we are doing and we are, I think, conceivably working in a field which in time will include the study of all patterned communication in all modalities" (ibid. 275). No wonder, then, that Dean MacCannell could claim, in his loving and pensive necrology of Goffman: "Those of us in the areas of semiotics . . . can regard him as a forerunner" (1983:1; cf. Vester 1989; see also Riggins 1990).

By "contour," I meant above to suggest the peculiar, if constantly shifting, interlacement—in part intellectual, in part intimate—of the contemporary American semiotics community, which I have elsewhere positioned within the wrappings of a global "Semiotic Web" (Sebeok 1985, Ch. 10; note that this metaphor is now also used as the title for a continuing series of yearbooks, the fifth of which appeared in 1991, and which I continue to coedit with Jean Umiker-Sebeok, who was also the *rapporteuse* of our Amsterdam forum; see further our prefaces to these volumes, commenting on the rationale for our use of this expression).

A case in point: I coedited the transactions of the 1962 conference with Margaret Mead's daughter, Mary Catherine Bateson, whose father was Gregory Bateson, who, in collaboration with the above-named Jurgen Ruesch, wrote the (arguably) best general book to date on communication (1951). Bateson is presented by Lipset (1980, Ch. XII) as a "communication theorist." He was indeed a notably acute thinker about some of the deepest semiotic problems, including zoosemiotic. He took a leading part in our Amsterdam get-together, as well as in an earlier symposium (held at Burg Wartenstein, in 1965) which I had organized around the subject of zoosemiotics (Sebeok and Ramsay 1969:11–30); he also contributed a marvelous, oft-cited chapter, "Redundancy and Coding," to my first handbook on animal communication (1968:614–26).

Another case in point, this more to illustrate the wider, tentaclelike embrace of the American academic community: two participants in that Bloomington conference later became presidents of the Semiotic Society of America, established fourteen years afterwards; four of them became presidents of the Linguistic Society of America; and two of them became presidents of the Modern Language Association.

There are surprisingly many American scholars, situated in a multiplicity of academic fields, and some men of letters who clearly practice semiotics but who are not routinely so reckoned when formal tallies are drawn up. Among linguists, I take Kenneth L. Pike to be an unusually splendid exemplar, not only because he was the author of "a neglected contemporary American classic of 'cryptosemiotics' " (Sebeok 1988a:259), his monumental semiotic treatise *Language in Relation to a Unified Theory of the Structure of Human Behavior* (Pike 1967), but also because his name provides an opportunity for some further reflections about the relationship of autochthonous linguistics with its enveloping semiotic matrix. Not long ago, I had an occasion to review the ramifications, in historical perspective and worldwide, of the mutually coordinate or, as the case may be, hierarchical relationship between the two (Sebeok 1987a; cf. Baron 1979). There is no call to recapitulate this probe here in all its particulars, but I do want to cast a fresh glance at some of its strictly American reverberations.

All linguists resident in America (four of the following were immigrant expatriates) who have paid heed to the matter explicitly or at least implicitly—including Sapir, Leonard Bloomfield, Chao, Jakobson, Weinreich, Greenberg, Chomsky, Shaumyan, Irmengard Rauch, and Lamb—and whether using this or a cognate term or none, take it for granted, as most Europeans, notably Saussure, did or do, that linguistics is indeed subsumed under semiotics. (Note also that six presidents of the Semiotic Society of America since its founding in 1976 were linguists by profession: in order of service, Henry Hiż, Allen Walker Read, Irmengard Rauch, I, Naomi Baron, and Linda Waugh.) Bloomfield remarked that "linguistics is the chief contributor to semiotic" (Sebeok 1987a:7). Chao distinguished languages from "quasi languages," citing zoosemiotics as one, gestures another such category, and in general following the semiotic terminology of Charles Morris (1968:116, 195). Chomsky, who wrote a sagacious article titled "Human Language and Other Semiotic Systems" (1979), later alluded to a "science of semiology," in the framework of which it is tempting to draw an analogy to rules of grammar (1980:253). Greenberg asserted that "the special po-

sition of linguistics arises" from the fact that it is "a part of the
nascent subject of semiotics, the science of sign behavior in general" (Sebeok 1988a, Ch. 16).

Jakobson (1981:766) spoke of "semiotics, which incorporates
linguistics as its fundamental part," and he accused linguists
"who insist on excluding from the sphere of semiotics signs
which are organized in a different manner than those of language" of "egocentrism" (1980:19; cf. Eco 1987). Irmengard
Rauch has returned to this subject in several of her papers (most
recently in 1987), and she also coedited the proceedings of a
conference (Rauch and Carr 1980) where this was a principal
topic for discussion. Lamb not only claimed that "pure linguistics, properly conceived, leaned quite naturally to semiotics"
(1984:9; cf. also Sebeok, Lamb, and Regan 1988) but named the
instructional unit he founded in 1982 at Rice University the Department of Linguistics and Semiotics. Sapir viewed language
as but one of the "specialized forms of symbolic behavior" (Sebeok 1987a:7), and there is no doubt that he was "thoroughly
committed—first and last, early and late—to a triadic view of
the sign," or that his "allegiance to the principle of mediation
is explicit everywhere in his . . . studies" (Berthoff 1988:3).
Shaumyan defined linguistics as "a part of semiotics that deals
with natural sign systems, that is, with natural languages"
(1987:18). Weinreich spoke of semiotics as the study of signs and
sign systems "of which language is but one variety" (1980:390).

Such views were also consonant with those of many U.S.-
based philosophers, as wildly dissimilar in outlook as Carnap,
who classified linguistics as "the descriptive, empirical part of
semiotic" (1942:13); Cassirer, who dogmatically asserted that
"linguistics is a part of semiotics" (1945:119); Langer, who in
her "general theory of symbolism" (1942:116) distinguishes
between "verbal and non-verbal formulation"; Maritain (see
especially 1957; and cf. Deely 1956); Urban (1939:229—"Communication by language is . . . but one phase of a more general
phenomenon"); Ransdell, who published an article titled "Semiotic and Linguistics" (1980); or even Whitehead, who delivered
a series of lectures at the University of Virginia on symbolism
(1927; Ch. 7 is entitled "Language"), and who discoursed at
length on the question, "What is 'significance'?" (1919:12; Ch.
I).

Morris, who understandably considered "the term 'language'
. . . vague and ambiguous in current usage" (1946:36), coined

the expression "lansign systems" for sign-sets of the kind in question, and proposed (as it turned out, to no avail whatsoever) to call the individual members of these systems "lansigns." The foundations for a semiotic linguistics were laid by Peirce himself (see also below); they were seldom better understood and complemented than by the American philosopher Ransdell (1980; for an American linguist's assessment, cf. Rauch 1987; and see also Shapiro 1983 and Pharies 1985).

Here I should also mention the extraordinarily absorbing researches of Watt with various sorts of writing systems, especially his sequence of papers—soon to be expanded and consolidated into a book—on the semiotics of the alphabet (1975, 1980, 1981, and 1988). That the alphabet is an intricate semiotic system no one can doubt; however, while it turns out to be distinctly different in some respects from any natural language, it is nevertheless, as Watt affirms (1988:234), "amenable to description in terms of a grammar." Too, I clearly understood for the first time from these studies that, "while the letters are (mostly) used to stand for segmental phonemes of a language, they themselves most resemble not phonemes, but morphemes" (ibid. 200). Script in general, and the alphabet in particular, is triply linked to the semantic coverage, to the morphemic units, and to speech (as distinct from language).

More generally, it is essential to distinguish between two oppositions: verbal vs. nonverbal and vocal vs. nonvocal (Sebeok 1988a:45–52). Human sign languages, such as the American Sign Language (ASL), are verbal + and vocal −. In his discussion of a "semiotic view of sign languages," Stokoe attends to and expands on these distinctions by dividing anthroposemiotics (see below) into a major and minor branch.

> The minor branch will now be sign language. . . . What the proposed new classification adds to the picture is the important fact that a minority of mankind, those with severe hearing impairment, especially those born deaf, may have as a primary semiotic system a language which uses as its prime symbols visible actions of the same kind used by many other creatures for signalling and used by the majority of mankind as supplementary or subsidiary semiotic devices. (Stokoe 1972:16f.)

There exists a huge literature on the ASL (Klima and Bellugi 1979; Wilbur 1979), including its art forms, notably in silent poetry and song, and purported "signing" interactions by means of ASL in alloprimates (Sebeok 1987b), as well as about other sign languages around the globe.

A highly unusual model for the fusion of the verbal with the nonverbal, called "semiotic extension," is the one developed by the psychologist McNeill (1979:98–100). This consists of a daring and productive elaboration of some ideas of L. S. Vygotsky by way of Peircean sign-theory. McNeill presents a sophisticated bifurcated model for the organization of action: first, the sensory-motor idea must encompass the other content, which is "the information that differentiates (specifies) the speech program which is accessed via the sensory-motor idea." Second, "the sensory-motor idea must be related to the other content." As to the ontogenesis of semiotic extension, McNeill shows (ibid. 237) how the object of an indexical sign must simultaneously be regarded as "the sign vehicle of an iconic or symbolic sign." Levelt (1989:94) comments on semiotic extension: "It is probably no accident that the thematic roles of space and physical action extend to time and . . . to other domains of experience," i.e., that our categories of experience develop ontogenetically from a matrix of "sensory-motor" ideas, notions pertaining to physical motion and action.

At the 1962 Bloomington conference, a Yale psychologist, George F. Mahl, was mainly responsible for the second, meticulously detailed and documented, principal presentation (Sebeok et al. 1972:51–124). This dealt with "psychological research in the extralinguistic area," including the functional relationships between the extralinguistic phenomena and the nonlinguistic states and processes in speaker-and-listener interaction in the communication. Mahl's voluminous collected papers about nonverbal and vocal behavior during clinical psychological interviews were published in 1987. He has many astute observations about posture, gesture, and proximity, the interrelationships of verbal and nonverbal behavior, and the role of speech disturbances that are or are not associated with fear and anxiety during self-revelatory talk.

After this abridged *tour d'horizon* of major resident linguists' and kindred perspectives on semiotics, let me return to Pike and his book. A quintessentially American contemporary linguist, Pike engaged in evangelistic activity on behalf of the Summer Institute of Linguistics and the Wycliffe Bible Translators. His interests have ranged from phonetics to discourse structure, rhetoric, and semantics. Eventually, however, "leaving [his] own discipline . . . because some of us need to explore this trail," he declared a wish to satisfy an ambition of "showing the relationship between the structure of verbal and nonverbal behavior," "to meet the need, to some degree, for a unified theory of verbal and nonverbal behavior," or to "elaborate communication without sound" (1967:5f., 35, 72)—in a word, which he nowhere employs despite his evident familiarity with Peirce's *Collected Papers* and especially with the two main semiotic treatises of Charles Morris, and his having published several articles in *Semiotica*—he turned to semiotics.

Unlike, however, most of our aforementioned linguist colleagues, Pike has actually attempted concrete semiotic anatomizations of certain social events, rigid in form or ceremonial, and "repeatable in general type with recognizable recurring elements" (ibid. 72). One of these was a keenly observed church service (ibid. 73–97), another the "family breakfast scene" (ibid. 122–28), and a third a football game (ibid. 98–119).

The last mentioned has since been at least twice surpassed: once by another American-born linguist and accomplished signtheorist, John Lotz, whose passionate semiotic analysis of football games I read and discussed with him not long before his untimely death, but the completed manuscript of which has not been located among his papers (Sebeok 1988a:231–52); and later by the witty English ethologist Desmond Morris, in a fascinating, all-embracing account of soccer (1981). Pike's distinction between official game and spectacle also found an echo in Goffman's distinction between players and participants in *Encounters*, his quasi-semiotic study of several types of interactions (1961:36, n. 30).

Eugene Nida's fundamental studies of semantic elements, "on which others can build," were emphasized by Read (1973:174). His semiotic studies, confined to the verbal level, are preeminently oriented to translation theory and its applications; they have continued in this domain, culminating in a volume on the componential analysis of referential meaning (1975).

In the light of the foregoing paragraphs, these alternative arguments, and more, could now be entertained:

• that the story of linguistics be subsumed as a vast chapter integrated within the far more comprehensive chronicle of general and applied semiotics;

• that linguistics, offering a window to the mind, is therefore a branch of the cognitive sciences (which, as I would argue, may be tantamount to semiotics);

• or that semiosis, inclusive of universal grammar, being a criterial attribute of our biological endowment, is part and parcel of the sciences of life;

• or else that the age-old inquiry into verbal signs, being so empirical and rigorously formalized, constitutes an autonomous discipline demanding independent treatment.

For the purposes of this essay, I opted to exclude American linguistics as such but to embrace those among our linguists who, like Pike, have made distinctive and seminal contributions to nonlinguistic semiotics. This does not contradict the dogma that all linguists are semioticians (not true vice versa); but some are clearly "more equal than others."

The incursion of trained linguists—or, much worse, those but half-baked—into other, nonverbal or syncretic, at any rate, into anthroposemiotic domains, has sometimes proved unavailing or counterproductive. Yet at other times the use and application of linguistic models has been found to be of considerable heuristic value. Consideration of just one example of each kind of outcome may be enlightening.

The field called in some quarters *kinesics* illustrates what happens when linguistic categories are arbitrarily foisted onto areas of human behavior where they have little or no appositeness. *Kinesics* has been defined as "a term in SEMIOTICS for the systematic use of facial expression and body gesture to communicate MEANING, especially as this relates to the use of LANGUAGE (e.g. when a smile vs. a frown alters the interpretation of a SENTENCE)" (Crystal 1980:200; the term is alluded to in passing, under the lemma *Nonverbal Communication*, in the EDS 612). Sanguine researchers who minted this term and strove to authoritatively delineate its compass in the 1950s (although Mallery, Efron, and Ruesch in this country and a host of Europeans had solidly preceded them in the study of body motion as a form of communication) acted on the conviction that the "exhaustive techniques of linguistics" (Birdwhistell 1970:xi) were eminently germane. As Crystal had, however, correctly pointed out, "it is highly unlikely that kinesic behavior has sufficient structural complexity, discreteness, or semantic organization to warrant its analysis in the same terms as linguistic behavior; and spurious terminological identity is best avoided" (1974:270). An even worse mistake arose from this group's naiveté about "exhaustive techniques of linguistics" (whatever that euphoric phrase might have meant): for they not only committed themselves to the unmotivated and, as it turned out, false assumption that the rest of bodily motion was organized much as is the output of the speech apparatus (i.e., consisting of an arbitrary coordination, out of a narrow selection of producible acoustic signals, of vocal signs with the entire *Umwelt* as to their field of reference), but they chose a *particular* descriptive schema (the so-called Smith-Trager model) which was even then on its irreversible way to oblivion.

However, in quite another sphere of investigation, endosemiotics (discussed further below), the use of another linguistic model, to wit, generative grammar, has proved extremely productive. The term *endosemiotics* (Sebeok 1985:3; 1990a) was coined in 1976 for the study of semiosis in such subsystems of the body as organ assemblies, organs, tissue, cells, and cellular organelles; among other subfields, it encompasses what has lately come to be called *semioimmunology*.

One of the profoundest biological puzzles, clearly a biosemiotic problem, namely, how an antigen is recognized and how a structure exactly complementary to it is then synthesized, has focused on the ability of the immune system to make a specific adaptive response to an indefinitely large spectrum of natural and man-made molecules and to distinguish protein molecules made by ego from almost identical proteins of nonego (autoimmunity). Gene pieces, inherited by individuals, can be assembled into 10^8 to 10^{10} antibody genes; subsequent exposure to antigens induces mutations that result in the production of even more antibody molecules.

Some immunologists have characterized the repertoire of the B lymphocytes as "complete," meaning that the system can respond by forming specific antibodies to any molecule existing in the world, including molecules never before confronted or even invented. This technical use of "completeness" brings to mind an adage of Wilhelm von Humboldt's, one that was later embraced (although never explained) by Chomsky—who called it in his early writings "creativity," or sometimes "open-endedness"—about the capability of languages to "make infinite use of finite means." Jerne, in a 1984 Nobel address permeated with semiotic terminology, then proposed this analogous idea:

"The immense repertoire of the immune system . . . becomes a vocabulary comprised not of words but of sentences that is capable of responding to any sentence expressed by the multitude of antigens which the immune system may encounter." Further, he said: "As for the components of a generative grammar that Chomsky mentions, we could with some imagination equate these with various features of protein structures" (1985).

He then proceeded to elaborate these, concluding that he finds it astonishing that the immune system embodies a degree of complexity comparable with language, especially that one cognitive system has evolved with, the other without assistance of the brain (which, strangely enough, excludes lymphocytes). The context for the reexamination of the immune system in such terms began with the elaboration of the idiotype network theory of Jerne himself, who realized that its receptors and specific secreted products (antibodies) recognize not only the external world of antigenic determinants (epitopes) but also antigenic determinants on the immune receptors themselves (idiotypes). In brief, Jerne's semiotic insight was that corresponding to most—perhaps all—of the epitopes of the external universe there are corresponding internal images, or iconic symbols, within the organism's immune system.

We see, then, from these contrastive little homilies about semioimmunology and kinesics that the application of one linguistic model or another in selected corners of semiotic concern may at times provide illumination, at other times yield no insight at all, or worse, temporarily mislead. Such is saliently the case in practically the entirety of traditional zoosemiotics, based, in America as elsewhere, on the twin fallacies that animal signaling systems were in some vague sense the evolutionary antecedents of language and that the latter evolved for purposes of communication—cogently contradicted by Chomsky, Popper (discussed in Sebeok 1987b), and others (discussed in Holenstein 1982 and 1986:197–202).

Given that linguistics as a whole is to be excluded from this account, what about other massive logocentric endeavors, notably literary semiotics? First, let me register my preliminary concurrence—especially in view of the fact that his observation contradicts much received opinion—with Godzich (1978:389f.), who stressed that the preoccupation of semioticians is with semiotics, and that although literary texts figure prominently among their concerns, they are rarely at the center of them, so that the view of literature which emerges from semiotic practice is very much in the nature of an "offering," a secondary by-product of an autotelic construction effort.

This view notwithstanding, it is the case that "many poetic features belong not only to the science of language but to the whole theory of signs, that is, to general semiotics" (Jakobson 1960:351). As far back as 1974, Bailey and Chatman had already compiled a bibliography of twenty pages of entries under this specific rubric for the United States and Canada alone; indeed, as Wellek says in his incomparable compendium of American criticism during the first half of this century, many in this country "aim at an all-embracing structure of universal poetics and finally at a science of semiotics" (1986:156). So Riffaterre's first American book was devoted to the semiotics of poetry, wherein he showed that "the basic semiotic mechanism is that any sign system can structure another of a higher level of complexity and become a mere code serving to signify something else" (1978: 157).

Scholes has fearlessly ventured in just this direction, by way of a series of lively practical demonstrations of semiotic technique, with a glossary of semiotic terminology attempting to knit together the loose ends of his book (1982). (Again, note that five of the sixteen presidents thus far of the Semiotic Society of America can be reckoned literary semioticians: Thomas G. Winner, Michael Riffaterre, Jonathan Culler, Robert Scholes, and Nancy Armstrong.)

Since midcentury, until at least the advent of the era of so-called poststructuralism ("deconstruction," "grammatology," the unfortunately designated "pragmatism," and the like), there has appeared a veritable avalanche of explictly or implicitly semiotic works that bear on textual matters. Concomitantly with—or perhaps despite—the coming of these novel approaches, whole fresh semiotic subdisciplines have sprung up, with a distinctively American flavor, or at least with a strong input from the Western shores of the Atlantic, dealing with many genres of, or approaches to, semiotics of discourse in the broad sense.

Here are just a few random (and incommensurate) samples, listed in no special order, with a few representative references:
• semiotics of the theater, comprehending both the playscript and the spectacle text, together with other performance elements (Carlson 1988a, 1990), and applications thereof to specific dramatists (such as six plays by Eugene O'Neill [Kobernick 1989]) or to a single drama (such as *Othello* [Calderwood 1989]);
• semiotics of puppetry, which "integrates many semiotic streams, codes, and channels," including "colors, costumes, gestures and body movements, dance, music, physical traits, and staging, as well as language" (Sherzer and Sherzer 1987:1f.; see also the 1983 special issue of *Semiotica* "Puppets, Masks, and Performing Objects from Semiotic Perspectives," Vol. 47);
• semiotics of television, including TV ads (Fiske, an Australian scholar, now at the University of Wisconsin-Madison, with Hartley, 1978, Ch. 3 and passim);
• the analysis of narrative strategies employed in everyday conversations (Tannen 1984, Polanyi 1985) or in specialized conversational interactions, as between doctors and their patients (West 1984), trial judges and the jury "in explicit and subtle verbal and 'nonverbal' ways that never show up on the 'dry' appellate record" (Blanck, Rosenthal, and Cordell 1985:90), and the like;
• the semiotic problems involved in "intertextuality" as an approach to literary texts, painting, music, ethnography, film, etc., for instance, assembled and edited by Morgan in a special issue of the *American Journal of Semiotics* (Vol. 5, No. 4, 1985; or O'Donnell and Davis 1989); see also my analysis of intertextuality in the Spielberg film *E.T.: The Extraterrestrial* (Sebeok 1986a:183–88, first presented in 1984 at the meeting organized by Morgan on which this issue was more or less based);
• semiotic approaches to ethnomethodology, a specialized discipline usually classified with the social sciences, utilizing text-and-talk, indeed, its own system of signification expressed in its own poetic idiom (Flynn 1991);
• the semiotics of tourism: "all over the world," says Culler (1981:128), "tourists are engaged in semiotic projects, reading cities, landscapes, and cultures as sign systems." Especially noteworthy in this regard is Jules-Rosette's comparative exploration (1984) of the messages of tourist art as a semiotic system in certain areas of Africa. Overall, this field of investigation has engaged the attention of American authors as diverse as

MacCannell (1976a), in his scintillating book *The Tourist*, and
Percy (1981:46–63), besides Culler; an outlandishly imagined relation between an allegedly "real" territory, in the case in point
"America," and its "simulacra," that is, the grid of iconic signs
that stands for it, if "it" truly exists, is depicted in Baudrillard's
America, a singularly fatuous and inadvertently funny vertigo of
interpretation (1988:11);
• the fundamental semiotic structures of design and the meaning of visual signs and symbols used in, for example, graphic
design (Frutiger 1989; Gottschall 1989; Thompson 1988), information graphics (Wildbur 1989), or, more generally, the visual
display of quantitative information, as developed in the outstanding books by Tufte (1983, 1990); Martin Krampen's *tour de
force* special issue of *Semiotica*, "Icons of the Road" (Vol. 43, Nos.
1–2 [1983]), is especially valuable for showing how such an
analysis can be firmly grounded in Peircean semiotic theory;
• closely tied to the preceding is the matter of the theory and
practice of notational systems (Goodman 1968; Krampen 1986a),
the common ones among which include dance notation (Maletic
1987), musical notation (the art of which was itself formerly
called *semeiotiké*; see Sebeok 1985:48), space notation, notation
systems in logic (e.g., Roberts 1973), mathematics, chemistry
(Mounin 1985:177–88), and the like;
• the nature of medical descriptions in terms of a hierarchical
model of information (Blois 1984);
• the *facultas signatrix* characteristic of the aging and the aged
(Sebeok 1977a:189; Stafford 1989), or of severely retarded persons
(Price-Williams and Sabsay 1979);
• legal semiotics, an internationally proliferated subfield, in
which, for instance, a semiotic theory of narrativity may usefully
be deployed (Tiefenbrun 1986; Kevelson 1988);
• urban semiotics, or the study of the city as a social symbol,
which has emerged in the main from European work but is now
pursued in the United States as well (Gottdiener and Lagopoulos
1986, to which the former contributed Chs. 9 and 13 and coauthored the introduction).
How to deal with such matters here without getting bogged
down in a morass of specialization? What, for instance, is one
to make of the protean American critical pluralist and philosophical synthesizer Kenneth Burke (Fiordo 1978; Hymes 1968;
Wellek 1986, Ch. 14)? The writings of Burke—which, in some

respects, can be compared with Peirce's (Feehan 1989:258–65)—
bristle with modern technicalities, drawn, among many other
fields, from semiotics. In his suggestive essay "What Are the
Signs of What?" (1966:359–79), further clarified elsewhere,
Burke argues, in an antinominalist stance, that things are the
signs of words, not the other way around; and that language is
symbolic action (Heath 1986, Ch. 4). The system of symbolism
he invented resembles nothing as closely as Cassirer's concept
of symbolic form (1953–57), although Burke thinks Cassirer (like
Bergson) is more "Scientistic" (i.e., post-Kantian), while his own
views are more "Dramatistic" (i.e., in an older scholastic tradition of medieval realism) (ibid. 23).

In a proper compendium of American semiotics, one would
want to judiciously sift writings such as Burke's from those of
less semiotically saturated *littérateurs*, so that one would presumably meet the standards of one of Eco's hypotheses for the
make-up of a history of semiotics, requiring "an impressive rereading of the whole history of philosophy, and maybe many
other disciplines" (1983:80), notably, I think, the history of
humanistic criticism. An encyclopedic undertaking of that
magnitude cannot, however, be conceived short of a massive
interdisciplinary collaborative endeavor.

Eco justly notes that "there are certain poets or novelists who
have investigated the life of signs or sign-behaviour more lucidly
than many theorists did," and aptly alludes to Proust (ibid. 81).
From the American side (having already mentioned Poe; see also
Jakobson 1981:7–17), I would adduce here, first and foremost,
the case of our eminent, very recently deceased, contemporary
author of half a dozen outstanding novels—more reminiscent,
some think, of Camus than of Proust—the late Walker Percy.

Percy began to publish essays on semiotic themes in 1954, and
he continued to pay serious attention to such issues thereafter;
fifteen of his philosophical essays, including "Semiotic and a
Theory of Knowledge," were collected in a book (1981, Ch. 11).
He facetiously wrote me (August 13, 1982): "I am figuring that
since you venture into literary forms such as dialogues with
Maeterlinck [cf. Sebeok 1986a, Ch. 8], you can forgive a novelist
for trespassing into semiotics."

In 1980, Percy took a month off to participate *in statu*, as it
were, *pupillari*, in the First International Summer Institute for
Semiotic and Structural Studies, at the University of Toronto.

He was thoroughly comfortable in the pertinent works of St. Thomas and Maritain, Peirce, Cassirer and Langer, G. H. Mead and Morris, indeed, with the contemporary semiotic scene here and, increasingly since 1986, in the Soviet Union. While his own contributions to semiotics flowed outside the academic mainstream and, as such, gained him but modest scholarly renown, they were original and interesting (they have been analyzed in detail by Thornton and W. H. Poteat [Broughton 1979:169–218], by P. L. Poteat [1985, esp. Chs. III and IV], and with especial sensitivity by his fellow physician Robert Coles).

Percy's essay "A Theory of Language" (1981:288–327) contained a fascinating critique of transformational grammar. For one thing, he proposed an alternative that "is founded on a general semiotic," which he defined, in his personal triadic manner, as "the science of the relations between people and signs and things" (ibid. 307). In the same essay, however, he also fastened upon and reviewed "Peirce's theory of abduction . . . as a valid and possibly useful strategy in approaching language as a phenomenon" (ibid. 320). He went on to contrast this with Chomsky's views (cf. 1980:136, 139f.)—which Percy judged "odd and . . . wrongheaded"—of this pivotal Peircean concept (cf. Fann 1970; Eco and Sebeok 1983, passim).

Structural and functional triads, as against dyadic couplings, seemed to allure Percy (cf. "Toward a Triadic Theory of Meaning," 1981:159–88, 199). He was evidently inspired by Peirce's "radical theory of signs which undertook to give an account of those transactions in which symbols are used to name things and to assert sentences about things" (although he followed Morris as well as, with modifications, Ogden and Richards). He deemed Peirce's efforts to have been "heroic and unavailing" (ibid. 187), but the latter adjective surely no longer describes the state of this affair. Rather prematurely and, I think, uncritically, Percy grasped at an idea proposed by Norman Geschwind, who allegedly uncovered in the cortex the neurophysical substrate for the triadic structure of the symbolic act (ibid. 326f.).

Intriguing to me is the opposition Percy drew (alas, after Ludwig Binswanger's existential analysis school of thought, not its semiotically far more sophisticated primary source) between *Umwelt* and *Welt*: he held that the first-mentioned, constituting the environment of a sign-using (by which he meant "nonspeaking") creature, contrasts with that of the world of a speaking organism

in that "there are gaps in the former but none in the latter"
(1981:203). The former, he said (overlooking the social dimension
that informs such speechless vertebrate creatures as killer
whales, lions, wolves, the African Great Apes, etc.), "only no-
tices what is relevant biologically," as opposed to humans, who
dispose of the "entire horizon symbolically." "Gaps that cannot
be closed by perception and reason," he added, "are closed by
magic and myth."

In fact, all animals, man included, do have their *Umwelt* (corresponding to Husserl's [1913, Subsection 28] "my natural world-
about-me"), that is, an internal model of a universe (*Welt*) "as
is"; but humans have a *pair* of interlaced models, the hierarchically superior of which ("secondary modeling system" in Soviet
semiotic parlance, or approximately Husserl's "ideal worlds-
about-me") has an added syntactic component. This alone enables the construction of an infinity of possible worlds (Sebeok
1986a:13f. and 1988d). (I unearthed a letter from Percy, dated
April 19, 1982, asking: "Tom, could you refer me to a statement
in English of von Uexküll's notions about *Welt*, *Umwelt*, *Innen-
welt*, und so weiter?")

Except for Percy's above-named pre–twentieth–century antecedents, and for G. H. Mead (who, alas, died in 1931, eight
years before I began my studies at the University of Chicago),
this landscape is now beginning to edge into my lifespan's ken:
among his modern sources, besides my teacher Morris, I knew
Cassirer, Maritain, and Langer. The former two are, of course,
"U.S. semioticians" by co-optation only, and this in a double
sense: both Cassirer and Maritain were born and worked mostly
elsewhere, and semiotics was the central, long-term preoccupation of neither. These basics of their nearly contemporaneous
biographies notwithstanding, each spent years in his adoptive
country, where each wrote, or reworked, pieces of considerable
import about semiotic topics.

As to Cassirer, Hamburg (1949:81) had already called attention
to his anomalous position concerning semiotics, or rather, by
certain standards, the lack of it, in suggesting that

> whereas the import of symbolic media for the *intelligibility* of re-
> ality is certainly not a new discovery and has been realized by
> philosophers from Plato to Dewey, the thesis that a symbolic re-
> lation obtains for any possible (culturally encounterable) context

in which we perceive or observe a "world," expresses what is most distinctive in Cassirer's conception of philosophy.

A comparable extension of the philosophical concern beyond the cognitive to other types of signifying and modes of sign-usages has been advocated more recently by positivistic thinkers, who are intent upon establishing a more secure foundation for the discipline of semiotics [sic]. Unfortunately, Cassirer himself nowhere explicitly differentiates his own type of inquiry from the kind of sign-analyses carried on by, e.g., Carnap and Morris.

I should now like to impart fleeting personal glimpses of Cassirer, Maritain, and Langer, the briefest of anecdotes, really, since much more rounded sketches of each of them, by those who knew them better, are available, and their contributions, at least of the two men, have of late been pored over by many. Such vignettes scarcely portray semiotic theories or applications, but they illustrate the processes and illuminate the people who impel them.

On Friday, April 10, 1981, having barely landed in Hamburg, where I had flown to take part in the Third German Colloquium of the Deutsche Gesellschaft für Semiotik, I received a phone call from Klaus Oehler, the organizer, my friend and my host, asking me to accompany him immediately to a wreath-laying observance beneath a bust erected in memory of Ernst Cassirer. This piece of sculpture stands in the foyer of the University of Hamburg's *Philosophenturm* (the same building where my office was located during my visiting professorship in 1966). Cassirer had been Professor of Philosophy (that is, he had occupied the same chair that a foremost German specialist on Peirce, Oehler, now holds) at the University of Hamburg from 1919 until his dismissal and departure for Oxford and then to Göteborg in 1933. Those standing around at this ceremony included members of the German Society's board, plus a scattering of senior American semioticians. I was taken aback when I was unexpectedly called upon to make some commemorative remarks, but it turned out that, fragile as this link may have been, I was the only one present who had ever come face to face with Cassirer. This affair prompted a number of impromptu recollections.

I recounted that I had attended Cassirer's lecture "Structuralism in Modern Linguistics" in the fall of 1944. He delivered it, at Jakobson's invitation, before the Linguistic Circle of New York, at the New School for Social Research, some weeks before his sudden death, on April 13, 1945, on the campus of Columbia University. Cassirer and Jakobson had chanced to cross from Göteborg to New York on the same freighter, *Remmaren*, May 20-June 4, 1941. What I remember vividly even to this day is that these words, adapted from Genesis 27:22, pressed on my mind throughout Cassirer's lengthy lecture: "The voice is Cassirer's voice, but the hands are the hands of Jakobson." After his lecture, in the course of which Cassirer stressed the word *semiotics* (*sic*; already in 1923:18 he had written about "*Symbolik und Semiotik*), Jakobson and I, in the company of a few others, dined with him. The linguist and the philosopher each gave an animated account of their daily conversations aboard ship, and I concur that "these talks no doubt influenced [Cassirer's] interest and work on structuralism" (Krois 1987:30, 222f., n. 86). On the other hand, I never could find any trace of Cassirer's reciprocal influence on Jakobson's thinking. Between this odd couple, Jakobson, then at his cerebral pinnacle, was doubtless the dominant personality, although Cassirer in his younger days could be quite self-assured in public.

Not long after Hitler came to power, Cassirer's senior colleague, Uexküll, read a paper tinged with the classic semiotic flavor of his *Umwelt-Forschung* at a Hamburg Congress of Psychology, on a piece of research he had recently concluded on the cognitive maps of dogs. As these are constructed of and demarcated by scent-signs, he asserted that a dog takes everything located within its olfactory field for its property. Cassirer opened the discussion by recalling that Rousseau had said that the first man who erected a fence and declared "This is mine" should have been beaten to death. "After the lecture of Professor von Uexküll," he then expanded, "we know that wouldn't have sufficed. It was the first dog which should have been beaten to death." This bandying about territoriality was attacked in next morning's *Völkische Beobachter* by Herr Goebbels himself, under the punning headline: "Kötereien eines deutschen Professors!"

Cassirer—whom Uexküll, a profoundly original idealist yet empirical semiotician, deemed the greatest living German philosopher (see also Schilpp 1949, passim), one who shaped an entire generation of students in neo-Kantian ways of thinking— left for Vienna at the beginning of May 1933. In his *Essay on Man*, a condensed American reworking of his *Philosophy of Sym-*

bolic Forms, Cassirer's argument is avowedly, although meta-
phorically, based on Uexküll's biosemiotic principles extended
into the human world: man's acquisition of the "symbolic system," he contended, transforms the whole of our existence; accordingly, he designated man *animal symbolicum* (1944:26).

Uexküll's impact on the "American" Cassirer (1944:23f.) cannot be overestimated, even though a careful study of the writings
of the senior scholar will, I am convinced, show that Cassirer
(and generations of *his* followers) failed to grasp the fundamental
idea of his "functional circle" (a construct made up of signs
arranged in a negative feedback circuit), or his independently
innovative fashioning of a new pragmatic, sensory semiotics
(he also, more mysteriously, rechristened Uexküll "Johannes").
Readers can verify this adverse judgment for themselves by reading the works of Uexküll; for further general particulars on Cassirer, who is currently undergoing a kind of mini-revival in this
country, see Krois's splendid book (1987); and as to Cassirer's
brand of semiotics, see Verene's authoritative lemma (1986). The
secondary sources about Cassirer are staggering, as the nearly
500-page annotated bibliography by Eggers and Mayer (1988)
testifies. (An edition of Cassirer's complete works, including his
many unpublished remarks on semiotics, is in preparation under
Krois's direction.)

When L'Ecole Libre des hautes études was founded in New
York in February 1942, Jacques Maritain became its first vice-
president, then succeeded Henri Focillon in 1943 as its second
president. At the time, I was a graduate student at Princeton
University, but during the same year I also commuted to give a
course at the Free School and to audit many courses there. It
was there that I got acquainted with this amiable, admirable,
prolific, and many-sided *spirituel*.

Let it be avouched up front that the glaring omission of Maritain from the *Encyclopedic Dictionary of Semiotics* was in no way
due to editorial negligence, but to the last-minute dereliction of
the would-be author of the entry. Luckily, this embarrassing gap
has now in part been filled by Deely's paper "Semiotic in the
Thought of Jacques Maritain" (1986).

Although it is difficult for me to remember the exact circumstances over a span of forty-five years, I do recall the sexagen-
arian philosopher inviting me, with his customary graciousness,
to accompany him early one morning on a stroll from his apart-

ment at 30 Fifth Avenue through Washington Square en route
to Mass at (I think) St. Joseph's Church. He inquired about my
studies during that walk. I responded by telling him something
about my growing desire, instigated by Morris and reinforced
by Jakobson, to explore the doctrine of signs, especially verbal.
That appeared to engage his interest. He asked me if I had read
"Jean" Poinsot, a name that meant nothing to me. He then ad-
monished me—as I later recounted in a piece in the *Times* (Sebeok 1986b)—to peruse the *Cursus Philosophicus* of "the profound
doctor" Poinsot. I am sure I heard the name of Poinsot for the
first time in the streets of New York that day.

All this chitchat, however, meant little to me then. Its significance fell into place only some fifteen years afterwards, in
the context of my reading Maritain's "Language and the Theory
of Sign" (1957). Although I had casually studied some of Maritain's demanding philosophical books at the Aquinas-saturated
University of Chicago and in Princeton, I had no way of knowing
then that, increasingly since the late thirties, he had been pon-
dering about the theory of signs deeply, and that he was just
seeing through press an article, "Sign and Symbol" (1943), itself
a revised English version of a 1938 article, "Signe et symbole,"
which appeared in the *Revue Thomiste*, a journal then unfamiliar
to me. In 1956 he expanded this original French article, which
in turn was republished in English in a book edited by his friend
Dr. Ruth Nanda Anshen the following year. (For further particulars of this convoluted bibliographic yarn, see Deely 1986:
139.)

In 1957, I got hold of the Anshen compilation to consult an
article by Jakobson (Ch. IX) and was amazed to find Maritain's
piece "Language and the Theory of Sign" in the very same volume (Ch. V). It provided the key to our conversation back in
1943 (also dovetailing with another I had, in the 1970s, with the
Portuguese linguist José G. Herculano de Carvalho, likewise
about Poinsot—but that episode is extraterritorial). At the very
outset of his meditation, Maritain struck to the heart of semiotics'
epistemological mission:

> No problems are more complex or more fundamental to the con-
> cerns of man and civilization than those pertaining to the sign.
> The sign is relevant to the whole extent of knowledge and of
> human life; it is a universal instrument in the world of human

beings, like motion in the world of physical nature. . . . signs have
to do with all types of knowledge. They are of considerable importance in the psychic life of nonrational animals.

In a virtually unknown and scarcely obtainable follow-up to
his essay "Sign and Symbol" (which excuses the extended quotations below), he intriguingly dealt with a distinction between
what he called the logic-sign and the magic-sign, which "not
only makes men know things, it makes things be. It is an efficient
cause in itself; hence all the procedures of sympathetic magic"
(1956:62). Among other observations, he noted (ibid. 59):

Animals make use of signs; they live in a kind of magical world.
Biologically united to nature, they use signs which belong to a
psychic regime which is entirely imaginative. The intellect in
primitive man [in the sense of Lévi-Bruhl, who had been his
teacher] is of the same kind as ours. It may be even more alive
in him [the noble savage again, now situated in a semiotic context]
than in some more civilized people. But the question here is that
of its status and the existential conditions under which it operates.

Elegantly insinuating causality into the argument, Maritain then
adds (ibid. 61) that, in his opinion,

we here find ourselves confronted with a refraction in the world
of imagination or with a nocturnal deformation of the practical
sign as a quality of sign, or considered in order of the relationship
itself to signification. That is to say, in the order of formal causality,
wherein the sign is by its essence the vicar of the object. Let us
not forget that this relationship of sign to signified is in its own
order singularly clothed. The motion toward the sign or the image, St. Thomas says, after Aristotle, is identical with the motion
toward the object itself: *"Sic enim est unus et idem motus in imaginem
cum illo qui est in rem"* [So it is that movement toward an image
is one and the same with a movement toward the thing imaged
(trans. John Deely)].

Astonishingly, Maritain finally turns to Poe as well as to Mallarmé (ibid. 63) to sustain his argument that, when "the sense
of the dignity and mystery of words dissipates" in the course
of history, "poetry may possibly be tempted to return to magic
and to crave for 'the power of words.' . . . " He then finishes

with this paragraph, which movingly prefigures the sort of modern skepticism to which I intend to come back at the end of this essay:

> A curious and tragic phenomenon where something great and invaluable is looked for and missed, namely the genuine dignity of words, which refers to truth, not to power, and where by dint of refinement the civilized mind retrogresses to that magical notion of the sign which was normally in the child-like state of mankind yet is for mankind in its adult state, but a pathological symptom.

I have always been perplexed that Maritain remained, in America and elsewhere, essentially unrecognized outside his parochial tradition, and even within, as a serious contributor to semiotics (e.g., Hudson and Mancini 1987 make no mention of the fact). Jakobson, his erstwhile confrere at the Ecole Libre and his cocontributor to the Anshen volume, never cited him, either (as far as I know), in his lectures or in any of his writings. In October 1948, Maritain gave a series of lectures at the University of Chicago (these were to appear, in 1951, as *Man and the State*), and he returned for more lectures in 1956. Morris and Maritain apparently failed to meet, and neither seems to have been aware of the other (despite the fact that Morris had an article on mysticism in the ever–surprising Anshen volume [Ch. XI]).

The rich Dominican vein in semiotics (Deely 1988)—running from Aquinas, with his threefold emphasis on the *modi significandi*, the *suppositiones*, and the abundant use of semiotic concepts, to the vast elaboration and consolidation of the latter by Poinsot, and onwards to the New World through Maritain to John Deely and a very few others—has been insufficiently mined by the general semiotics community here or abroad. That mother lode of pure gold is far from exhausted. Now that I myself have turned septuagenarian, I wish I had grasped Maritain's credo sooner and better, for I have become convinced that the tradition in which he labored mutually harmonizes with and enriches what I have elsewhere termed the "major tradition" in semiotic studies (e.g., Sebeok 1988a:63).

Susanne Langer has long been regarded as the American "philosopher most influenced by Cassirer" (Krois 1987:12). Morris put her down, too, together with Wilbur M. Urban, as a "follower" of Cassirer (1946:189). She herself has told us as much: "In many years of work on the fundamental problems of art," she says she found Cassirer's philosophy of symbolic forms, however elusive, "indispensable; it served as a key to the most involved questions" (1962:58). In 1946 she translated Cassirer's little book *Language and Myth*, characterizing it in her preface as imbued with "a final flash of interpretive genius" (x).

After World War II, because of the easy accessibility of her attractive paperback *Philosophy in a New Key*, Langer became something of a campus celebrity, but her work, while never regarded as trivial, seldom seems to have been taken for more than "a point of departure" by such professionals as Morris (1946:50). Thus Charles S. Stevenson (in Henle 1958, Ch. 8) dissected her arguments, ascribing "a symbolic function to the arts," viz., music, "that other writers have often denied to them" (ibid. 202), and judged them implausible. Stevenson (1958) tried to show, more generally (as Abraham Kaplan did earlier, in 1943), "that the importance of the theory of signs to all the arts, rather than merely to those commonly classified as representational, is seriously open to question" (ibid. 210). Similar difficulties, he stated, "arise in *any* theory of signs" (ibid. 219), yet he concentrated his specific criticisms on Langer's views alone. Years later, Morris, while completely ignoring Langer's thesis, found Stevenson's arguments not to be compelling (1964:67).

In mid-May 1969, Langer was a featured speaker at a symposium held at the Smithsonian Institution, where I was also a guest. She read a paper titled "The Great Shift: Instinct to Intuition" (Eisenberg and Dillon 1971, Ch. 10), the indicant concept of which turned out to be how she thought language began—"with symbolic utterance" (ibid. 325), she asserted. She held that "speech is not derived from animal communication; its communicative and directive functions, though all-important today, are secondary; its primary function is the symbolic expression of intuitive cognition" (ibid. 326; she had made the same point in 1962, Ch. 2).

In other words, language evolved, in her view (though the terminology here is mine; cf. Sebeok 1986a:10–16), as a uniquely human modeling system. In spite of its unfortunate oral delivery—Langer was tiny, dwarfed behind the lectern, and practically inaudible because of the placement of the microphone—I was enthusiastic about her talk (some participating biologists, I gathered, were, by and large, not) and told her so at one of the social functions we attended afterwards.

It is fascinating to note lurking in this very quotation a clue *in nuce* to Langer's equivocal position in American semiotics. Her frame of reference was sharply at variance with views promoted by simplistic physicalist technicians (some of whom are mentioned in Demers 1988, but there are others, especially Lieberman 1988) who strove to pursue an illusory comparison of language and animal communication systems. On the other hand, it is in line with critical doubts expressed by thinkers as different as Popper (1972:121), Chomsky (e.g., 1980:229f.), and many others (e.g., Sebeok 1990). This kinship is not at all surprising, considering Langer's intellectual lineage or the pervasive (although riven) impact of the neo-Kantians, via Wilhelm von Humboldt and Peirce or, as the case may be, Uexküll and Cassirer, on the parties involved.

The only comments known to me specific to Langer's "properly" semiotic project, which is said to focus on "the foundations of the theory of signs from within a highly differentiated philosophical matrix," are Innis's (1985:87–89). Clearly, however, her work merits detailed reconsideration in the near future, especially in its implications for aesthetics. But Innis's allusion to Nelson Goodman's ideas of notationality and similarity, to which, he alleges, "Langer's position . . . bears remarkable similarities" (ibid. 89), was stated with quite a different emphasis by Goodman himself: "I am by no means unaware of contributions to symbol theory by such philosophers as Peirce, Cassirer, Morris, and Langer. . . . I reject one after another . . . the views common to much of the literature of aesthetics" (Goodman 1968:xiif.). In his *Ways of Worldmaking*, Goodman acknowledged congruences between his different ways of "worldmaking" and Cassirer's effort to distinguish different "symbolic forms," but he adds: "Cassirer undertakes the search through a cross-cultural study of the development of myth, religion, language, art, and science. My approach is rather through an analytic study of types and functions of symbols and symbol systems" (1978:6).

Incidentally notwithstanding that Goodman, like Burke and Goffman, has generally steered clear of being pinned down by the "semiotics" tag, he did agree to become a plenary speaker, with a speech called "Routes of Reference," at the Second (Vienna, 1979) Congress of the International Association for Semiotic Studies. For eminent figures such as these, then, as in the weird sisters' riddling reply to Macbeth's query "What is't you do?" semiotics remains "a deed without a name."

A common ingredient of our national experience with semiotics is what I hereby propose to call the *Jourdain factor*: "Good Heavens! For more than forty years I have been speaking prose without knowing it." This first intruded itself to my attention the week after Christmas 1964 in Montreal, where I addressed an international symposium on Communication and Social Interactions in Primates. I began by proposing "to evaluate the structure of primate communication . . . against the background of other sign systems used by man . . . and elsewhere in the animal kingdom," and went on to introduce the term *semiotics* to a highly diverse audience of scientists (Sebeok 1967:363).

After my presentation, a gentleman came up to me and said: "I have been doing semiotics for years without knowing it." After identifying himself as Harley C. Shands, M. D., he invited me to lunch, which I accepted, the more so since I recognized his name as the author of a book (Shands 1960) I had recently read with much enjoyment and admiration. A few years afterwards, Shands used the word *semiotics* freely (e.g., 1968:60–63). Over the next decade or so, Shands became a frequent contributor to semiotics journals, and he published three books in the Approaches to Semiotics series. (He also became the sixth person, and the first and thus far the only physician, to be elected president of the Semiotic Society of America; alas, he died two months after assuming that office.)

Medicine was among the most venerable semiotic specialties to be elaborated in Western tradition (Sebeok 1986a, Ch. 4), but American clinical practice had drifted away from the other branches of sign interpretation. Although Shands was a busy teaching and practicing cardiologist-turned-psychiatrist, the tempo of his writing increased amazingly once he felt that he had the well-defined, sympathetic readership in semiotic circles he told me he lacked among his fellow doctors (his contribution to the scientific status of psychiatry was best assessed in Bär 1975:81–105). In this country, Shands's output at the interface of his craft with semiotics was exceeded only by that of the San Francisco psychiatrist Jurgen Ruesch, M. D. (cf. ibid. 1975:107–37).

Baer's new book (1988) was followed closely by his article

"Semiotics and Medicine" (1989), and the two together now provide a uniquely rich summative treatise on medical semiotics, indispensable for further researches in the history of medicine, focusing on the notion of symptom and how the latter is situated in the theoretical frameworks of Peirce, Bühler, Freud, and Greimas. Baer likewise provides convenient access to "the new semiotic paradigm first articulated by Thure von Uexküll" (1988:31) and expands this to accommodate the pertinent achievements of medical anthropology. Thure von Uexküll, who is himself a prolific writer on medical subjects, summarized his own views (1986) on problems and possibilities of a science of semiotic medicine, utilizing a nimble systematic amalgam of Peirce's approach with those of Jakob von Uexküll. Baer further develops a "logic of life" and presents an application of the principles of medical semiotics to what he conceives of as the ontogenetic stages of life, or its transformations.

Staiano's expert technical treatise (1986) offers an insightful exploration of the semiotic dimensions of the symptom by way of a case study based on her extensive fieldwork among the Black Caribs of Belize—how signs of illness are produced and assigned meaning among these people.

The subtle influence of the personality and publications of Shands eventually had trains of unanticipated reverberations in my life: as our friendship thrived, I began to study the *Corpus Hippocraticum*, the writings of Galen, and semiopathology in general. The two of us coorganized a national symposium on medical semiotics at the Wenner-Gren Foundation's New York headquarters, and we later took part in an international conference, "Semiotics of Anxiety," convened by Thure von Uexküll and sponsored by the Werner-Reimers Foundation in Bad Homburg (Sebeok 1988a, Appendix I). (This was also attended by Baer and Staiano.) It was directly as a consequence of this symposium that I was stimulated to start developing the notion of the "Semiotic Self." This eventually led me back to a long-interrupted dialogue with Milton Singer (see Sebeok 1989 and below).

As, under Shands's guidance, I kept hacking away at the periphery of clinical semiotics, my interest in "vital signs" grew, in the course of time blossoming into a series of lectures under that same title for the Johns Hopkins Medical Institutions (October 1–November 24, 1985), and then another for the Schools of Medicine, Nursing, and Liberal Arts at Indiana University-Indianapolis (September 11–November 20, 1986). These visits brought me into close and (I trust, mutually) productive contacts with many white coats—physicians, nurses, laboratory scientists—from whom I learned a great deal about endosemiotic processes, the arts of subjective and objective interpretation (of "subjective" symptoms and "objective" signs), and the varieties of professional interaction in clinical settings with fellow professionals and their patients.

Some years later, I met another extraordinary physician, F. Eugene Yates, the UCLA medical engineer who coined the term *pharmacolinguistics*, later emended to *pharmacosemiotics*. Among his other foundational contributions to the problematic of self-organizing systems, Yates published two important companion articles explicating the transition from kinetics to kinematics, showing that "science has been permeated with semiotic issues all along" (1985:359; cf. [with Kugler] 1984).

Albert E. Scheflen, M. D., the late professor of psychiatry at Albert Einstein College of Medicine (who was closely associated with Birdwhistell, Bateson, Kendon, and, although less so, Shands [see, e.g., 1974], and in whose company I spent 1966–67 at the Center for Advanced Study in the Behavioral Sciences), the Washington neurologist Richard M. Restak, the San Francisco psychiatrist Frank A. Johnson, and the Chicago psychiatrist Philip Epstein are four more among an ever-increasing number of physicians, here and abroad, who are moving back toward their semiotic roots through various but converging paths. Scheflen (1967:118), reviewing the problems of psychoanalytic language in relation to semiotics, called for the making of "a glossary . . . to the methods of semiotics in general," which, to a degree, is a *fait accompli* some twenty years later. He also forecast that "a future task for semiotics is to gain an integrated picture of various types of context," and said that the opportunity to go about research in this way—that is, in pragmatics—has "provided the breakthrough to modern semiotics."

It should be noted that the most productive convergences may be with specialties other than psychiatry. These range from semiotic approaches to the genetic code, to the brain code, and particularly to the metabolic code and to the immune code (for details, cf. Sebeok 1990b). In addition, other health sciences are significantly linked to semiotics, none more so than nursing

(Donnelly 1987), a profession from which I have, in recent years, drawn half a dozen outstanding graduate students.

Yates's observation about the saturation of science by considerations of *significance* is amply borne out by writings (especially recent) of the distinguished American quantum physicist and cosmologist John Archibald Wheeler, a student of Bohr and Einstein. Wheeler's preoccupations with "physics as meaning" (1984:137) were clearly influenced by Peirce (personal communications). At the heart of Wheeler's "meaning-circuit model" of existence lies the postulation that semiosis in a community of observer-participants

> past, present and future is brought into being by the machinery of the world. However, it goes on to interpret this very world of past, present and future, of space and time and fields, to be— despite all its apparent continuity of imagination, immensity and independence from us—a construction of imagination and theory and troweled and plastered over countably many elementary quantum phenomena. . . . (From Wheeler's report to the New York Academy of Sciences, 1986)

In short, physics, in Wheeler's grand conception, is the offspring of semiosis, "even as meaning is the child of physics" (1984:123). The mathematician perhaps most preoccupied nowadys with the "physics of meaning," René Thom, recently coined the neologism "Semiophysics" to label the search for significant forms, and attempted to elaborate a "general theory of intelligibility" (1990:vii). Some other physicists, too, implicate semiotics in science, as does, for example, Giorgio Careri (1984:156), writing in the context of the idea of order:

> But let us not forget that science considers every instant in time to be identical to any other instant in time, and any point in space to be equal to every other point in space. It is astounding to discover how much of reality can be understood by this outlook. Still, our senses pick up other events, events that cannot be arranged within such a simple measurable framework, thanks merely to the yardstick and the clock. For these events, the signs are the most appropriate expressions, and so the correlations among these signs can be perceived as a sense of immeasurable order, for example, in the unity of a work of art.

The view that the practitioners of fundamental physics (or high-energy physics or particle physics) contrived a language— to be sure, one of great power and precision—in order to talk about the—or *a*—world, or that physics is therefore not the discovery of a ready-made world, is generally accepted by the community of physicists. This is at present but a marginally controversial view, which Muriel Rukeyser, in "The Speed of Darkness" (IX, St. 2), neatly summed up so: "The universe is made of stories, not of atoms."

This judgment was recently discussed in a provocative book, *Inventing Reality: Physics as Language*, by Bruce Gregory, who explains at the outset how he uses the word *language*: "I call any symbolic system for dealing with the world a language." "Physics *is* a language, a way of talking about the world," Gregory claims (1988:vi), or, as I would prefer to put it, it is a very special set of semiotic systems, their "vocabulary" consisting of particular domains of mathematics suited to Newtonian physics in terms of forces and changing positions with time, or with quantum mechanics.

Gregory's book was anticipated (among others) in the second edition of Johann Bernhard Stallo's *The Concepts and Theories of Modern Physics* (1881, 1884; my references are to Percy Bridgman's edition of 1960), where Stallo explained that his critique of contemporary physical theory was based on the sciences of "comparative linguistics" and of "the modern theory of cognition" (read: the sign-handling or semiotic propensity; ibid. 10). These led him to the conclusion that thought deals not with things as they are, or are suppposed to be, in themselves, "but with our mental representations of them." Thus they are *"symbolical"* (1960:156f.; italics in the source).

As far back as January 5, 1960, in his inaugural lecture for the Collège de France, Lévi-Strauss, as is well known, bounded the scope of anthropology so as to be tantamount to that portion of semiotics which linguistics hasn't arrogated for itself, a delimitation he amplified by affirming that, since human beings communicate through signs and symbols, for anthropology, which is a conversation among human beings, anything interposed between two objects is sign and symbol. In 1962, Margaret Mead alluded to "face-to-face communication, multi-modal and complex, within specified cultural and social settings" (Sebeok et al.

1972:285) after the ethnographer Weston La Barre's report at the same conference made much the same proposal (ibid. 191–220).

How these and other influential scholars budged semiotics in the two ensuing decades or so "from the periphery of exploratory anthropological concern into the core of the field," at least in Anglophone areas, was dexterously traced out by Umiker-Sebeok in a wide-ranging review article (1977). Although she felt that "efforts toward a creation of a semiotic theory of culture have just begun," a decade or so later Karp trenchantly confirmed that "the best recent work in anthropology" has moved "toward a semiotics of social situations" (1986:35).

In 1979, Umiker-Sebeok herself, jointly with Irene Portis Winner, coauthored and coedited a special issue of *Semiotica* (Vol. 27:1–290 and AtS 53), "Semiotics of Culture," along four complementary lines:

> (1) by the juxtaposition of the semiotics of nature with certain so-called distinctively human, or cultural semiotic processes; (2) by the historical or theoretical comparison of traditions of cultural semiotics emanating from Eastern and Western Europe and from North America; (3) by considering the semiotic implications of some of the central methodological issues with which the ethnosemiotician is concerned; and (4) by direct applications of a particular semiotic approach to specific cultural texts from both primitive and modern societies. (Ibid. 1)

Singer, alluding in his important book to the "tilt of culture theory to semiotics" (1984a:48–52), argues for a *semiotic anthropology*. While the phrase *semiotic ethnography* (Herzfeld 1986; Karp 1986:31) is found here and there, the neologism *ethnosemiotics* eventually began to prevail (MacCannell and MacCannell 1982, Ch. 4), although this composite, too, soon acquired multiple meanings: it is now sometimes used as a term for the investigation of indigenous systems of meaning, but occasionally also in reference to the decoding of indigenous systems (Herzfeld 1987:199). Competing expressions, such as *symbolic anthropology* or *semantic anthropology*, are sporadically advocated, but other American anthropologists, such as Mertz, Parmentier, and their associates (1985), are content to continue, in clean-cut fashion, to employ *semiotics* without any redundant qualifying prefix. (A special issue of *Semiotica*, titled "Signs in the Field: Semiotic Perspectives on Ethnography," edited by Michael Herzfeld and with an important afterword by James W. Fernandez, was published in Vol. 46:99–330, in 1983.) Fernandez (pp. 323f.) there answers his own question, "Why semiotics?" by positing semiosis "at the center of the human condition," because it deals with intelligibility, which, he says, always involves a negotiation between the self and the other.

Singer is one of the few American anthropologists of his generation to have enjoyed technical training in semiotics: he wrote his dissertation under Carnap on the history of the formalization of logic and mathematics just at the time Morris's and Carnap's *Encyclopedia* monographs (see below) were in galley, and he also served, in 1938–39, as Bertrand Russell's research and teaching assistant in his Chicago seminar "Words and Facts" (published, in 1940, as *An Inquiry into Meaning and Truth*). He began to make use of his training in 1951, when he joined Robert Redfield in a cooperative interdisciplinary project to compare civilizations. His reassessment of Lévi-Strauss's "structuralism" and Radcliffe-Brown's "structural functionalism" (1984b) culminated in a theory of cultural symbolism based on a Peircean semiotic rather than a Saussurean semiology. The application of Peirce's doctrine of signs to an anthropological theory of cultural symbolism generated a semiotics of American identity, a semiotics of Indian identity, and, more generally, a semiotic anthropology. The recent tribute, edited by Lee and Urban (1989), displays a range of studies, especially on the theme of the "semiotics of identity," showing Singer's influence on many of his colleagues and students.

Although in this country archeology has lagged behind the rest of anthropology in receptiveness to semiotic models (for a general survey, see Gardin 1988), this has changed of late: in the fall of 1987, a multinational conference, "Symbolic, Structural, and Semiotic Approaches in Archeology," was convened at Indiana University, the proceedings of which are now in preparation (for publication envisaged in 1991). By contrast, folklore, including especially "folkloristics" (McDowell 1986), is, and has been for some time, richly permeated with semiotic ideas and practices, boasting of a literature far too extensive to cite. (Note that a prominent folklorist, Richard Bauman, was elected presi-

dent of the Semiotic Society of America for 1981, and see his
presidential address [1982]; further, consult Stoeltje and Bauman
[1988] on the semiotics of folkloric performance.)

The somewhat nebulous concepts of "popular culture" and
"traditional culture" are usually defined in complementarity to
"elite culture," or simply subsumed under "culture" in general
(Winner 1987). These terms, however, are not at all replacements
for *folklore*; in fact, they are grossly misleading, on account of
their association with "the products of the entertainment in-
dustry, quick fashion-building and other phenomena seen rather
as opposite to rather than part of" the former (Honko 1990:7).
This notwithstanding, their study has also been penetrated by
semiotic notions, while once again the Jourdain factor, as cited
by Berger (1987:359f.) in this very context, reared its head.

It is likewise intriguing to follow the latter-day convergence
(ambiguous, to be sure) of semiotics with such kindred, but
arguably more conservative, disciplines as geography, practitioners of which, we learn, acknowledge the contributions of
Cassirer, Langer, and other figures familiar to us (Foote 1985:
164); and with history, which, we are told, provides "the materials and the evidence for a possible doctrine of signs that,
rather than close in on itself, opens out toward the infinite"
(Williams 1985:321). Articles such as "Semiotics and History,"
by Haidu, and "Semiotics or History," by Marike Finlay-Pelinski,
began appearing in *Semiotica* in 1982 (a second special issue on
semiotics and history will also soon appear, as Vol. 83, Nos. 3–
4 (1991), the first having occupied Vol. 59:209–385).

An uncommon example of "a semiotic history" is Nye's (1983)
reconstruction of Thomas A. Edison, amounting to a semiotic
critique of conventional biographical methodology. "The first
principles of historical semiotics," Nye (20) tells his readers,
must be cognizant of the facts that "(1) documents produced in
the past, no matter how complete, render discontinuous tran-
scriptions of their objects of signification," and (2) the "meaning
of any transcription is not a fixed solidity, but varies according
to which code it is understood to be a part of." Too, semiotics,
Dean MacCannell comfortingly averred in 1986 (195), "provides
the only logical base for rebuilding the field of sociology."

In connection with ethnology, sociology, and history, Hymes
(1978:403f.) thought that "it is difficult or impossible for the semiotic work to interact fruitfully with [these] particular disci-

plines," but if so, "that would be unfortunate for both sides of the relationship." He further conjectured that "the semiotic formulations have something to offer the particular disciplines in freshness of perspective. . . . "

Eco's celebrated observation about semiotics being the discipline studying everything which can be used in order to lie is paralleled on the level of international relations by the Goffmanesque works of Jervis. In his fascinating 1970 book, Jervis laid the foundations for a thoroughly semiotic theory of deception as an integral part of international relations, and went on to apply the concepts and principles he developed to nuclear politics, including strategic planning (1987). The relevance of semiotics for war-and-peace studies is manifest from Jervis's intricate political analyses, which can, of course, be equally useful on national or parochial levels.

Semiotics and its various techniques are necessarily implicated in lying or deceit, as becomes amply clear from such recent books on the subject as Bowyer's *Cheating: Deception in War & Magic, Games & Sports, Sex & Religion, Business & Con Games, Politics & Espionage, Art & Science* (1980), Ekman's *Telling Lies: Clues to Deceit in the Marketplace, Politics, and Marriage* (1985), and a collection of papers on human and nonhuman deceit (Mitchell and Thompson, 1986). I have also discussed the topic in my "Notes on Lying and Prevarication" (terms which aren't synonymous for me; Sebeok 1985:143–47). To give just a single technical example, in dock pilferage by gangs of longshoremen, one holdsman is designated "the signaller": "The signaller's hand signals, as incomprehensible to the outsider as a tick-man's telegraph, allow him to work as effectively at pilfering as at unloading" (Mars 1982: 104). In the juicy argot of the American underworld, the noun *sign* refers to evidence of moonshine traffic, and the verb *to signify* (sometimes *to wedge*) refers in street usage to the act of manipulating people by playing the opinion of one person in authority against the opinion of another.

Considering the medical provenance of Western semiotics, Dr. Shands's "Aha!" response was hardly astonishing to me. More so perhaps was Mary Douglas's acknowledgment of the Jourdain factor in the course of her very interesting discourse on the future of semiotics (1982). As this eminent social anthropologist reminds us in her speculative essay (prepared, as a matter of fact, under Harley Shands's instigation),

The future of semiotics will not be confined to the contribution
it can make to academic fields where the interpretation of meaning
is the daily routine. There are grounds for thinking that several
branches of philosophy and cognitive psychology would benefit
from a more theoretical and sustained input from semiotics than
they receive so far. (1982:201f.)

Douglas elaborates upon this point by way of an example from
the field of economics, inviting us to consider the distinction
between semiotic analysis of ratiocination and rational behavior
according to utility theory. She thereby shows how, in the
growth of a long, slow wave of "criticism of the fundamental
assumptions of Western thought, semiotics has a unique part to
contribute."

I was, however, taken quite unawares by Sidney J. Levy's
opening remarks in his elegant keynote lecture at the First International Conference on Marketing and Semiotics (Umiker-
Sebeok 1987:13–20), in the course of which he said: "If I am a
semiotician, I discover that with the surprise of the fellow who
was delighted to learn that he spoke prose" (ibid. 13). In his
conclusion, he spoke of an intellectual voyage, a "venture on
the Semiotic Seas" (ibid. 19), evoking an image of semiotics as
"an adventure" on which our good neighbors from elsewhere
like to embark. Indeed, it was Barthes (1988:4) who, in a 1974
lecture given in Italy, conjured up the same image when he told
his audience that, for him, semiotics was neither a cause nor a
science, discipline, school, or movement, but "an adventure."
Levy, whose J. L. Kellogg Graduate School of Management at
Northwestern University boldly hosted this conference, is one
of the world's authorities on marketing.

If, as some economists do, we picture the human mind as a
"consuming organ" (Schelling 1984:343), we must ask: *what* does
the mind consume? The principal lesson that was driven home
by this conference was that it is signs that the mind consumes,
and the realization that marketing (including advertising, product design, and other adjunct endeavors) is focally concerned
with bartering not "objects" but the entities we familiarly call
signs and symbols (cf. Mick's 1986 survey; see also id. 1988). So
can one consider marketing a species of professionally applied
semiotics?

But just what constitutes "applied semiotics"? As far as I

know, this construction originated with Charles Morris, who
wrote (1946:220): "The application of semiotic as an instrument
may be called *applied semiotic*." Semiotic(s) as a whole, he proposed, can be pure, descriptive, or applied; the latter, he specified, "utilizes knowledge about signs for the accomplishment
of various purposes" (ibid. 353f.). This was one in an array of
strategic trichotomies posited by Morris. These became popular
in other fields (including marketing) where such distinctions
were severally turned to practical account, but commonly in a
rather mechanical fashion. Rulon Wells (1967:105) shares the
widespread disbelief about the feasibility of these abstractions,
but he notes that "something like them has actually been done
in practice. Perhaps, though," he adds, "what has been done
in practice is not to abstract perfectly, but to focus."

A version was incorporated into the anonymous (but actually
authored by a Berlin colleague, Roland Posner) programmatic
introduction to the initial issue (1979) of the journal of the
Deutsche Gesellschaft für Semiotik, which devoted a long paragraph explicating "Angewandte" or applied "Semiotik," as opposed to "Allgemeine," or general, and "Vergleichende," or
comparative, semiotics. The former is made to cover an enormous expanse of topics, which, in sum, seems to comprehend
much of what Morris would rather, I suspect, have included
under descriptive semiotics, that is, what the majority of those
of us who profess to do journeyman semioticians' work actually
do. One can't be sure, because Morris's categories are, in this
respect, not at all clear-cut.

A more refined schema appeared in the inaugural issue of the
American Journal of Semiotics (1981) by the Polish logical semiotician Jerzy Pelc, who consecrates over four pages (27–31) to applied semiotics. This comes into play, he says, "when the method
of interpretation is applied not to a single thing, event or phenomenon but to a certain complex thereof, a set forming a whole,
particularly a systematized whole" (ibid. 27). His first example
is literature. Although his tripartition—theoretical, methodological, and applied—differs somewhat from the Germans' as
well as Morris's, this illustration, indeed all his examples, are
virtually the same as the ones enumerated by the former.

In recent months, Jean Umiker-Sebeok undertook the preparation of an *American Directory of Applied Semiotics*, covering both
Western hemispheres and, eventually, the Old World. Her proj-

ect, which is in the final data-gathering stage, "seeks information about individuals, centers, businesses, and projects . . . which utilize the concepts, methods, and empirical data of semiotics for professional problem-solving in business, education, law, or medicine." Judging by the great number of responses returned thus far (summer of 1989), of the last four substantives "education" seems to have been widely and broadly interpreted by recipients of her questionnaire to embrace not only pedagogy as such but a wide variety of artistic and humanistic subjects normally taught in universities.

To put it mildly, then, there is little consensus about what constitutes applied semiotics. There are similar difficulties, of course, with "applied anthropology" and "applied linguistics" (to say nothing, *mutatis mutandis*, of applied physics, chemistry, biology, and the like), even though there are independent U.S. learned societies to accommodate the devotees of several. Their fields of application are generally domain-oriented, although *which* domains are matters of taste.

In applied anthropology, the fields of practice are most often educational, medical, or urban; in applied linguistics, the teaching and learning of foreign languages or of the mother tongue are central but sometimes also include a host of so-called hyphenated fields, such as psycholinguistics, sociolinguistics, clinical linguistics, as well as the planning of national language policy. (To complicate matters, I was recently asked to contribute an article on semiotics to an American anthology of applied linguistics on the editor's bizarre presumption that the former was a branch of the latter.)

At the 1986 meeting of the Semiotic Society of America, we organized a round-table discussion, "Presenting Semiotics to the Professions." The fields of application represented were business, education (both secondary and postsecondary), government, mass communications, medicine, nursing, law, and museology. The content of applied semiotics, it seems, emerged there by inductive enumeration of topics rather than by abstract definition.

The circumstances in which the products of application are manifested, at least in the United States, are usually threefold: policy, action, and, most of all, information (in the vulgar sense)—that is, semiotics as a "resource." Accordingly, I have asked myself, as others wanted to know: can any work that I have done be considered unambiguously *applied* semiotics? Why so?

To begin with, I exclude from this rubric the entirety of my various semiotically informed writings on animal communication and in text analysis, such as on the sacred discourse and *einfache Formen* (in the expression of André Jolles) of an ethnic group I studied in the Soviet Union; a logos of Herodotus's *History*; a film by Spielberg; the Sherlock Holmes canon; the last words of President Grant; experimentation (however crude) with forms of expression other than the monograph or essay to convey scientific knowledge (in dialogue, say, or in verse); analysis of particular sign phases, such as "icon," "index," "symptom," or "fetish"; Japanese monkey performances; and modes of artistic expression in the world of animals. I would also hesitate to include under applied semiotics the "to-be-continued" series of compilations on aspects of "unverbal" semiosis Jean Umiker-Sebeok and I jointly launched about fifteen years ago, covering thus far speech surrogates, such as drum and whistle systems (1976), aboriginal sign languages of the Americas and Australia (1978), and monastic sign languages (1987).

There remains only one assignment I have undertaken which meets all three of *my* criteria for applied semiotics, to wit, a mingling of *policy* and *action* with *information*. This is the piece of research reported in Sebeok 1984a (an emended version of which appears in Sebeok 1986a as "Pandora's Box in Aftertimes"). The *policy* aspect has been under consideration by the U.S. government, under the direction of the Department of Energy, for more than two decades: how to dispose permanently of high-level radioactive wastes? However, their successful isolation over long periods of time does raise a subsidiary set of problems, such as how to ensure not only that the wastes remain unaltered by natural events and processes, but also that they be unaffected by future activities of humans, whether direct (say, a breach of the depository facility with a concomitant release of waste) or indirect (i.e., offsite), not to mention war, terrorism, or sabotage. Any action of this nature would have a significant potential for increasing the radiological dose to our descendants from the repository. To deal with this potential, a Human Interference Task Force, with a wide range of expertise among the members (political science, sociology, environmental sciences, law, nuclear regulation, nuclear engineering, anthropology and

archeology, psychology, public policy, materials science, clima-
tology, to name only some), was created by the Department of
Energy in 1980, and I was soon co-opted to represent semiotics.

I have often been asked why I agreed to serve on this Task
Force. There were three principal considerations that played a
part in my decision to do so.

• First, being the father of three daughters, I have a personal
stake in the information-transfer system of chemically coded
messages that determine the course which the development of
future generations of organisms is to pursue.

• Second, as I contemplated the historiography of semiotics
(including linguistics), I realized that all previous efforts have
concentrated on either diachronic tasks (historical linguistics,
ritualization, etc.) or synchronic tasks (communication and signification, etc.) (Sebeok 1988a, Ch. 2), but never before on the
shape of things to come. A stint in futurology offered something
of a challenge.

• Third, from the outset, I looked at this exercise as being one
indubitably in "applied" semiotics. Some important implications
of this third criterion were severally foregrounded by the ten
other contributors to a special issue of the German journal *Zeitschrift für Semiotik* (Posner 1984, Sebeok 1990d) devoted to com-
municating with future generations.

As to action, this is how matters stood in 1989: a comprehensive budget bill was enacted not long ago by Congress, designating southern Nevada's Yucca Mountain site as the prime
candidate to host a site for the deposit of spent nuclear fuel.
Further studies of this site, at a cost estimated at far in excess
of a billion dollars, are provided for in the current legislation.
Such study should include further investigation of ways and
means to implement the prevention of human interference with
the burial. A Nuclear Waste Technical Review Board—a quite
prosaic version of the "Atomic Priesthood" (Sebeok 1984a:24)
which I proposed in my original report—is now established and
charged, among other mandated responsibilities, with the mon-
itoring of site-characterization activities.

Before leaving for now the topic of applied semiotics, let me
divulge one wholly unforeseen turn of events, making semiotic
application doubly sure: the MoMing dance company, directed
by the Washington choreographer Liz Lerman for the Dance

Exchange, advertised among its coming attractions for 1987 twin performances titled "Atomic Priests: Coming Attractions" and "Atomic Priests: The Future." Developed by Lerman and the company, the libretto is in large part based, "with music by Mike Vargas and [the] Henry Purcell," on my "Communication Measures to Bridge Ten Millennia." Michael Silverstein of the University of Chicago, who chanced to see this piece enacted, wrote me that "it was quite a moving experience." A review in the *Village Voice* characterized it as "a chilling and engrossing piece, made even more so by the vivid performing of everyone involved"; another reviewer, in the February 1988 issue of *Dance*, thought that it looked

> like a post-holocaust *Star Trek*. The people we see range from their twenties through their eighties and evolve in occupation from business-suited twentieth-century bureaucrats to mysterious elders executing rituals in a clearing in the distant future. Pictographs intending to warn serve mainly to tantalize, and priestesses distribute a deadly host. The elders . . . teach the young survivors to dance by guiding their bodies, as a Balinese teacher would.

Thus far, I have been able to view the show only on tape (supplied by courtesy of Lerman). I found it to be a pair of soberly satirical pieces, cleverly blending more or less verbatim citations from my text with original music and dance, rendered with wit and gentle humor.

Morris (1946:219, 353), following a terminology suggested by Carnap (1942:12–15), contrasted applied semiotics with two other kinds, the former named "pure." Morris went on to explain that pure semiotic(s)—an expression seldom encountered nowadays—"elaborates a language to talk about signs. . . . " If anyone qualifies as having spun pure semiotics, it is surely Charles Sanders Peirce, for whom the notion of applied semiotics (at least in the senses illustrated above) would perhaps have appeared absurd, if only because "there is no absolutely definitive semiotic analysis of anything" (cf. Ransdell 1986:679). And if Emperor Augustus was right in designating a "classic" by the quantitative hundred-year-survival rule, Peirce has just about made it. In Pope's compressed couplet, that rule reads:

"Who lasts a century can have no flaw, / I hold that wit a classic, good in law."

In 1936, Alfred North Whitehead expressed his belief to Charles Hartshorne that "the effective founders of the American Renaissance are Charles Peirce and William James. Of these men, W.J. is the analogue to Plato, and C.P. to Aristotle, though the time-order does not correspond, and the analogy must not be pressed too far" (Lowe 1990:2:345). Joseph Lancaster Brent III, in the manuscript of his life of Peirce (1960; revised in 1990, Ch. 1, p. 6), characterizes him as "one of the most brilliant and possibly the most brilliant and original mind[s] of his place and time. . . ." Echoing this impression, Bertrand Russell (1959:276) wrote of Peirce that "beyond doubt . . . he was one of the most original minds of the later nineteenth century, and certainly the greatest American thinker ever." American semioticians all but universally, and foreign semioticians increasingly, espouse Peirce as their undisputed *fons et origo* of the doctrine of signs. Max Fisch (in his introduction to Sebeok and Umiker-Sebeok 1980:7) has called Peirce "the most versatile intellect that the Americas have so far produced," but his student, Joseph Jastrow (1930:135), recognized Peirce, already in the early 1880s, as "one of the most exceptional minds that America has produced. . . . Peirce's lectures impressed the student as an amazing exhibition of mental ability." He is also said to be "the most original mind that the United States has yet produced," "more nearly like Leibniz than any other American philosopher with respect to the range, variety, and ingenuity of his intellectual contributions," and "the founder of what is still this country's most distinctive philosophical movement" (Nagel 1982:303). In short, the Peircean paradigm is now firmly regnant. Peirce, in a letter to a friend composed November 15, 1904, wrote this in part of himself:

> I am by nature most inaccurate. . . . I am quite exceptional for almost complete deficiency of imaginative power, & whatever I amount to is due to two things, first, a perseverance like that of a wasp in a bottle & 2nd to the happy accident that I early hit upon a METHOD of thinking, which any intelligent person could master, and which I am so far from having exhausted it that I leave it about where I found it. (Brent 1960:181; 1991)

Lamentably, Peirce has lately become a rather conspicuous figure, besides genuine scholarship, of hagiography. Like Aristotle, he has a learned organization named in his honor, with a journal now (1990) in its twenty-sixth volume: the *Transactions of the Charles S. Peirce Society*. Subtitled *A Quarterly Journal in American Philosophy*, it publishes many articles on semiotic—or, to be precise, "semeiotic"—topics. However, the only consequential American biography of Peirce thus far remains Brent's all-too-long-unpublished but capital UCLA dissertation, dated 1960, on which Conkin's published biographical sketch (1976: 193–265) and other brief accounts are also based; Brent 1991 is a revised and updated version of his dissertation (for a recent attempt at a biography in German, see Walther 1989).

Then there is the curious incident of *The Maltese Falcon*. In this beloved Dashiell Hammett novel (although not in the perhaps even more beloved movie), there is embedded a parable about a man named Flitcraft, who comes to live under an assumed name: Charles Pierce. In a lengthy commentary about the Flitcraft passage, Steven Marcus (1974:xviii-xix, n.) says: "It can hardly be an accident that the new name that Hammett gives to Flitcraft is that of an American philosopher—with two vowels reversed—who was deeply involved in just such speculations" about

how despite everything we have learned and everything we know, men will persist in behaving and trying to behave sanely, rationally, sensibly, and responsibly. And we will continue to persist even when we know that there is no logical or metaphysical, no discoverable or demonstrable reason for doing so.

If Marcus is right, and the near-congruence in names is not just a coincidence, Hammett must, however implausibly, have read Peirce before 1930!

Here, a couple of terminological observations need to be interpolated. Notoriously, and possibly ruinously, semioticians— or *semiotists* in Rauch's rendering (e.g., 1987), and in Safire's— haven't thus far been able to reach unanimity as to their own self-designation or in firmly naming their field of endeavor. Thus dedicated Peirceans are proud to identify their totem group by their unyielding use of *semeiotic*; Fisch (1986:322) even stresses that Peirce "never" used *semiotics*, although he evidently did compose that very lemma *sub voce* in the *Century Dictionary*. Morris consistently used *semiotic* but permitted the publication of his collected writings on the theory of signs in a series titled Approaches to Semiotics (see my terminological note to Morris 1971:9–10). In like manner, Saussureans generally display their colors under the banner (when in English) of *semiology*, even though the Swiss master's better-suited—although for obscure reasons unsuccessful—coinage *signologie* (Engler 1968:46) was also available (cf. Lady Welby's *significs*; for other *signum*-derived words, see Sebeok 1987d).

The denotation of each of these academic jargon terms is, no matter how leaky, the "same." But each harks back to a different tradition and, being overburdened by complex emotional resonance, carries different connotations. Dialectal divisions of this nature are confusing for the public, of course, and have impelled some practitioners to concoct (even as recently as in Landowski 1988:79f.), and then attempt to impose, *post hoc* divergences in denotation. *Semiotics*, with its foreign-language cognates, now appears to have the best chance for survival (see further Sebeok 1985, Ch. 2). (It is incongruous that Culler [1986, Ch. 4], for example, heads the section of his book that deals with Saussure's *semiology* "Semiotics: The Saussurean Legacy.")

Another seemingly homely case in point may be adduced from a study of such an ordinary and extensively studied nonverbal social act as a handshake (Hall and Hall 1983). As these authors noted in their fascinating analysis, the semiotic aspects of the physical execution of shaking hands, which is in fact an exceedingly complex interaction ritual in humans (though it occurs in animals too), has acquired at least these labels: tie signs; emblems; tactile modes; collapses, openers, and closures; tactile holds; metasignals; access rituals; and greeting behavior. Plainly, the Edifice of Semiotics is still as badly in need of a housecleaning as it was in 1975 (Sebeok 1985:156–64), when I first called attention to this nomenclatural clutter.

The domestic and European secondary literature about Peirce and his voluminous writings, published or still in manuscript, not only is staggering but continues to accrete at almost an exponential rate. Much of this literature appears to be exegetical in character, and—since Peirce was a polymath of extraordinary scope—is but tangential to semiotics in a superficial sense. I say "in a superficial sense" because Peirce's monumental opus is topically fragmentable—in spite of its long span of composition between 1857 and his death—only at the risk of losing vital affinities within the whole, and with its semiotic core. In the septuagenarian Peirce's own words of self-appraisal, quoted from a lengthy letter to Lady Welby (December 23, 1908),

> it has never been in my power to study anything,—mathematics, ethics, metaphysics, gravitation, thermodynamics, optics, chemistry, comparative anatomy, astronomy, psychology, phonetics, economic, the history of science, whist, men and women, wine, metrology, except as a study of semeiotic. . . .

Russell (1959:277) recognized that "Peirce had a thorough grasp not only of mathematics and of the scientific developments of his time, but also of the histories of science and philosophy." Carolyn Eisele has drummed into many of us a different lesson: that, for one thing, "the key to understanding the connections between his diverse undertakings was his mathematics" (Dauben 1982:314). Yet his mathematics "contains much material of the first importance for semiotic" (Ransdell 1986:674). Indeed, as Esposito (1980:ixf.) correctly observed, Peirce "was to a considerable degree a *systematic* philosopher," who conceived of his calling as "an ensemble of investigations." The entire ensemble is subsumed within the framework of a tripartite "General Semeiotic" (consisting of speculative—i.e., philosophical, theoretical, or "pure"—grammar, critical logic, and speculative or philosophical rhetoric, sometimes dubbed methodeutic).

In recent times, cis-Atlantic books and essays tangent to semiotics tend to be reverentially peppered with citations from Peirce. Like the little old lady from Jersey City who went to see *Hamlet* on Broadway for the first time and reported her disappointment because the play seemed to her to be little more than a string of hackneyed expressions, these countless Peircean *obiter dicta*— my all-time favorite being the one about "this universe is perfused with signs, if it is not composed exclusively of signs"— delude by virtue of their easy conversance.

Take as one example his now well-nigh ubiquitous icon/index/

64   Thomas A. Sebeok

symbol trichotomy. As I have previously insisted (Sebeok
1988a:110f.), such categories "can scarcely be understood when
wrenched out of the total context of [Peirce's] semiotic." For they
are but one set among a veritable cascade of triadic relational
structures subsumed under firstness/secondness/thirdness:
qualisign/sinsign/legisign (cf. Short 1982), rheme/dicisign/ar-
gument, I/it/thou (cf. Singer 1984a), abduction/induction/de-
duction (cf. Eco and Sebeok 1983), mind/matter/God, language/
expression/meaning, sign/object/interpretant (the latter further
cloven into immediate/dynamical/final) (Sebeok, in Deely et al.
1986:35–42), possibility/actuality/necessity, unity/plurality/to-
tality, and so (with many variations) on and on.

Firstness/secondness/thirdness is Peirce's most cardinal underlying trichotomy; from this flows his pragmatic definition of
meaning—the conceivable results of any conception. In a vivid
illustration, we can say, for example, that an infant early on
becomes aware of an entity, which is its caretaker, viz., its
mother. The initial "meaning" of mother is milk, warmth, or
the like. In this instance, the neonate embodies firstness, the
mother secondness, and milk, warmth, etc., thirdness. The fullest, most detailed, and critical discussion thus far of the entire
range of Peirce's semiotic trichotomies will be found in a monograph (1987–88) by the learned Toronto philosopher Savan.

At the core of Peirce's sem(e)iotic one finds not at all, as is
sometimes polemically claimed, the sign but sem(e)iosis (cf. Fisch
1986:330; roughly, so also later in Morris, Eco, Rey, Landowski,
etc.), unless the sign has been antecedently defined in terms of
sem(e)iosis. But then the essence of his notion of sem(e)iosis
involves irreducible tripartitions in relationship or action, which
require a comprehensive rather than a piecemeal appreciation
of such categories.

Although there is no substitute for reading Peirce's texts in
the original, there now exist several excellent accounts of Peirce's
doctrine of signs, or major aspects of it, among which I would
single out these from North America: Tursman (1987), Savan
(1987–88), Short (1982, 1988), and Ransdell (1986 and especially
1991); for the beginner, Sebeok and Umiker-Sebeok (1980) might
also be helpful (and see passim Sebeok 1981b, 1985, 1986a, and
1988a.) Furthermore, both Semiotica (19:157–366, 1977) and the
American Journal of Semiotics (2:1–263, 1983) have dedicated entire
issues and more to Peirce's sem(e)iotic.

Recognition and advocacy, as far back as 1952, of Peirce's pioneering role in structural linguistic analysis, especially in the domain of linguistic operations with meanings, was among Jakobson's many great merits. While Jakobson continued to dwell on this, and to give perspicacious glimpses of Peirce as a genuine forerunner of modern linguistics, he left elaboration of his insights to some of his students and others. Accordingly, this topic became the theme of my 1975 presidential address to the Linguistic Society of America. At least two books by other American scholars (Shapiro 1983 and Pharies 1985) later took the subject up in more, yet still far from exhausting, detail. The fullest treatment to date is Joëlle Réthoré's immense University of Perpignan dissertation *La linguistique sémiotique de Charles S. Peirce*, soon to appear, it is hoped, in an English edition in the United States.

In 1878, in his famous "How to Make Our Ideas Clear," Peirce began to develop his "pragmaticist" view of meaning, according to which the meaning of a message is the behavior it induces, its truth-value depending on whether that behavior has consequences beneficial to the interpreter. It turns out that Peirce's view of meaning is in excellent conformity with the theory of evolution, particularly in regard to the linkage between the individual and his *Umwelt*. In my opinion (and in this area, as in theology, there are only opinions), his is the only satisfactory theory of meaning in the murky history of semantics so far.

Peirce's theory of truth, which reaffirms how thoroughly semiotic his conception is, was articulated in MS 283 (a copy of which was kindly provided to me by Nathan Houser). This passage was evidently composed in 1906, and I reproduce it at some length not only because it sheds light on several aspects of Peirce's thought but because it so keenly captures the flavor of his language and argumentation:

Mr. Ferdinand C. S. Schiller [the British pragmatist philosopher] informs us that he and [William] James have made up their minds that the truth is simply the satisfactory. No doubt; but to say "satisfactory" is not to complete any predicate whatever. Satisfactory to what end?

That the truth is the correspondence of a representation with its object is, as Kant says, merely the nominal definition of it. The truth belongs exclusively to propositions. A proposition has a subject (or set of subjects) and a predicate. The subject is a sign;

the predicate is a sign; and the proposition is a sign that the predicate is a sign of that of which the subject is a sign. If it be so, it is true. But what does this correspondence, or reference of the sign, to its object, consist in? The pragmaticist answers this question as follows. Suppose, he says, that the angel Gabriel were to descend and communicate to me the answer to this riddle from the breast of omniscience. Is this supposable; or does it involve an essential absurdity to suppose the answer to be brought to human intelligence? In the latter case, "truth," in this sense, is a useless word, which never can express a human thought. It is real, if you will, it belongs to that universe entirely disconnected from human intelligence which knows the world of utter non-sense. Having no use for this meaning of the word "truth," we had better use the word in another sense presently to be described. But if, on the other hand, it be conceivable that the secret should be disclosed to human intelligence, it will be something that thought can compass. Now thought is of the nature of a sign. In that case, then, if we can find out the right method of thinking and can follow it out,—the right method of transforming signs,—then the truth can be nothing more nor less than the last result to which the following out of this method would ultimately carry us. In that case, that to which the representation should conform is itself something in the nature of a representation, or sign,—something noumenal, intelligible, perceivable, and utterly unlike a thing-in-itself.

Truth is the conformity of a representamen to its object. *its* object, *its* object, mind you. The International Dictionary at the writer's elbow, the Century Dictionary which he daily studies, the Standard which he would be glad[,] sometimes, to consult, all contain the word *yes*; but that word is not true simply because he is going to ask on this 8th of January, 1906, in Pike County, Pennsylvania, whether it is snowing. There must be an action of the object upon the sign to render the latter true. Without that, the object is not the representamen's object. If a colonel hands a paper to an orderly and says "You will go immediately and deliver this to Captain Hanno," and if the orderly does so, we do not say the colonel told the truth; we say the orderly was obedient, since it was not the orderly's conduct which determined the colonel to say what he did, but the colonel's speech which determined the orderly's action. Here is a view of the writer's house: what makes that house to be the object of the view? Surely not the similarity of appearance. There are ten thousand others in the country just like it. No, but the photographer set up the film in such a way that according to the laws of optics, the film was forced to receive an image of this house. What the sign virtually has to do in order to indicate its object,—and make it its,—and all it has to do is just seize its interpreter's eyes and forcibly turn them upon the object meant: it is what a knock at the door does, or an alarm or other bell, a whistle, a cannon-shot, etc. It is pure physiological compulsion, nothing else.

So, then, a sign, in order to fulfill its office, to actualize its potency, must be compelled by its object. This is evidently the reason of the dichotomy of the true and the false. . . .

From the outbreak of World War I to about the death of George H. Mead in 1931, semiotics in the United States was at a low ebb. Peirce-as-a-semiotician vanished from view, to be revived only in England in the early 1920s through the good offices of C. K. Ogden and I. A. Richards (cf. Russo 1989:116f.). He began very slowly to resurface here when his *Collected Papers* started to appear in that decade, followed by Morris's generous although limited endorsement (1946:290; reinforced in Morris 1970:18–22, 40–42, 55f.):

His classification of signs, his refusal to separate completely animal and human sign-processes, his often penetrating remarks on linguistic categories, his application of semiotic to the problems of logic and philosophy, and the general acumen of his observations and distinctions, make his work in semiotic a source of stimulation that has few equals in the history of this field.

Of course, it was not the "pragmaticist" Peirce but the pragmatist Mead who, through his lectures, including Morris's own notes and Mead's unfinished manuscripts left behind, influenced him at the outset, although later Morris came to perceive a significant, because independent, convergence between the two. Morris (1970:35) stressed that "Mead's analysis of the gestural sign (whether linguistic or nonlinguistic) made fundamental the behavioral nature of the interpretant toward which Peirce's semiotic had developed." Mead, unlike Peirce (cf. Short 1982:308, n. 10), had a technical theory of meaning, which was triadic in character, involving "gesture, adjustive response, and resultant of the social act which the gesture initiates" (1934:80, and Ch. 11 passim), but, according to Morris (1970:36), "Mead's most important contributions to semiotic are his behavioral analysis of the language symbol and his elaboration of the key role of such symbols in the development and maintenance of the human self and the higher levels of human society."

In passing, it should be noted that Mead's views played a decisive role in the development of the sociology of symbolic interaction (including Goffman's formation—after all, he too studied at Chicago), surveyed by MacCannell (1976b). This is as good a place as any to also mention the fascinating book of Duncan (1968), with its portentously double dedication: to Kenneth Burke, "Master Symbolist of Our Time," and to Mead, "Founder of the Chicago Tradition in Symbolic Analysis"; as well as a collection of essays by Blumer, which likewise rely chiefly on the thought of Mead, "who, above all others, laid the foundations of the symbolic interactionist approach" (1969:1).

Nor should one forget the voluminous writings, as a spinoff of this same tradition, of Victor W. Turner, a Scotsman who also taught at Chicago from 1968 to 1977, and who argued that "the relationship between symbolic behavior and social life was semiotic" (Babcock and MacAloon 1987:7); it was the "distinctive and influential feature of *his* symbolic anthropology that it was a 'grounded' semiotics" (meaning, I suppose, "empirically grounded") (ibid. 11).

Yet another unexpected idiosyncratic offshoot of Mead's principle, that *"the meaning of any utterance or any sign is the response to that utterance or sign,"* is incarnate in Morse Peckham's book *Explanation and Power*, the central theme of which is that *"all human semiotic behavior is semiotic transformation"* (italics in the source), leading him to conclude that, hence, "we cannot determine either the point at which sign behavior emerged in the history of the species or the point at which it emerges in an infant living in the present" (1979:xv, 139f.).

Semiotic(s) as such began to transpire publicly and acquire a measure of definition in this country only in 1938, with the publication of Morris's *Foundations of the Theory of Signs* (1971:13–71), although after the early 1920s, commencing while training with Mead, its author progressively immersed himself in the theory of signs. This monograph first appeared as a part of the *International Encyclopedia of Unified Science* (Neurath, Carnap, and Morris 1955), to which Morris also contributed a programmatic article, "Scientific Empiricism" (1:63–75), as it were presaging, in respect to semiotic(s), the ensuing *Theory*. So, for instance, Morris remarked that the "modern version of formal logic developed in the hands of philosophic rationalists who were themselves mathematicians. It arose out of the cross-fertilization of the medieval approach to logic in terms of a general theory of signs and the methods of modern mathematics," a union the origins of which he ascribes to Leibniz (ibid. 66).

Morris goes on to cite Peirce's view that logic rests on a general theory of signs (ibid. 67), and then to define science as "a body of signs with certain specific relations to one another, to objects, and to practice," adding that it is "at once a language, a knowledge of objects, and a type of activity," leading to the interrelated study of the tripartite division of syntactics/semantics/pragmatics, which he dubs a metascience. He continues: "Discussion of the specific signs of science must be carried on in terms of some theory of signs, and so semiotic, as the science of signs, occupies an important place in the program—indeed, the study of the actual language of science is an instance of applied semiotic" (ibid. 70). Carnap's companion monograph, *Foundations of Logic and Mathematics* (ibid. 139–213), included an important syntactic and semantic analysis of mathematics and logic as contributions to Morris's conception of a more comprehensive semiotics of the language of sciences, which is further complemented by Leonard Bloomfield's well-known monograph *Linguistic Aspects of Science* (ibid. 215–77).

It might be worth recalling here in connection with the latter that the editors had originally commissioned another scholar, Manuel Andrade, to write on linguistics. Andrade, one of Franz Boas's most original students and an exceptional teacher, became, under the spell of Carnap and Morris, far more interested in semiotics than was Bloomfield. He did write his monograph, but Carnap and Morris wanted him to make some editorial emendations which Andrade would not accept. Then, in a fit of depression or temper, he tossed his manuscript into the fire in front of a horrified Morris (who told me this story). Shortly after this incident, Andrade unexpectedly died of a coronary thrombosis, and his students (among whom I, though a relative beginner, was the closest to him at that time, for I was uniquely slated to write my dissertation under his guidance) were unable to coherently reconstruct his very resourceful and fertile train of thought and argument. The editors then asked Bloomfield to write a hurried substitute piece, which they published in the *Encyclopedia* (but which had originally appeared in 1939).

The *International Encyclopedia of Unified Science*, resulting from the efforts of "the unity of science movement," embodied the confluence of divergent intellectual currents to which semiotics conduced, both explicitly—especially via Carnap and Morris (e.g., 1971:17f.)—and, perhaps even more so, implicitly. I had adverted in my paper "Ecumenicalism in Semiotics" (Sebeok 1977a:180–206) to the involvement of semiotics with this movement, broadly speaking and comprehending General System Theory. Roy R. Grinker, a Chicago M. D., launched a series of conferences in October 1951 "for the purpose of approaching a unified theory of behavior or, as we sometimes grandiosely stated, of human nature" (Grinker 1956:v). Ten or more of them had taken place by 1956, although the transactions of only four of these saw print (ibid.). Jurgen Ruesch was a dominant figure from the introduction to the end (ibid. ix-xi, 340–61). Among many interesting active discussants, one also finds such stellar names as Karl Deutsch, the political scientist; Alfred E. Emerson, the zoologist, and one of my Chicago professors; Charles Morris; Talcott Parsons, the sociologist; and Anatol Rapoport, a mathematician and general system theorist.

In the fourth (and last published) conference, Morris (ibid. 350) discussed Parson's remarks on boundary relations between sociocultural and personality systems and Ruesch's analysis of various types of boundaries, asking what makes them *a* system, and continuing in part:

> Now there are certain symbols, which we may call common symbols, which are common features of the cultural system the personality system and the social system. It seems to me that these symbols which are common to the discriminable subsystems make of them a human action system.
>
> If you hold a theory of signs in which a sign or symbol always involves some change in the organic state of the person for whom something is a sign, then these common symbols would also involve changes in the biological system. Therefore, whether you want to consider the total human action systems formed from just the three subsystems so far mentioned, or whether you also bring in the biological system, is largely a terminological matter. In any

case, it is these common symbols that make human action "a" system, and which anchor the human system upon the biological system. . . .

Asked to give an example, Morris went on (ibid. 351) with an earlier example, "policeman":

It pertains to all of them. It has a meaning in the communication system, and it has a meaning in the social system in that it defines a role; it also has a meaning in the personality system in that if a person becomes a policeman and now symbolizes himself as a policeman, he has become a policeman. He is then not merely performing that role in the social system but has become a changed person.

"I like that very much," Parsons exclaimed.

Sometime in the mid-1950s, Morris unexpectedly phoned me to ask if I would sit in for him at one of the later conferences, at which my long-time collaborator on psycholinguistic matters, Charles E. Osgood, was to be the main presenter. I did, but I found his talk repetitive and the discussion on the whole unfocused as well as unproductive.

The Chicago meetings were paralleled by a similar but more ambitious series of group ventures in New York City, some of the transactions of which were published under the continuing title *Cybernetics: Circular Causal, and Feedback Mechanisms in Biological and Social Systems*. The aim was "in the study of man [to] find eventual unification of all the sciences" (von Foerster 1950:9). At least five volumes of transactions were edited by Heinz von Foerster, an Austrian teaching in the Department of Electronic Engineering at the University of Illinois. A cumulative index appeared with transactions of the tenth conference (1955:85–100), in which you won't find the word *semiotics*, but you will find numerous entries, such as "language," "significance," "symbol," and so forth, leading to a host of issues of burning interest to present-day workers in semiotics.

The participants were distinguished figures, including, from time to time, two great mathematicians, John von Neumann and Norbert Wiener, and, from our cast of characters mentioned elsewhere in this book, Warren S. McCulloch (as the chairman), Gregory Bateson, Yuen Ren Chao, Margaret Mead, Walter Pitts,

I. A. Richards, Claude E. Shannon, and more than a dozen other permanent or floating partakers. The materials are too diffuse and extensive to attempt a summary here, but they seem to have centered on conceptual models supplied by the theory of information, with extension to "problems of language structure" and the notion of circular causal processes across many fields (1952:xiiif.).

The eighth conference (1952), for example, highlighted these topics: "Communication Patterns in Problem-Solving Groups" (leader: Alex Bavelas); "Communication between Men: Meaning of Language" (I. A. Richards); "Communication between Sane and Insane: Hypnosis" (Lawrence S. Kubie); "Communication between Animals" (Herbert G. Birch); "Presentation of a Maze-Solving Machine" (Claude E. Shannon); and "In Search of Basic Symbols" (Donald M. MacKay). Any of these topics could be comfortably accommodated, with perhaps a shift of jargon, in a get-together of semioticians.

Doubtless of less interest to semioticians on the whole, but of considerable archival value for this account and to me personally, are the proceedings of another series of New York–area conferences (Ithaca, Princeton) held in the mid-1950s, edited by Bertram Schaffner, a medical doctor of the University Seminar on Communications at Columbia University, simply titled "Group Processes." The participants were, by and large, comparably distinguished (with a couple of future Nobel Laureates); too, there was some overlap with the former, e.g., included was the ubiquitous Margaret Mead. Presentations at the second conference (1956) featured a "Kinesic Analysis of Filmed Behavior of Children," by Ray L. Birdwhistell, and the classic paper "The Message 'This Is Play,' " by Gregory Bateson.

There exists a very large, separate literature on General System Theory, launched and abetted by Ludwig von Bertalanffy, who stated that "the idea goes back some considerable time: I presented it first in 1937 in Charles Morris's philosophy seminar at the University of Chicago" (1968:90). I was a sophomore there at the time, but I met up with Bertalanffy a few years afterwards. In 1954, the "movement" jelled into a formal Society for the Advancement of General Systems Theory, under the prestigious auspices of the American Association for the Advancement of Science. A series of yearbooks was launched in 1956, of which there are seventeen volumes in my library. Many now-familiar figures dart in and out among the contributors, including several more eventual Nobel Laureates, as well as our own Kenneth L. Pike, two well-known Soviet linguists, G. S. Ščur and V. A. Zvegintsev, and the Polish cognitive scientist (and whilom *Semiotica* contributor, now at Iona College) Maria Nowakowska (1986).

The ecumenical strivings of a weighty segment of the American semiotics community will thus be seen as, at times (especially in the 1950s and 1960s) and in part, having coincided and interlocked with the membership of the several and various "unified science" and/or "general systems" movements, which were led and promoted by the cream of the American academic establishment. The same professors—Morris being a notable exemplar—or physicians or foundation executives tend to reappear, often wearing different guises. A collaborative position paper offering a semiotic perspective on the sciences was put forward by Anderson and five other authors in 1984. For a valuable commentary on "unified theory" in relation to semiotics, in part in reaction to the aforementioned, see also Floyd Merrell's paper (1987) delivered at a State-of-the-Art Conference on semiotics held at Indiana University in October 1984 (most of the transactions of which unfortunately remain unpublished). See, however, for its momentous theoretical consequences, Merrell's important new American trilogy (1991a, b, c), which came to my hands too late to assess for the purposes of this book.

Charles J. Lumsden, an American physicist by training, now a professor of medicine in Canada, was the junior codeveloper with Edward O. Wilson of behavioral ecology, also known as sociobiology, which is sometimes presented as the culmination of a search for "the grail of a unifying theory of biology and the social sciences" (Lumsden and Wilson 1981:ix; see also Wright 1988:111–92), or at least as a field that "will come increasingly to occupy the social sciences as the links between biology and the study of culture are more powerfully forged" (ibid. 362).

In view of their crusade for unification, it is not surprising that Lumsden (1986:202), while conceding there may be "much merit in semioticians' views that the understanding of mind, culture, and society will ultimately depend on a rigorous understanding of symbol and communication in their discipline," argues that, if semiotics is to be successful in these endeavors, "it must become an evolutionary science." Thus far I agree with

Lumsden, and his further demand that "human sociobiology must realize the semiotic imperative," but without at present following him further into the tulgey woods of gene-culture co-evolution.

As Richard Parmentier perspicaciously pointed out in the course of his review (1989:118f.) of a NATO-sponsored conference, *Semiotics and International Theory: Towards a Language of Theory* (Evans and Helbo 1986), "any effort to construct semiotics as a universal metalanguage must confront the fact that semiotics is itself a semiotic system," viz., that semiotics carries its own pragmatics. Not by any means all, or even many contemporary American, semioticians are nowadays involved with the unified science or general system movements. "Semiotics," Parmentier concludes, "thus abandons its hegemonic pursuit of metascientific status only to occupy the more secure position of well-disciplined exemplar."

Even in his twilight years, Morris identified with Peirce, who, he said, felt himself to be only "a pioneer, or rather a backwoodsman, in the clearing and opening up" of semiotics. Morris felt essentially the same way about his own work (ibid. 8). In the ensuing years, the global impact of Morris, accrued through his books and teaching (although he remained a prophet with least honor at his own institution in Chicago), was impressive— how much so was borne in on me vividly in the course of my later travels in Asia and Europe, especially in Japan and the Soviet Union.

Morris's tripartition of semiotics into syntactics, semantics, and pragmatics—endorsed repeatedly by Carnap (1942:8–11)— became dogma which is generally more observed outside than inside semiotics, because its technical operational use appears minimal. Withal, as Martin observed (1978:xiv), "no clear or compelling reasons seem to have emerged for its overthrow."

By 1953, an excellent, informative, substantial book appeared about Morris's life and works by the Italian (but Texas-linked) semiotician Ferruccio Rossi-Landi, praising and displaying his *mentalità enciclopedica e classificatoria* (ibid. 26). Another subtle interpreter of Morris was the German (but American-trained) philosopher Karl-Otto Apel, who wrote about his semiotic(s) in 1959, as well as in his critical introduction (1973) to the German translation of Morris's 1946 book. These publications underscored the fact that Morris was, by and large, always more appreciated abroad than in this country (although some dissertations about him, by Eakins in 1972, by Fiordo in 1976, were produced on campuses in Iowa and Illinois).

Charles Hartshorne, who was a colleague of Morris's from 1931 to 1955, and with whom I was casually acquainted at Chicago, is chiefly known among our community as the senior coeditor of Peirce's *Collected Papers*. (It is less well known that Hartshorne contributed a valuable book [1973] to ornithosemiotics.) He never attended Morris's seminars on semiotics and did not familiarize himself with his writings on this subject. However, after he left for Emory University, D. S. Clarke became his student (in the early 1960s), in consequence of which Clarke came to write his *Principles of Semiotic* (1987), as well as to compile a historical anthology of semiotics (1990).

It was Morris, my first teacher in semiotics at Chicago, soon to be followed by the now sadly all but forgotten Ethel M. Albert at Northwestern University, who introduced semiotics to the American university curriculum, and probably worldwide.

I have written, for the time being, all I want to about Morris in my "Vital Signs" (see Appendix below) and above, but to all that I add one diagnostic observation: that, in proportion that the reputation and stock of Peirce have risen, those of Morris have declined. I believe this is due to the fact that Morris embraced behavioral psychology so explicitly. Interestingly enough, Mead's theory of reciprocal, behavioral expectations is inconsistent with modern behaviorism, and closer to the standpoint of Peirce (who, although ever the staunch opponent of materialism, has been called, by some perverted extension of that term, as by Conkin 1976:219, "a complete behaviorist"). Note how these two intersecting curves parallel the contemporaneous pair delineating the ascent of cognitive psychology and the descent of behaviorism (but cf. Skinner 1977, and especially his critique of Susanne Langer on pp. 3f.).

Morris made no direct contributions to either descriptive or applied semiotics (as opposed to what he called the pure variety). He defined the former (1946:353, 219) as semiotic(s) which "studies actual signs," giving as examples statements about "what signs signify to certain persons, how signs are combined in a specific language, the origin, uses, and effects of specific signs," and so forth, such statements, or ascriptors, constituting "a natural science" in contrast to logic.

Five years after Morris died, Ruth Garrett Millikan published an ambitious book (1984) in which she attempted to develop a semiotic theory in continuity and harmony with the natural sciences. She dedicates her book to Morris, "the memory of whose warm enthusiasm enabled [her] to persevere," regretting that he "did not see the rough ideas he so generously encouraged in a young acquaintance grow into a strongly naturalist view and then engender a theory of signs."

In this respect, as in many others, Roman Jakobson, my second teacher in semiotics (Sebeok 1988a, Ch. 13), was the converse of and stood in complement to Morris. When he landed in America (in June 1941, as I mentioned, in the company of Cassirer), Jakobson already had behind him half a lifetime's accomplishments in several branches of this domain. Yet Eco did not exaggerate when he wrote that ransacking his immense bibliography "to seek out an item explicitly devoted to semiotics may be disappointing," and that "despite his frequent use of the word 'semiotics,' some of the pages which have most influenced the development of this discipline fail to mention it" (1987:111–13). The reason, Eco assumes, that Jakobson never wrote a book on semiotics is that "his entire scientific existence was a living example of a Quest for Semiotics."

Jakobson was, in fact, "semiotically biased from his early years." As he himself told an interviewer (1978:66): "I associated with young painters during my adolescence, I had long talks with them about the relation between painting and poetry, between visual signs and verbal signs. This is how interest in semiotics came into my life." In response to Pomorska's probing (Jakobson and Pomorska 1983, Ch. 5, "Semiotics"), "because you have in fact studied literary and artistic phenomena as signs throughout your scientific activity in all domains of language and art . . . [o]ne would think that this would have exhausted questions of semiotics," Jakobson reaffirmed his early interest in the relationship "between the pictorial sign as an element of painting and the verbal sign as an element of language," and he referred to the Prague Linguistic Circle: "Of all the semiotic types and all the forms of art, language and the verbal art remained the fundamental and favored topics of the Circle between the wars."

He went on to tell her that "Peirce devoted his life to founding [the] science [of semiotics] and to tracing its first, vast program, which even today answers the needs of modern thought." With his accustomed erudition, he then cited and discussed early Slavic verse as an "eloquent example of the supreme role of language in its multiple and creative relations with other systems of signs," which "gives us a lesson in general semiotics." As he had done before, he repeated that "we must now clearly undertake a comparative study of language and all other groups of signs, a study that has been planned over the course of centuries by a whole succession of thinkers. One would have to be myopic not to agree." Finally, as for the question of

> which genres of signs enter into the frame of semiotics, there can be only one answer: if semiotics is the science of signs, as the etymology of the word suggests, then it does not exclude any sign. If, in the variety of the systems of signs, one discovers systems that differ from others by their specific properties, one can place them in a special class without removing them from the general science of signs. The number and range of concrete objectives that present themselves to semiotics argue for their systematic elaboration around the world.

I was early among his pupils whom Jakobson encouraged "to try semiotics," which, by the early sixties, "was no longer an impossible dream; it was," Eco confirms, "the result of a successful quest." In other words, while Jakobson made no direct contributions to pure semiotics in Carnap's and Morris's sense, he was responsible, like no one else before him, for animating and electrifying, both here and abroad, a large gamut of topics in descriptive semiotics (most particularly in the domains of language and several of the arts; cf. Jakobson and Pomorska 1983:152).

In his 1952 Bloomington lecture, Jakobson also declared his engagement with communication engineering; in particular, he seemed for some years to be under the spell of Shannon and Weaver's mathematical theory of communication (1949). This induced him, in 1960, to become deeply involved in a "Symposium on the Structure of Language and Its Mathematical Aspects," where he cited Shannon in support of his statement about the "semiotic definition of a symbol's meaning as its translation into other symbols," referring to Shannon's definition of information as "that which is invariant under all reversible encoding or translation operations," or, briefly, "the equivalence class of all such translations" (*Structure* 1961:251). This was a neat way to bring under one umbrella Peirce's interpretant, Jakobson's translation theory, and Shannon's information theory. However, Jakobson's interest in information theory (as well as cybernetics) cooled considerably over time, and, except for remnants of fossilized terminology, it appeared to leave no permanent trace. The same is true of current American semiotics overall.

Thus I was singularly fortunate in having Morris and Jakobson as my two immediately successive companion guides through the thickets of semiotics. The Denver-born Morris, soaked in logical positivism and scientific empiricism of the Vienna Circle, and the Moscow-born philologist, who spent the second half of his life ensconced among our Ivy League institutions, were both quintessentially capacious and cosmopolitan in outlook. While Morris became increasingly concerned with questions of axiology (esp. in 1964), Jakobson grew ever more interested in mathematics and the natural sciences, especially in their mutual relations with semiotics (1973, Ch. 3).

The conceptual basis for Prague School theory, as Galan has demonstrated, was semiotics, its advent in 1934 effectively marking a final break with that of Russian formalism (1985, Ch. 4). While some of this movement had its roots in a native Czech semiotics of art, its bulk stemmed from Russia (Bakhtin's views, among others) and Saussurean linguistics. The Prague School structuralists, Galan notes, "were eager to test the tools of semiotic analysis on material from the . . . arts—film, theatre, the visual arts, music and even ethnographic artifacts like folk costume" (ibid. 82). In the creation of this semiotic esthetics, Jakobson rapidly took a leading role; in due course, it came to constitute a large part of the baggage that he eventually imported to this country.

Jakobson's first of many lectures at Indiana University took place in 1944, and that was "The Theory of Signs." Not unexpectedly, but to the bafflement of our Department of Psychology, then headed by an old-fashioned radical behaviorist, J. R. Kantor (famed for his *An Objective Psychology of Grammar*), it was heavily flavored by Old World estheticism. It was burdened, moreover, by the speaker's thick Russian accent (in those days, *signs* and *science* were homonymous for him). I noticed Kantor fidgeting throughout Jakobson's presentation, and he immediately rose to his feet shouting when the speaker had ended: "Why, this is nothing but medieval philosophy!" Jakobson promptly jumped to *his* feet, shouting back: "No, no! It goes back to Plato and Aristotle!"

Initially, Jakobson was interested in Morris, but their relationship failed to flourish, perhaps because his intrinsic buoyancy was incompatible with Morris's Zen placidity, or perhaps because of profound differences in their respective traditions. The one thing they certainly shared was a focus on Peirce, and I have some reason to believe that it was Morris who first drew Jakobson's attention to Peirce. At any rate, as I recounted in my "Vital Signs" (see Appendix below), by 1952 he was deeply engaged, to the point of a ruling preoccupation, in Peirce's "visionary theses" (Jakobson and Pomorska 1983:154).

One of the remaining puzzles centers on the reconciliation of Jakobson's consistent binarism—a cornerstone of all his pursuits, in and far beyond linguistics—with Peirce's patent trinarism (Eco and Sebeok 1983:1–10). Jakobson himself never came publicly to terms with this apparent contradiction, which since his death has been probed by several scholars, among them, with notable skill and textual corroboration yet inconclusively, Andrews (1990).

Another of Jakobson's characteristic tenets, which he upheld to the last, was that the "number and range of *concrete* objectives that present themselves to semiotics argue for their systematic elaboration around the world. However," he cautioned that "one should reject all the unsuitable efforts of sectarians who seek to narrow this vast and varied work by introducing into it a parochial spirit" (ibid. 158; my emphasis). Many of us know who the "sectarians" were that he put the rest of us on guard against, and the location, to this day, of their deflating headquarters.

The Prague School's fields of attention enumerated (though not exhaustively) by Galan above are all multifariously tilled by specialist practitioners in this country, as they are selectively cultivated in workshops throughout the world. I have already alluded to semiotics of the theatre. Let me briefly touch upon the remaining four and mention some related matters, starting with the semiotics of music.

One of Morris's students, from his seminar the year after the one in which I participated, was Leonard B. Meyer, who became one of this country's foremost musicologists. His work displays the influence of, among others, Peirce, Colin Cherry, and Chomsky (e.g., 1967:261f.). It is pervasively concerned with modes of signification, which he calls the formal, the kinetic-syntactic, and the referential, insisting that "any account of musical communication that pretends to completeness must find a place for all three" (ibid. 43). Although semiotics is implicit in Meyer's distinguished body of writings, it has constituted the pivot of Robert S. Hatten's since 1982, when he defended his erudite and programmatic dissertation, titled "Toward a Semiotic Model of Style in Music: Epistemological and Methodological Bases," at Indiana University, concluding, "one may say that whereas semiotics exhausts style, style does not exhaust semiotics, which must ultimately embrace the vastness of music as meaning" (ibid. 213). (Note also that *Semiotica* 15:3–82 [1975] and 66:1–330 [1987], as well as WEB 1986 [1987:405–581], by various hands, were devoted to this seemingly illimitable subject.)

Speaking of the theatre and of music, an inexplicable hiatus on the American scene is semiotics of the opera, a form of great interest from Eastern and Western Europe to Japan but curiously ignored over here. Perhaps the most complex of syncretic objects, involving the literary, musical, and scenic arts, with inputs from a still wider array of codes (as noted in Sebeok 1985:79), this is an area of concentrated international researches at this time, which deserves the careful attention of young scholars in this country as well.

On the other hand, semiotics of the dance, including the ballet (Shapiro 1981), directly linked as these are not only to music but also to nonverbal communication, as well as to explorations of notational systems, is an area that does flourish here (Hanna 1986). An innovative genre of interest has been an extension of semiotic techniques of analysis to the art of mime, ranging from Marcel Marceau to Pilobolus and Mummenschanz (Royce 1987).

Another complex syncretic art form and an important early testing ground for descriptive semiotics, the cinema, continues to be as extensively plowed here as elsewhere (Williams 1986, Polan 1989).

As to what Galan calls "the visual arts," modern semioticians tend also to take account of forms that aren't usually considered to be "high arts," embracing, to be sure, drawing, painting, etching, sometimes photography (à la Svetlana Alpers, Barthes, Lindekens, Metz, Susan Sontag, etc., and more specifically Tomas 1982, 1983, and 1988), but also cartoons and the comics and such exotic practices as the craft of tattooing (Parry 1933; Glynn 1982:131f.; Sanders 1988, 1989) and other kinds of body scoring and cosmetic decoration (Morris 1977:222–29, 317). Sculpture, the plastic arts in general, and/or architecture may be included as well. I take all such forms to fall under what Meyer Schapiro (1970:488) has called "the art of representation constructs," involving elements such as the prepared surface, the boundaries, the positions and directions, the format of the image-sign, and so forth.

An unusually happy research program was launched by Marvin Carlson, creatively syncretizing architectural semiotics and theatre semiotics into unitary structures: this singularly imaginative approach initially resulted in a jewel of a semiotic analysis of the Old Vic of London (1988b) and has since grown into a full-length book (1989) with many other exemplars.

In 1984, *Semiotica* devoted a special issue (52:3/4), guest edited by Mihai Nadin, to "The Semiotics of the Visual: Defining the Field." Semiotics of the visual arts, perhaps more so than other branches, has traditionally dealt in dialectic fashion with such core problems of semiotics as art and illusion, the artist and his/her subject (or model), and the relation between art and its societal context. The role of semiotics in painting, moreover, is controversial in an interesting way with respect to the notion of conventionalism in pictorial representation, engaging on opposite sides sophisticated scholars such as Gombrich (1981) and Goodman (1968). Hasenmueller (1984:335) fastens on the classic question whether the resemblance between images and the world is natural or conventional, and stresses that Gombrich's resolution, that resemblance is rooted in empirical parallels, as against Goodman's position of extreme relativism, "is crucial for semiotics." Wollheim (1987:361, n. 23), too, sharply distinguished recently between two views, calling them "mainstream semiotics" (descending from Peirce) vs. "radical semiotics" (practiced by Goodman, but also György Kepes and Rosalind E. Krauss in this country). With semioticians of the former persuasion Wollheim claims to have "no particular dispute," only with the "radicals," "who hold that all signs, including pictures, are conventional. . . . " Assessments of these two traditions of semiotics are found in Preziosi (1989), where they are seen as mutually implicative.

Works on the semiotics of sculpture, in the orthodox sense, are rare, excepting for the plastic characteristics combined with the ritual transformations wrought by masks (Crumrine and Halpin 1983; see esp. Ch. 16, and p. 209, for a discussion of their symbolic function and "semiotropic effect") and the totem pole or canoe carvings and decorations and the like of Northwest Coast Indians (codified extensively in ethnographic accounts). Some semiotic aspects of the arts of floral arrangements and bonsai may also be studied under this heading. Octavio Paz (1990:18, 20) remarks, apropos the famous, awe-inspiring Mexican statue known as the Great Coatlicue: "What we call a 'work of art' . . . is perhaps no more than a configuration of signs. Each onlooker combines these signs in a different way and each combination expresses a different meaning. The plurality of meanings, however, is resolved into just one *sense*, which is always the same: a meaning that is inseparable from sensory experience." Furthermore, as captured by his elegant semiotic formulation, an expression like a Mayan god covered with "attributes and signs is not a sculpture to be read like a text but rather a sculptured text. . . ."

By contrast, architectural semiotics, properly, as Preziosi considers it to be, "a facet of a broader area of inquiry generically termed visual semiotics . . . is integrally related to the semiotic study of the nature, functions, usage, ideological status of cultural artifacts of many kinds—from megalopolitan formations to graphic notations" (1986:44f.). Studies have proliferated, in "a rich and complex mélange," in the Americas, as elsewhere, representing "developments out of (and implications for) general semiotic theory. . . . " (Preziosi, a linguistically adept archeologist, was president of the Semiotic Society of America in 1985.)

Galan lastly refers to "ethnographic artifacts," especially—in tacit but obvious reference to the pioneer analyses of P. G. Bogatyrev, suggestively amplified by Henry Glassie (1973)—to "folk costume." Indeed, there exists a fair amount of literature on sartorial signs, or the semiotics of clothing (comprehending the fertile field of semiotic application to uniforms: see, e.g., in general, Joseph 1986, and, on the semiotics of Boy Scout uniforms, Mechling 1987), including a 1981 book by the American novelist Alison Lurie, who entitled her opening chapter "Clothing as a Sign System." (In July 1989, at ISISSS '89, there was held a Colloquium on the Body and Clothing as Communication.)

There are many explorations having to do with the semiotics of bodily artifacts (Golliher 1987), as well as of a wide variety of corporeal extensions, including, for instance, such enticing domains as gardens in general (Moore, Mitchell, and Turnbull 1989) or, more specialized, Japanese gardens (Casalis 1983). Umiker-Sebeok drew my attention to a discerning article by Michael Pollan on the semiotics of lawncare in America, which appeared as the lead piece in a 1989 issue of the *New York Times Magazine*. The writer, who is at work on a book on gardening, compares gardening with lawncare:

> if lawn mowing feels like copying the same sentence over and over, gardening is like writing out new ones, an infinitely variable process of invention and discovery. Gardens also teach the necessary if rather un-American lesson that nature and culture can be compromised, that there might be some middle ground between the lawn and the forest—between those who would complete the conquest of the planet in the name of progress, and those who believe it's time we abdicated our rule and left the Earth in the care of its more innocent species. The garden suggests there might be a place where we can meet nature half way. (P. 44).

Nor have the semiotic aspects of the lexicon and practices of American wine-drinking (Lehrer 1978) or the culinary practices of the Japanese (Loveday and Chiba 1985) been neglected, although such articles merely foretoken a vaster and richer area awaiting exploration.

Foote reviews four characteristic aspects of semiosis of the perdurable material expressions, as opposed to the dissipative manifestations of vocal signs and other kinds of nonverbal ones, informally launching a kind of "distinctive feature analysis" (as this kind of exercise is called by linguists) which could usefully be generalized much further to remaining types of semiosis (1988:245f.). I once gave an example of this (in Sebeok 1985:29f.), to wit, in reference to a comparative analysis of the advantages and disadvantages of channels used for communication in and across all species and inside the body. Foote relates the use of objects in semiosis to "human action in sustaining memory, and with effacement of memory" (ibid. 263), which is particularly pertinent to the notion of the second or so-called semiotic self (Sebeok 1988a, Appendix I, amplified in Sebeok 1989).

A particularly nice example of a semiotic analysis of an artifact that became the medium for expression in a major civilization, that of the Andean Incas, is the Aschers' fine study of the code of the quipu (1981). Another pertinent paper, that of Blanchard (1983), is devoted to a study of discrete objects as pictured in various phases of Greek art and in the Homeric epic; Blanchard, appropriately enough, takes as his motto this quotation from Arnauld and Nicole's 1662 *La logique*: "When one looks at a certain object only as representing another one, the idea of that object one has is the idea of a sign, and this first object is called a sign."

A mundane object was chosen by Seligmann (1982) for his semiotic analysis, namely, the door, in its denotative as well as connotative aspects: how, in North American culture, does the door serve as an adjunct to initiating, terminating, or avoiding social contact, and more? Solomon's popular induction into the mysteries of semiotics (1988) largely converges on signs of concrete objects, ranging from suburban cottages to teddy bears, food and dress.

The semiotic dimension of ideology and, conversely, the ideological dimension of semiosis, in their American facets, were reconnoitered by Armstrong (1986). Her essay is devoted mainly to the issue of gender, i.e., feminism, and to what she calls "cultural studies," including several subtopics, such as "the historical struggle among various cultural formations to resist or to achieve cultural hegemony," leisure theory, and aspects of recherché debates swirling around "postmodernism." An entertaining analysis of ideology in action is found in Casalis's meticulous, poker-faced account (1975) of the rhetorical practices of *Penthouse* magazine. Rhetorical signifiers and ideological signifieds are indissolubly united for this author, like, in Saussure's famous simile, the "front" and the "back" of a sheet of paper.

Armstrong's essay did not touch on the topic of semiotics and Marxism, which was later dealt with in a separate study by an Italian semiotician, Augusto Ponzio (1989), who explored the relationship of the two, although exclusively in a limited European context. Claims that semiotics can be illuminated by the intellectual history and pretensions of Marxism, indeed, propositions that there can exist a Marxist semiotics at all, seem nowadays fraught with heavy irony. To paraphrase Raymond Aron from "The Opium of the Intellectuals," the poetry of Marxist ideology has been brought down to the prose of reality. In view of the to all appearances irreversible political and economic developments—accompanied by a dramatically improbable iconography (such as the "Goddess of Democracy" effigy of the Statue of Liberty in Tiananmen Square), itself well worth detailed semiotic scrutiny—convulsing the Soviet Union, former Soviet bloc countries, and China today, such suggestions, which nowadays find little or no proficient reception in America, appear but a perverse academic frivolity.

Fantasies of a Marxist semiotics were put forward in multifarious accommodations and shapes by, among others, Adam Schaff in Poland in 1962, L. O. Reznikov in the Soviet Union in the late 1960s, and Georg Klaus in the DDR even as late as 1973. Today these would be greeted with bored indifference throughout Western Europe, and with amused incredulity or downright contempt in Berlin, Budapest, Bucharest, Prague, Sofia, Moscow, or Tartu, and, though for the moment perhaps more cautiously, in Beijing, Wuhan, or Nanjing. At any rate, not even the most extreme segment of the fading radical American intelligentsia has ever put so grotesque a program on the table. In sum, it would be fair to conclude that semiotics has by and large escaped from Marxist ideology relatively unscathed, and did not substitute economic or political formulas for creative thinking. The pertinence of all this to a book such as mine became even more arresting when Václav Havel, addressing a joint meeting of the U.S. Congress in February 1990, spoke of his "one great certainty: Consciousness precedes Being, and not the other way around, as the Marxists claim"—in other words, that ideology, or a semiotic system of beliefs, creates the "real" world, not vice versa! However, comparisons between communicative exchanges and economic exchanges (e.g., of money) have been attempted several times and can have "semiotic utility" (as in Vaughn's 1980 paper, esp. p. 140) as much for their similarities as for their differences.

In May 1987 I delivered a series of lectures on various semiotic topics in Buenos Aires (Sebeok 1988e). After one of my early lectures, I was challenged by a reporter, "What do you think of Argentina?" Since I had barely landed and had not formed any views at all, I quipped: "Argentina seems to me a two-class

society." "What do you mean?" she pressed. "Half of your people are psychoanalysts, the other half analysands." Later, I was
to discover that Argentine analysts were, in fact, split up into
many bitterly rivalrous factions—several Freudian groups, at
least two Lacanian, a scattering of Jungian, and so forth. But all
of them, so I was told, were "interested in semiotics."

This is not the place to discuss the flaws of psychoanalytic
theory or practice; anyhow, there is nothing I could add to Adolf
Grünbaum's compelling critique (1984), except perhaps to de-
plore the outlandish preoccupation of a few American semioticians with the cold leftovers of the French psychoanalytic bazaar.
In contrast to the lack of manifest interest in Marxism on the
part of most of the U.S. semiotics enterprise, clear voices of
engagement on its part with one psychoanalytic school or another are being raised—which is not to say that this theme is
anywhere near the point of main attraction, or has ever been its
cynosure.

Eugen Bär's series of four essays, each originally published in
Semiotica, gathered in augmented form under the title *Semiotic
Approaches to Psychotherapy* in 1975, and provided there with an
illuminating preface by Harley C. Shands—significantly headed
"The Credo of an Unbeliever"—is, I think, absolutely indispensable. Bär's chapters focus, respectively, on Lacan, Jung,
Shands, Ruesch, and Scheflen. Elsewhere (1983) Bär added a
piece on Freud, from whom, Shands says, each of the aforementioned "made his own effort to integrate into the lessons
learned directly or indirectly . . . the important influence of the
communicational process."

However, as Shands also points out, two facts are immediately
evident: first, that the work of each of the three American-based
figures—Shands, Ruesch, and Scheflen—is complementary to
that of the other two; and second, that they as a group "show
very little trace of the kind of empire building that results in the
formation of many Freudians, Jungians, and Lacanians." The
Americans' orientation appears to be far more "ecumenical," a
mode which was violently attacked and polemicized by Lacan
as "Philistine." This reintroduces the notion of psychoanalysis
as an "ideology," the principal function of which "is that of
testing constantly for membership." The main link among "all
the represented authors is an assumption of the centrality in

human affairs of *communication* in a specifically cultural (spoken, gestural, ritual, political, religious) context," in brief, of the ubiquity of semiosis (Shands in Bär 1975:vii-xvii).

Since his 1974 dissertation on Freudian theory, in especial application to the tales of Edgar Allan Poe, Neal H. Bruss has continued to greatly elaborate—in part in response to the challenges of Grünbaum, and largely in the pages of *Semiotica*—what he has been calling "the semiological 'basic assumption' of psychoanalysis." This labor has climaxed in a book, *Freud's Semiotics* (forthcoming).

By contrast, Kaja Silverman's book *The Subject of Semiotics* (1983), while maintaining the centrality of semiotics, places her argument in a poststructural frame, lays a heavy emphasis on ideology, and privileges Lacan. On the other hand, Chaitin (1988:37) begins his essay by citing Lacan's distrust of semiotics, explains the reasons therefor, and in the end repositions Lacan's view vis-à-vis "the more sophisticated semiotics of the 1980s and 1990s." By this Chaitin (ibid. 61) means areas as diverse as "child-rearing practices, parliamentary institutions, literature, and labor relations," examined not from the point of view of the "meanings attributable to the signs used, not as the communication (whether violent or suggestive) of information or prejudice, but with an eye toward the reifying or liberating effects those discursive practices have on subjects" (which Silverman's book also focused on).

A fertile coupling of semiotics with psychoanalysis within the domain of sexuality, with, furthermore, a welcome evolutionary perspective, will be found in Rancour-Laferriere's ingenious and original book *Signs of the Flesh* (1985). For me, the appearance of this unique treatise (by a specialist, no less, in Russian poetics and semiotics) accentuates the paucity of informed writings in any language at the interface of semiotics and sexology. The institution at which I work also houses the Kinsey Institute for Research in Sex, Gender and Reproduction—and here I divulge that I have been trying for years to persuade my colleagues across the campus to turn some of their creative energies to the semiotic aspects of sexual behavior, but thus far to no avail. They have more important things on their plate . . .

Scholars in our domestic workshops have also enriched the literature of semiotics by philological articles, treatises, and edi-

88   Thomas A. Sebeok

tions dealing with ancestral figures, eras, or movements. *Semiotica* on occasion publishes special issues along these lines. Three recent representative collections edited by Americans dealt with, respectively, "Semiotica Mediaevalia" (ed. Jonathan Evans, in Vol. 63, Nos. 1–2), "The Classical [i.e., seventeenth-century] Sign" (ed. Susan W. Tiefenbrun, in Vol. 51, No. 1–3), and "Semiotics and Phenomenology" (ed. Richard L. Lanigan, in Vol. 41, No. 1–4).

Among noteworthy products by a single American author or editor (or a pair of editors) that have lately come to my attention, I would like to highlight the following three. Chronologically, the earliest among this trio is the edition of Philodemus of Gadara's *On Methods of Inference* (1978), by Phillip Howard De Lacy and Estelle Allen De Lacy. Most of this unique work, which presents the Epicurean view of semiosis, was recovered from a papyrus and is here presented with their excellent translation and commentary. Having already mentioned above, as well as reviewed elsewhere (Sebeok 1986b), John Deely's extraordinary (therefore controversial: see Deely 1988) edition, with his translation and interpretive commentary, of Poinsot's *Tractatus de Signis* (1985), I need not dwell on its merits again here. In a different genre, there is Wellbery's *tour de force* study (1984) of the (primarily) German Enlightenment in its pre-Kantian phase reinterpreted in the light of modern semiotics, from which he then draws valuable insights to yield a perspective on our contemporary semiotic preoccupations.

There are, of course, numerous insightful American essays of a philological character—too many to list exhaustively—bearing on historical figures or groups of interest to or variously claimed for semiotics: Augustine, R. Bacon, Bachelard, Berkeley, Buber, Collingwood, Condillac, Dewey, Heidegger, Hobbes, Hume, Locke, Lull, Mallarmé, Mukařovský, Peter of Spain, M. Polanyi, Reid, J. Royce, Schütz, Suárez, Wittgenstein, the Conimbricenses, East Europeans or Soviets, to name but a few (in general, consult the SSA Proceeding volumes and the EDS). Chapter 4 of Culler's book on Ferdinand de Saussure (1986 [1976]:105–50) offers a lapidary review and assessment of the Saussurean semiotic legacy, further exemplified in his later treatment of Barthes's "semiology" (1983:70–77).

I have deferred to the end of this section touching on the

amorphous but sprawling theme of the sustained impact of European semiotics upon American semiotics prospects in the twentieth century, overlying the knotty, reticulate patterns of the preceding century. Clearly, this impact is most discernible in the *oeuvre* of such discrepant overseas-raised and saturated preceptors as the German neo-Kantian philosopher Cassirer, the Russian philologist Jakobson, the French theologian Maritain, and the like. They, in turn, came to a position to relay the filaments of their respective traditions through countless arteries after, and in an important sense even before, their arrival on these shores and, in most cases, permanent settlement in this country. It is equally laborious to trace the polyphonic voices of such figures as, say, Louis Hjelmslev, Pierre Guiraud, or Roland Barthes, who were able to address us in person only occasionally, influencing us mostly through their publications.

Chronologically, C. K. Ogden and I. A. Richards, in tandem in *The Meaning of Meaning* (Russo 1989:110–45), as well as on occasion separately, first impinged upon American scholarly consciousness. Morris (1971:7), for example, professed that he "had been helped to identify the contours of a general theory of signs by *The Meaning of Meaning*." This book, with its several important appendixes (by Sextus Empiricus, Husserl, Russell, Frege, Gomperz, Baldwin, Peirce) and supplements (by Malinowski and Crookshank), had likewise found, as I have previously noted (1986a:63f.), all sorts of repercussions in my own writings.

Louis Hjelmslev's and Hans J. Uldall's "glossematics" (the tag was invented by the latter; and, by the way, in truth the two Danes sharply disagreed with one another, even about certain fundamental issues) has been credited by some as "the first coherent and complete semiotic theory." This is surely an irresponsibly concocted claim, although it may in part be true that "it has been a decisive factor in the formation of semiotics in France" (Greimas and Courtés 1979:137), at least among a restricted but vocal circle of Paris-area figures noted for their aggressive démarches, calling themselves L'Ecole de Paris. In turn, voices of this Paris-centered group echo in academic pockets here and there in the United States, chiefly in programs where Continental literary theory is emphasized (Schleifer 1987; Hendricks 1989; Larsen 1989), and in such workshops as Daniel Patte's—

who was chiefly responsible, at Vanderbilt University, for making available the English version of the first volume of the Greimas-Courtés *Dictionary* (1982).

But Hjelmslev's sway is held directly—that is, having entirely bypassed its Gallic-flavored literary applications—among a handful of American linguists, perhaps now exclusively by Lamb and his students. In a statement Lamb (1982:8f.) made about "certain lines of thought that were laid out by people who went before" him, he prominently named—besides Peirce, Saussure, and, more surprisingly, Benjamin Lee Whorf—Hjelmslev, "who said that all of linguistic structure is really nothing but a network of relationships."

The actual roots of L'Ecole de Paris, of which Greimas was the animator, are more circuitous by far. A full accounting would certainly implicate, in addition to Hjelmslev, at least Vladimir Propp, Claude Lévi-Strauss, and Pierre Guiraud. It would be quite erroneous, too, to equate its membership with French semiotics, even of Paris. There are numerous other outstanding professionals in and around that city who have little or nothing to do with that circle—Claude Brémond, Jean-Claude Gardin, Julia Kristeva, Alain Rey, Josette Rey-Debove, and René Thom among them, to name just a few, and to say nothing here of the momentous accomplishments of Lévi-Strauss. Each man and woman is recognized here for his or her contribution by the cognoscenti. I would just like to single out for mention a few additional figures, who seem to me particularly pertinent in this context.

One is Christian Metz, considered by many to be the fountainhead of modern film semiotics. His name has generated an immense secondary literature, including American. Most of his books are available here, beginning with his hefty, seminal *Language and Cinema* (1974), translated by Umiker-Sebeok. Carroll (1980), for one, has described Metz's work as having had "a significant impact on cinema studies in the mid-1970's," adding that it "remains the classic work of that period."

The second is Tzvetan Todorov, whose earliest semiotic work, about the *Decameron*, it was my privilege to publish as far back as 1969. With the linguist Oswald Ducrot, Todorov also produced a reference manual, very useful in its time, with critical entries relevant to semiotics (1979 [1972]:84–92). Among his many im-

portant books, however, the one which made the profoundest
impression on me, as it did on many other Anglo readers, was
his remarkable *The Conquest of America* (1984 [1982]), constituting
Todorov's refulgent meditations about, as it were, semioses of
confrontation in our hemisphere between the conquered Indians
and the conquering Spaniards.

At least a couple of other French authors, whose two quite
different, slender tomes were both translated from the French
and then published for American consumption, must be mentioned here. The author of the earlier of the two was Roland
Barthes, a luminous, prolific, and utterly captivating gentleman
of letters (and, from the beginning in 1969 to 1974, also a hard-
working member of the editorial board of *Semiotica*). The title
the translators chose for the English edition was *Elements of Semiology* (first published in France in 1964, and then in New York
in 1968). Typically original and idiosyncratic, this attractively
provocative essay was so indelibly imprinted on its insufficiently
attentive Anglo-American readership that many took it as tantamount to not simply the latest word—*dernier cri*—out of Paris
but the first and final judgment on semiology, a.k.a. semiotics.
When, years afterwards, I was invited by the editor of the *New
York Times Book Review* to undertake a critical assessment (Sebeok
1986b) of a highly technical and obscure seventeenth-century
treatise on signs, I was strictly instructed to open with an explicit statement that semiotics, "now a chic undertaking," did
not commence just a couple of decades earlier with "the semi-
journalistic works of Roland Barthes." For a clear and useful
appreciation of Barthes's "Semiology: The Sign, Relations and
Functions" and its reverberations, see the account by Lavers
(1982:219–28).

The other book, Pierre Guiraud's *Semiology*, came out in Boston
in 1975 (original French edition, 1971), with a shrewd, knowledgeable foreword by Frank Kermode. Kermode says:

Semiology has now a strong theoretical foundation, which M.
Guiraud lucidly describes; but no one, I think, would claim that
it is fully formed. In particular there is still a good deal of reasonable doubt about its use, at the present stage of its development, in the analysis of the arts, including literature. . . . It is still
conceivable that it may turn out to be one of those disciplines

which are of value not because the practitioners ever reach their
objective—in this case a generally applicable science of signs—
but by reason of casual and accidental discoveries made along the
way.

Guiraud's simple, straightforward exposition, Kermode notes,
will enable his readers "to read with more understanding the
most interesting attempts yet made—which I take to be those
of M. Roland Barthes—at such an analysis" (viii). Those of us
who knew the late Guiraud as a great philologist, linguist, many-
sided contributor to semiotics (Calvet and Valdman 1989), and
wonderously cynical and urbane Frenchman can imagine his *Je
m'en fous* pout and shrug, so well pictured by Rick Stafford in
Laurence Wylie's delicious *Beaux Gestes: A Guide to French Body
Talk* (1977:22)!

Over here, the most carefully heeded living European semiotician is not French but Italian: Umberto Eco. Eco, whose minute anatomization of Jakobson's semiotics (1987) I have already
cited, rightly regards Hjelmslev as "invaluable for the whole
development of structural semantics" but also recognizes his
limitations in a global perspective (e.g., 1984:21). Eco has made
his own overall position quite clear: "Many semioticians assume
(and I rank among them) that Peirce in fact outlined . . . a project
of a general semiotics" (ibid. 6f.). It would be stimulating and
instructive to chart the course of Eco's gradual ascendancy in
America (which he visits frequently) since 1976, when his first
major work, *A Theory of Semiotics*, appeared in English at Indiana—since then, all of his books have become available—but
this pleasurable task must be postponed for a future occasion
(see also Proni 1988).

Although probably less well known to the American public
than Eco, other prominent Italian semioticians abound. After
all, as I wrote in my foreword to Segre's latest book, "Italy is the
country where the European rinascimento of semiotics has its
true roots and whence some of its best work continues to reso-
nate worldwide, via some very fine translations" (1988:vii). In
addition to Segre's, I should at least mention that, in two of my
series alone, there have hitherto appeared seven further books
written or coauthored by Eco, one by Corti (1978), one by Valesio, who teaches at Yale (1980), one by Pagnini (1987), with

one each soon forthcoming by Giorgio Fano, Emilio Garroni, Giovanni Manetti, and Marco de Marinis.

Veering now toward a quite different region of Europe, namely, the Soviet Union, writings by several members of the justly celebrated Tartu-Moscow School of semiotics have also impinged heavily upon American scholarship, although not to the same extent as the Italo-French ones, or necessarily affecting the same academics. For those who cannot manage Russian, two nicely complementary American readers, in addition to a number of outstanding British efforts, have facilitated access to this enormously rich and creative literature: the one by Baran (1976), the other by Lucid (1977; republished in 1988 with a new foreword [v-viii] by Sebeok); a special issue of the journal *New Literary Theory* (Vol. 9, No. 2, 1978) also featured Soviet semiotics. Stephen Rudy, in his essay "Semiotics in the U.S.S.R" (1986; see also the relevant lemmata in the EDS), provides indispensable additional edification on this subject. So does Igor Chernov's (who is a pupil of Lotman) new "Historical Survey of Tartu-Moscow Semiotic School" (in Broms and Kaufmann 1988:7–33). One should also read the original articles by Bogatyrev, Egorov, V. V. Ivanov, Lekomceva, Lotman, Oguibenine, Piatigorsky, Revzin, Revzina, Syrkin, Uspensky, and other Soviet scholars scattered throughout the pages of *Semiotica*, from Vol. 1 (1969) onwards. I would particularly single out V. N. Toporov's prize-winning article "On the Semiotics of Mythological Conceptions about Mushrooms" (53:295–357), which, with a preface by Wendy O'Flaherty (289–93) and an afterword by Jakobson (359f.), graced an entire special issue of this journal.

A key concept of the Tartu-Moscow School has to do with primary and secondary modeling systems, actually an Aesopic euphemism created for *semiotics* in 1964, when the use of this term was prohibited by "scientific" commissars, but which eventually took on a curious life of its own. The concept has been widely discussed in the West, stimulated my own critique of these twinned concepts (Sebeok 1988d), and ultimately led to the production of a massive collaborative tome exploring many aspects of the whole subject of modeling in semiotics (Anderson and Merrell 1991).

Specialists in the field are of course aware of the many and varied contributions of East European semioticians. In quantity,

high overall quality, and sheer diversity, these have been and
remain today impressive indeed. In Poland, for example, an emphasis is evident, emanating out of the Warsaw-Lwow school of
logic (Buczyńska-Garewicz 1987), sparked by Franz Brentano's
student Kazimierz Twardowski and his followers, who included
Tadeusz Kotarbinski (whom, memorably, I met at a Romanian
resort in 1967) and Alfred Tarski (at whose house in Berkeley I
dined in 1959 in the company of Jakobson and Quine). In Czech-
oslovakia, they led up to, flowered during (Galan 1985), and
followed (Tobin 1988) the heyday of the Prague School project,
with prominent figures such as Jan Mukařovský (ibid. 265–73
and passim), who was concerned with the semiotic ramifications
of artistic perception and experience.

Other workshops continue to flourish in Bulgaria, Hungary,
and Romania. These certainly widen the horizons of ethnography, philosophy, poetics, and ultimately semiotics around the
world, and *a fortiori* in the United States in ways too intellectually
swarming and divaricated to detail here. (For details, see the
relevant entries in Sebeok and Umiker-Sebeok 1986.)

II.

The university is perfused with signs, if it is not
composed exclusively of signs.

—Peirceonal communication

From this shifting kaleidoscope of people and ideas—the names
and labels that take shape, shimmer, dazzle, although ofttimes
fade away—I would like to turn next, albeit briefly, to the or-
ganizational aspects of semiotics, the external expressions that
have molded its development in teaching and research in the
United States.

We know something about Peirce's seminars at Johns Hopkins

from 1879 to 1884, for instance from Jastrow's enthusiastic account (1916):

> The fertility of his resources imparted a breadth to his treatment that brought the student to a constant leadership of a rich mind. His knowledge never gave the impression of a burden, but of strength. His command of the history of science was encyclopedic in the best sense of the word. . . . [His] sense of masterly analysis accomplished with neatness and dispatch,—all seemingly easy, but actually the quality of the highest type of keen thinking— remains as the central impression of a lecture by Professor Peirce. (Ibid. 723)

It has been asserted that Allan Marquand was his sole Ph.D. candidate (in 1880). But among others who participated in Peirce's seminars, one should surely mention at least Joseph Jastrow, Christine Ladd(-Franklin), John Dewey, J. McKeen Cattell, O. A. Mitchell (credited by Peirce for having introduced the quantifier into formal logic), and Thorstein Veblen.

Perhaps the most enduring monument to Peirce's students is the 1883 volume he collected, *Studies in Logic by the Members of the Johns Hopkins University*. Marquand's dissertation, "The Logic of the Epicureans," was based on the Philodemus fragment; as for the paper Marquand read on this same subject at a meeting of the Metaphysical Club (January 13, 1880), Peirce was the commentator of record (although the De Lacys seem not to have known this work). Dewey's dissertation on Kant has vanished. We are, alas, ignorant of what the semiotic complexion of Peirce's seminars was like.

In my "Vital Signs" (see Appendix below), I stated my belief that "the very first sequence of courses in semiotics, so labeled, in any curriculum anywhere" was offered by Charles Morris, beginning in the late 1930s, at the University of Chicago. I identified the only classmate of mine (of a handful) I can still remember: the teenage mathematical prodigy Walter Pitts, who was to become Warren S. McCulloch's collaborator (and to whom, McCulloch wrote, "I am principally indebted for all subsequent success" [1965:9]).

I think that only three of us—the prolific science author Martin Gardner, the preeminent musicologist Leonard Meyer, and I— survive from among Morris's Chicago seminarians. When Morris moved to the University of Florida, he discontinued his semiotic seminars, and the teaching of a subject thus identified in university catalogs ceased until Ethel M. Albert briefly revived the practice at Northwestern University in the late 1960s.

Albert, who died after a long and debilitating illness in the late 1980s, is named in the Northwestern catalog as a professor for 1966–67, and her 1968 vita update identifies among her areas of "current" research "semiotics: theoretical models and methodology for comprehensive analysis of continuous discourse." The bulletin for the previous year listed the topics of three successive graduate "seminars on semiotics": discourse analysis, systematic lexicography, and animal communication. The identical sequence appeared as late as the 1979–80 catalog, but Albert's name had vanished by then, as does any more recent mention of semiotics. Edward T. Hall's seminar in proxemics is first listed at Northwestern in 1968–69.

Nowadays, the teaching of semiotics—as distinguished from semiotically informed teaching—is common in American institutions, sometimes in separate departments, such as at Rice; sometimes in other programs, such as at Brown and Indiana universities; and often *ad hoc* (cf. Rauch 1978; and Appendix III, "Teaching Semiotics," in Sebeok 1988a:272–79). Brown University, for example, has for decades offered an undergraduate concentration in semiotics through its Center for Modern Culture and Media.

"Semiotically informed teaching" is a subject I cannot deal with here beyond noting that it has pervaded certain important American liberal arts curricular reform movements, for example, those built around the so-called Great Books program. This is illustrated by Scott Buchanan's programmatic injunction of the late 1930s, in the same year, during the heyday of President Robert Maynard Hutchins, that I entered the College of the University of Chicago:

> The liberal arts are chiefly concerned with the nature of the symbols, written, spoken, and constructed, in terms of which we rational animals find our way around the material and cultural world in which we live. . . . There are concrete data and artificial products that must be distinguished from the abstract principles and ideas which govern them. There are many connections that

these aspects have with one another, and it is the business of the liberal artist to see these apart and put them together. (P. 227)

Ironically, it was the retrospective semiotic of Galen and Aquinas, later of Maritain, that was involved in this and kindred efforts, which, on the other hand, explicitly rejected Peirce, James, and Dewey, as well as Chicago's Carnap and Morris.

The *American Journal of Semiotics* devoted an entire recent issue (Vol. 5, No. 2, 1987) to semiotics and education, guest edited by Donald J. Cunningham, which should be read by all concerned with recent pedagogical trends in this area in this country. Elsewhere, he says that education is a field in which semiotics has had, until lately, relatively little impact, but it is clear from his survey (1987) that this situation is rapidly improving.

A decade ago, an exciting vision of Paul Bouissac (University of Toronto) was realized by the creation of the International Summer Institute for Semiotic and Structural Studies. Its basic purposes are to provide graduate and postdoctoral students and others with a set of courses and seminars in the various branches of semiotics, and to foster interdisciplinary exchanges by bringing together, for a reasonable length of time, specialists who share a common interest in the advancement of semiotics. The institute has typically alternated estivally between Canada and the United States (with occasional hibernal excursions to another continent, viz., to India); campuses which have hosted one or more institutes in this country include Indiana University (twice in Bloomington, once in Indianapolis), Northwestern University, Vanderbilt University, and the University of Hawaii (each with one).

In passing, I should allude to the International Semiotics Institute, formally established in Imatra, Finland, in July of 1988, having as its primary aims the consolidation of pedagogical resources worldwide and the facilitation of the movements of students among different institutions that offer semiotics courses in whatever guise. According to present plans, the day-by-day functions of the institute are to be carried out through over half a dozen regional centers, with the one to service North America located within the Indiana University Research Center for Language and Semiotic Studies. This center within a center is directed by Donald J. Cunningham.

It should also be recorded that a sophisticated course of instruction in semiotics was introduced in the mid-1960s in the elite Brookline High School for sophomores, juniors, and seniors, under the leadership of Donald W. Thomas (1976). The curriculum is supported by four readers especially designed for these classes. This project still continues, although it is unclear at this time how far, and with what success, it has spread beyond Massachusetts to other states in the union.

On July 28–30, 1975, the First North American Semiotics Colloquium was held at the University of South Florida (see Sebeok 1977a). It was there that the idea of forming a Semiotic Society of America was propounded. The following year, September 24–25, the society's initial meeting took place at the Georgia Institute of Technology in Atlanta, with over one hundred registrants, under the presidency of Henry Hiż. The most important piece of business conducted there was the adoption of the society's constitution, essentially as it was drafted by (our 1980) president-to-be Allen Walker Read. The SSA has held fifteen more annual meetings since (frequently together with rump sessions of the Charles S. Peirce Society), peregrinating from the East (Buffalo, College Park, Providence, Reading) to the West (Denver, San Francisco, Snowbird), to the Midwest (Bloomington [bis], Cincinnati, Indianapolis), to the Southwest (Lubbock, Norman), and to the South (Nashville, Pensacola).

Proceedings of nine of these meetings have been published so far, chiefly on Deely's editorial initiative, lately in volumes approaching eight hundred pages per annum. Other serials of the SSA have included the now-fugitive issues of the *Bulletin of Literary Semiotics*, replaced by the *Semiotic Scene*, replaced by the *American Journal of Semiotics* (currently in its seventh volume, successively coedited by Irene Portis Winner with Thomas G. Winner, then by Dean MacCannell with Juliet Flower MacCannell). Now published by Indiana University Press, this is the society's, and therefore America's, official learned publication in semiotics. In 1989, the *Semiotic Scene* was revived, under the editorship of Terry J. Prewitt; this new series is intended to supplement the AJS.

In 1977, *Ars Semeiotica: International Journal of American Semiotic* was launched, under the nominal patronage of Charles Morris, at the University of Colorado. On May 11 of that year, Morris wrote: "International in character but with the due recognition of the place of American contributions in this field—so I have long wished for contemporary semioticians to be. In my work I have had this emphasis for over fifty years." In 1982, after its fourth volume, *Ars Semeiotica* folded without fanfare into a Greek-German venture, *Kodikas/Code*, where, bereft of its identity, it soon afterwards vanished.

Regional or local organizations have sprung up here and there. The largest among these is the Semiotic Circle of California (Rauch 1986), which had its third meeting in 1988. The Fifth Congress of the International Association for Semiotic Studies is scheduled to be held in this country in June 1994, hosted by the University of California at Berkeley.

About thirty books have appeared to date under the umbrella title Advances in Semiotics from Indiana University Press. This series includes both of the principal complementary anthologies commonly used by beginning students in the United States: Innis (1985) and Deely et al. (1986). Plenum Press brings out another series, Topics in Contemporary Semiotics; among its eight volumes to date, it has featured Krampen et al. (1987), often used as a companion volume to the preceding pair of readers. In 1986, Plenum also published *The Semiotic Sphere* (Sebeok and Umiker-Sebeok 1986), assembling twenty-seven chapters on the state of the art in as many countries around the globe.

The Semiotic Web, a continuing series of yearbooks under the imprint of Mouton de Gruyter, began appearing in 1986. Both the *Sphere* and the *Web* are produced, under the editorial care of the Sebeoks, at Indiana University's Research Center for Language and Semiotic Studies. The EDS was likewise prepared at the RCLSS, with the collaboration of a six-member international editorial board, and was published in Mouton's Approaches to Semiotics series (at the time of writing in its eighty-fifth volume, all of which were edited at the RCLSS).

Mouton de Gruyter, the publisher of *Semiotica*, since 1981 bestows the Mouton d'Or Award to recognize the single article published during the preceding year judged best by an independent international jury (Sebeok 1987c). Thus far, five out of the nine recipients so honored have been Americans: John N. Deely, William O. Hendricks, Judith Modell, Dorothy Davis Wills, and W. C. Watt.

III.

Que sera, sera.

—Jo MacKenna (Doris Day) singing to
Hank (Christopher Olsen), in Alfred
Hitchcock's *The Man Who Knew
Too Much* (1955)

At the outset of this book, I incautiously pledged "perhaps to
cautiously extrapolate from the known to the unknown," or in
other words to speculate yet again on *Dove va la semiotica?*—
where, in other words, is semiotics, particularly semiotics in the
United States, headed? Thus did Marrone (1986:149–51) pose
the question to me and several other colleagues in Palermo.
Curious myself, I attempted later to seek a consensual answer
elsewhere (Sebeok, comp. 1986), and later still, if both succinctly
and tentatively, to supply one myself (Sebeok 1988c).

Whereas modern practitioners of semiotics are content to
probe the perpetual and the universal, or, short of such lofty
pursuits, to dwell on and reassess their past, our distant cousins
the oracles of Greece, the haruspices of the Italian peninsula,
the augurs of Rome, like today's host of psychic readers, strove
to prognosticate the future. Their perceptions, illuminations,
predictions, their "pseudo-semiotic divinatory techniques" (Sebeok 1985:28), risk being embarrassed by time (the soothsayers
in *Julius Caesar*, like the witches in *Macbeth*, did turn out to be
right—but those were figures of fiction).

In cosmology, our ability to predict the future and retrodict
the remote history of the universe hinges on a crucial discovery
in 1929 by Edwin Powell Hubble, the American lawyer turned
astronomer, which makes it possible to relate in a systematic
manner the shift in the spectral lines of distant galaxies to their
distances, or, briefly, size to age. This paradigmatic model of
the dynamic expanding universe may be pictured as a theoretical
laboratory in which the beginning, the present, and the destiny
of our universe are seen not only as in flux but as radically
different, and in which the energetic world of elementary particle interactions can be seriously investigated. In fact, the 1965

detection of microwave background radiation left over from the initial hot fireball of the Big Bang helped sustain the theory in most dramatic fashion.

Forecasts about the shape of semiotics to come, too, depend on which "paradigmatic model," or theoretical gambit, one chooses for one's frame of reference. Inconveniently, we have nothing to lean on as solid as the Hubble constant. But for me the sign science has always seemed to be a branch of the life science, and semiosis the most pervasive, indeed, criterial, fact of all life on earth. The pluralistic laws of biology—which are not, to be sure, equivalent to the universals of classical physics, yet are high-level generalizations all the same—should therefore be applicable to semiotics. Semiosis, in short, is seen as a teleonomic process, its goal-directedness (cf. Short 1988:82) as the consequence of the operation of a program with an end in view. This is why the explanation of any semiosic "fact" can be modeled only in the form of a historical narrative.

However, the biosphere as a whole, its evolutionary processes, are intrinsically unpredictable. Even such a strong reductionist biologist as Monod came to a similar conclusion, namely, that

one of the fundamental characteristics common to all living beings without exception [is] that of being *objects endowed with a purpose or project*, which at the same time they exhibit in their structure and carry out through their performances (such as, for instance, the making of artifacts). Rather than reject this idea (as certain biologists have tried to do) it is indispensable to recognize that it is essential to the very definition of living beings. We shall maintain that the latter are distinct from all other structures or systems present in the universe by this characteristic property, which we shall call *teleonomy*. (1971:9; italics in the source)

For the best treatment known to me of both the explanatory and the nonexplanatory functions of models in biological theory, see Beckner (1959, Ch. III). Among those particularly pertinent to semiotics, cf. Beckner's discussion of the evolutionary models associated with the names of McCulloch and Pitts (see above), and of the feedback models of W. Ross Ashby and the cyberneticists. On the model of semiotics and biology—the science of the animate—of living organisms and their parts, according to Jakob von Uexküll, see Sebeok 1988a, Ch. 10; Thure von Uexküll 1989.

What, then, are the properties that characterize the living (Sebeok 1988b)? To begin with, the quick usually reproduce, that is to say, pass on to their offspring through copying and amplifying the voluminous messages (their form, not necessarily their material substance) that specify *them*—information that they themselves have inherited. Peirce called procreation "the most marvellous faculty of humanity" (CP 7.590), but it is a capacity shared with the power of semiosis: "Symbols grow. They come into being by development out of other signs. . . . It is only out of symbols that a new symbol can grow. *Omne symbolum de symbolo*, says Peirce about 1895 (ibid. 2.302), manifestly mindful of Rudolf Virchow's famous 1855 aphorism, *Omnis cellula a* [or *e*] *cellula* (Ackerknecht 1953:83, 251, n. 50). A comparable formulation also lies at the heart of Weizsäcker's thesis, to the effect that "information is only that which produces information" (1971:351).

Life, or genetic information, is, of course, a product of evolution through natural selection—the hereditary memory is modifiable; whether, however, according to conventional wisdom, such modification is always due to chance, or whether mutations are capable of responding to signs in their environment (for example, signs of stress), will doubtless be determined by experiments now underway.

Other features criterial of life that are sometimes adduced include organized, coherent, cooperative, and integrated complexity; uniqueness; unpredictability; interconnectedness with the rest of the biosphere; and evolution. For each such criterion, strong homologies can be found in semiosis, but Jakob von Uexküll went still further.

Two of the most salient features arising from Uexküll's synthesis are the elucidation of, first, the nature of the coupling between an observing organism and an observed organism, and, second, the mechanisms of mutual influence, or, more precisely, inviolable interdependence, between signs and behavior. This coalescence, synopsized and depicted in Uexküll's celebrated model of the "functional circuit" whereby every organism constructs its own subjective *Umwelt*, originated on earth with the evolution of the first cell.

Nothing exists for any organism outside its bubblelike private

Umwelt, into which, although impalpably to its observer, it remains, as it were, inextricably sealed. The behavior of every organism—"behavior" being defined as the sign trafficking among different *Umwelten*—has as its basic function the production of nonverbal signs for communication, and first of all for communication of that organism with itself. The *primal sign-relation* in the ontogeny of an organism is therefore realized as an opposition between *ego* and *alter*—self-recognition is the third fundamental property of living organisms. (There are multiple mechanisms for self-recognition, a major mode being the formation of antibodies in higher animals; see below.)

The interpretation of messages is, as we know, always context-dependent. The problem of embryonic development—that is, how one-dimensional information (the string of DNA) can become expressed in a three-dimensional organism (or really four-dimensional, since it is subject to patterned temporal changes)—is now likewise perceived and addressed in terms of contextual contingency, meaning that the present location of a cell and its present activity provide most of the information on what it is to do next. Thus biology turns into *topobiology*, "the study of . . . how cells of different types are ordered in time or place during development to give species-specific tissue pattern and animal form" (Edelman 1988:227f.).

This elemental binary schism subsequently brings to pass the *second semiosic dimension*, that of *inside* vs. *outside*. It is this secondary opposition that enables the organism to "behave," namely, to enter into relations or link up with other living systems in its surroundings. The coupling of the observed with the observer is thus, by definition, a phenomenon situated in this second dimension, where every "outside" becomes a denotatum (Morris 1946:347), a perceptual cue of an "inside." In other words, no "outside" exists beyond the impenetrable periphery of the *Umwelt*.

Jakob's elder son, Thure von Uexküll (1987 *et alibi*), has shown that whereas the functional circuit is based on a dyadic model for the generation of signs, for its productive function it is based on a triadic model, incorporating the equivalent of an interpretant. This double-track modeling posits the theory at once in the binary (Saussurean) tradition, on the one hand, and in the triadic (Peircean) tradition, on the other. It thus neatly reconciles the major with the minor semiotic traditions, even though the Ger-

man neo-Kantian scientist, who was by profession a theoretical
and experimental biologist, knew of neither (on the two traditions, see Sebeok 1977a:181–83).

The equivalent of the Peircean interpretant in this conception
is to be found in the specific character of the receptor in question.
The frame and the way in which the bifacial aspect of signs—
aistheton and noeton, signans and signatum, sign-vehicle and
designatum (Sebeok 1985:117f.), etc.—unfolds are dictated by
each organism's biological needs (such system-needs being usually called "homeostasis"), as spelled out by J. von Uexküll in
considerable detail, especially in his hermetic *Theoretical Biology*
(in German: 1920, 1928), so wretchedly translated into English
(in 1926) under C. K. Ogden's eccentric auspices. Only via this
semiosic operation can an organism attain the goals of its behavior.

Note an important consequence of this model: supposing that
a behavioral segment, say, in a chimpanzee, is registered by the
observing psychologist as a sequence of signing gestures to humans or other chimpanzees, and is interpreted by her as a string
of communicational sign-vehicles, then that behavioral segment
has to be, in the first instance, a product of that observer's subjective *Umwelt* (Sebeok and Umiker-Sebeok 1981; Sebeok 1987b).
In fact, what may constitute a "sign" in the *Umwelt* of the observed organism is inaccessible to the observer. The solution to
this seemingly intractable dilemma, according to Uexküll, pre-
supposes that the would-be observer of the behavior of another
organism begin by analyzing her own *Umwelt* before she can
undertake productive observations of the behavior of speechless
creatures. It is by way of such a comparative analysis that we
are led straight back into the heart of semiosis in our human
world.

Another kind of *Umwelt* theory was independently invented
in 1943 by Craik, who hypothesized that "the organism carries
a 'small-scale model' of external reality and of its own possible
actions within its head" (1967:61; cf. Bower and Morrow 1990:
48), and that the essential feature of thought is "not propositions
but symbolism" (1967:57). Craik's hypothesis has many surprising features, among which is his version of semiosis (ibid. 50f.),
or a kind of action cycle; for him, the Peircean interpretant becomes roughly coterminous with "translation" plus "reason-

ing," the basic materials for which he glimpses in inorganic
nature: "it is only the sensitive 'receptors' on matter, and means
of intercommunication . . . which are lacking" (ibid. 59). Craik
never mentions either Peirce or Uexküll, but he knew at least
the 1923 version of *The Meaning of Meaning* and, oddly, does
mention Mrs. Ladd-Franklin (ibid. 108).

After this short detour, we can return to some general considerations about future trends in American semiotics, though
attempt nothing so foolish as to provide a blueprint. The sad
fact must be registered, to begin with, that the contemporary
teaching of semiotics is severely, perhaps cripplingly, impov-
erished. The terminal reasons behind this were insistently
sketched out in C. P. Snow's Rede Lecture of 1959—itself anticipated in England by the likes of Matthew Arnold and Thomas
Carlyle—and can accordingly be ascribed to the utter, fright-
ening innocence of most practitioners of semiotics about the
natural order in which they and it are embedded.This whole
group is, as Snow complained, by absence of training tone-deaf
over an immense spectrum of intellectual experience: "As with
the tone-deaf, they don't know what they miss." Semiotics is
too important to be left in the hands of the "semiotician *ordinaire*"
(this phrase being Sidney J. Levy's unduly modest title, in Umiker-Sebeok 1987:13), for it will surely shrivel and wither unless
this lesson sinks in. (For a recent semiotically informed com-
pensating effort, see Paulson 1988.)

This is a good place to bring to mind again that our titans—
Peirce, Morris, and Jakobson—were thoroughly, if diversely,
seasoned in the scientific trends of their time. For many years,
when Peirce was asked to identify his profession, he called himself a chemist, but he had also written papers in mathematics,
physics, geodesy, spectroscopy, and experimental psychology,
among others. Jastrow (1916:724) made a point of noting about
an 1883 paper of Peirce's that "the trend was biological, the product required the schooling of discipline and the inspiration of
genius."

Morris's definition of semiotics (1946:223) is always and emphatically worth repeating: its scope, he affirmed, encompasses
"the science of signs, whether animal or human, language or
nonlanguage, true or false, adequate or inadequate, healthy or
pathic"; and as Jakobson (1973:44) remarked, in the perspective

of biology, in "the science of life which embraces the total organic world . . . the different kinds of human communication become a mere section of a much vaster field of studies."

These were essentially programmatic declarations, but they are being implemented daily, bit by bit, in laboratories all over America (and, of course, abroad as well). The results of such researches will certainly mold, continue to enrich, and inform our semiotics to come. Rudolf Jander (in De George 1981:225–50), an entomologist by trade, favors the term *biosemiotics* (cf. Th. von Uexküll 1991a), defined as "the application of general semiotics to living systems"; he argues further that all organisms, seedlings as well as chickens, "contain semiotic systems that mediate the observed semiosis" (245f.). (Jander's otherwise well-thought-out, stimulating scheme is unfortunately vitiated to a degree by his reliance on some bogus data, particularly about primates.) This underlying constitutional area of biosemiotics has happily been solidified with the creation, in Glottertal (Baden-Württemberg) on June 8, 1990, of an International Biosemiotics Society (IBS), incorporated under German law, with headquarters at the Klinik für Rehabilitation in Glotterbad.

Below, I shall mention, if sketchily, some biosemiotic particulars (for further details, see Sebeok 1990b). First, however, one practical chore that needs to be addressed by our students is either to define rigorously or to discard altogether from semiotic discourse such run-of-the-mill vocabulary items as "information" or "communication," on the one hand, and a host of *ad hoc* neologisms scattered through various recent theory-tied analytical dictionaries and similar aids for would-be beginning semioticians on the other.

A model of clarity for the former pair is persuasively provided by Wright in his chapters "What Is Information?" and "What Is Communication?" (1988, Chs. 9 and 17; 1989). Terminological chaos remains, however, a painful, special scandal of our generation of semioticians, and this needs urgently to be ameliorated (for some preliminary ventures in the rectification of terms, see Sebeok 1985:156–64; and for a more authoritative, though not necessarily always definitive, source, see the relevant lemmata in the EDS).

Semiosis is by no means unlimited (save perhaps in a metaphysical sense). Interpretants certainly had a demarcatable beginning on the protocellular level (Fox 1988:89–92) and, unless they carry on in robots and reproducing von Neumann machines beyond, will cease with the extinction of life.

Terrestrial semiosis—no one knows whether there is any other—began in the Archean eon (up to about 3,900 million years ago) and flourishes in the microcosmos, among the prokaryotic bacilli, cocci, and spirilla. All bacteria contribute to and draw benefits from a common gene pool. They form teams intertwined by localized semiosic processes. But the single most momentous fact about them is that they are not really discrete organisms: together they "constitute the communications network of a single superorganism whose continually shifting components are dispersed across the surface of the planet," and as a body they interact with eukaryotes in unremitting complex global commerce (Sonea 1988:40; 1990).

Microsemiosis is thus by no means confined to exchanges of signs in localized teams and throughout the biosphere, but it takes place abundantly as well in prokaryotic interactions with eukaryotes (plants, animals, protoctists, and fungi, that is, all organisms with nuclei, which can be thought of as bound-up packages of masses of DNA). Each bacterium is "part of a much larger network—a network that in some sense resembles human intelligence" (ibid. 45).

The asexual life cycle and resultant semiosis of the little amoeboid creature *Dictyostelium discoideum* continues to hold scientists spellbound for its complexity and elegance. These tiny organisms, independent in their natural habitat, synchronously aggregate when "hungry" into mounds of about 100,000 cells which commence differentiating into prestalk and prespore cell types, and then continue this process until it culminates in a fruiting body of dormant spores held aloft by dead cellulose-coated cells. This motile, now multicellular slug migrates toward light and an agreeable temperature to locate nourishment. The signans which carries the message "Agglomerate and find food!" (the signatum) is the cyclic AMP molecule—the same as Tomkins (1975) identified in the human metabolic code (see below).

The eukaryotes, notably plants and animals, serve our ancestral prokaryotes as both habitats and supplementary means of transportation. To do so efficiently, signs must continually flow between us, the colonized, and our colonizers, invisible to the naked eye: "As tiny parts of a huge biosphere whose essence is basically bacterial, we—with other life forms—must add up to

108   Thomas A. Sebeok

a sort of symbiotic brain which is beyond our capacity to comprehend or truly represent" (Margulis and Sagan 1986a:152). At
present, such, to be sure, is the case. But one of the most exciting
challenges for our students will be to uncover precisely how
signs are dispersed throughout the bacterial ensemble—this
view is aptly called the "unifying theory of intercellular communication" (Roth and LeRoith 1987:51)—to grasp semiosis on
a planetary scale, and to make plain the proper place of the
language-endowed animal enfolded within the vast, mainly silent biota.

Semiotic notions, it has been perfectly clear for some years,
have increasingly illuminated certain areas of basic biological
researches. To begin with, I should note that Yates (1991a) distinguishes microsemiosis from endosemiosis (cf. a sophisticated
discussion of the latter by Th. von Uexküll 1991b), confining the
former to "all those sign processes arising in complex cell operations (e.g., cell division, movement, secretion, metabolism,
maintenance, growth, repair), even including temporary, reversible suspension of most, or all life processes (encystation,
dehydration, freezing)," whereas the latter is employed to "address communication between cells or cell complexes."

As I deal with several branches of *endosemiotics* elsewhere in
more detail (Sebeok 1990b), it must suffice to but enumerate
here, with a few comments, some of these prospective research
opportunities for our successors:

• The genetic code, notably the far-reaching similarities in
structure between it and the architectonic model underlying the
verbal codes of all languages (Jakobson 1973:49–53). The genetic
code is universal, in the sense that the program of all living
entities is inscribed in the same "alphabet," and all organisms
decipher it by the same rules; the principles of a Chomskyan
universal grammar are likewise exceptionless—indeed, they
constitute the facultas signatrix itself.

• The immune code, now widely regarded (in a frontier field
that has been dubbed either *semioimmunology* or *immunosemiotics*)
as exhibiting not merely the properties of *any* semiotic system,
but rather one functioning, if well, in the manner of an unerring
open-ended generative grammar, capable of producing on the
order of 10^{11} different kinds of receptors (cf. Jerne 1985; see
above), designed to recognize, regardless of their shape or form,

"foreign" invaders (but when the system is not working well, diseases of autoimmunity, or mistranslations, occur).

• The metabolic code, an early study of which revealed Peircean thirdness, or symbolicity in the technical sense—the signans being the cyclic AMP molecule, and the signatum hunger (or the absence of carbon)—functioning at the interface of certain extra- and intracellular events (Tomkins 1975; and see further below).

• The neural code, as studied under the aegis of a relatively young discipline called *neurocommunications* (Whitfield 1984). Prosser (1985:118) rightly upholds that "communication is what neurobiology is about. The modes of communication include membrane conductances, patterns of neuronal spikes and graded potentials, electric coupling between cells, electrical and chemical transmission at synapses, secretion, and modification of neural function." The brain maintains direct channels with the lymphatic tissue via direct nerve links; it intervenes in the immunological activity in either a stimulative (+) or a retarding (−) capacity, e.g., in such emotional states as anger or joy. The signifier substances, called lymphokines, affect both the brain's bioelectric activity and the organism's psychological state.

Furthermore, against a background of "psychosomatic correlations" (Sebeok 1981b:260–65), new experiments conducted by psycho-neuro-immunologists seem to confirm that classical conditioning, according to the Pavlovian model, of specific lymphocytes can be achieved, such that a conditioned stimulus (in this instance, a saline solution) can be made to activate an immunological reaction normally reserved for an unconditioned stimulus (adrenaline).

It is worth noting, too, that the endocrine system and the nervous system, which are the two principal retes for the flow of communication within our bodies, are both specialized descendants of one common ancestor. Many of the molecules that served as messengers during the prokaryotic phase have maintained their essential structure even when their semiosic functions have changed over time. This explains many coincidences in semiosic processes throughout the five superkingdoms, as well as why endocrine messengers turn up so often in exocrine systems (the gastrointestinal tract, the bloodstream, the axon).

In 1975, a UCLA biochemist, Gordon M. Tomkins, published

110   Thomas A. Sebeok

a paper, now a classic of empirical semiotics as well, in which
he established that the cyclic AMP molecule is a *symbol*, a general sign in the precise technical sense of Peircean thirdness, in
that it "represents a unique state of the environment." Wright
has recently affirmed (1988:104) that this molecule has all the
attributes required for pragmatic meaning: there is a palpable
"symbol . . . ; something in the environment that the symbol
represents . . . ; and something alive that, upon processing the
symbol, behaves so as to reconcile its well-being with that environmental condition (by heading elsewhere)." As evolution
has progressed, cyclic AMP has hardly changed at all in meaning: it instigates *Escherichia coli*, within your gut, to search for a
more congenial environment when carbon is depleted; it provides social coherence in some species of hungry slime mold;
and it is a common second messenger in humans, denoting
different things in different contexts (ibid. 197). Tomkins has, in
short, unveiled the ancient origin of the symbol, not essentially
different in function from the symbols of human society. This
line of research must be continued and expanded to other semiosic entities.

   In fact, the phylogenesis of semiosis is now fairly well understood in its general outlines, although, of course, innumerable
particulars need to be ascertained and elucidated in the years
ahead. Semiosis emerged on earth with the appearance of pri-
mordial cells (some would argue for meaning inherent even in
the DNA molecule and in viruses, but this is doubtful). It informs
the microcosmos and the macrocosmos, leading to the evolution
of language as a modeling system, universally in the genus
Homo, and its manifestation as speech as a communicative device
in the adult and healthy form of our species *sapiens* (Sebeok
1986a, Ch. 2, *et alibi*). This was followed by other actualizations
of language, such as a sporadic assortment of speech surrogates
and script, and the ever-accelerating technology of the organi-
zational revolution (sketched in Beniger 1986).

   Likewise, the ontogenetic principles of semiosis in some species (e.g., some birds), including, notably, ours, are increasingly
coming to be understood. Colwyn Trevarthen's acute ethological
researches on the unfurling of the semiosic powers of infants,
especially in their early dyadic interactions with their mothers,
are a giant step in this direction (cf. 1990).

   The above are but a few critical domains of fundamental science where that intersects with the sign science, and where sensitive semioticians of tomorrow could well make productive contributions.

How animals communicate (*zoosemiotics*; Sebeok 1968, Sebeok and Ramsay 1969, Sebeok 1972, 1977b, and 1990e) has been of considerable interest to workers in semiotics since the early 1960s, including the special problems of how the speechless creatures communicate with humans and vice versa (Sebeok 1988b). The latter, however, is an area especially laden with misconceptions precisely when it is practiced solo by would-be inquirers untutored in semiotics and glaringly innocent of linguistics (Sebeok and Umiker-Sebeok 1981, Sebeok 1987b).

Our skeptical attitude is shared by many, such as Stephen Walker—to momentarily fasten on but one, chiefly since he is a psychologist with no discoverable hidden agenda—who begins his critique thus: "I should like first to emphasize that analogies between the demonstrated abilities of chimpanzees and the human use of speech [read: language] are extremely shaky" (1983:372). About the evidently widespread surreptitious use of human directions—briefly, the Clever Hans Phenomenon—Walker confirms that, as "practically all instances or sequences or combinations of gestures by chimpanzees or gorillas are made in the context of interactions with a human companion, there is virtually no evidence of this kind not vulnerable to the charge that the human contact determined the sequence of combinations observed" (ibid. 374).

There is a growing tendency to look at animal groupings, conspicuously insect societies, as information-processing systems; this, especially semiosis in honeybee colonies, has not escaped the attention of computer scientists interested, as many nowadays are, in parallel processing. While each individual bee converts signs in serial fashion, we now know that the colony operates as an ensemble in "parallel." This is a novel way of looking at zoosemiosis, from which members of the profession, viewing the human brain as an integrated social structure, have much to learn (cf. Seeley and Levien 1987).

How plants communicate (*phytosemiotics*; Krampen 1981b, 1986b) is a question that, in contrast with zoosemiotics, came seriously into the purview of the sign science less than a decade ago. We now know that phytosemiosic processes are enwrapped in zoosemiosic ones, which are thus hierarchically superior as

well as more complex (Uexküll 1987:5f.), and understand why
this must be so (Sebeok 1988b). We also know why human cells
understand the molecular messages of plants: for "many of the
chemicals that served as messengers during the unicellular phase
have maintained their essential structure, even as their communicative functions have changed" (Roth and LeRoith 1987:54).

Messages (besides, of course, energy and materials such as
food) are produced by plants, transformed by animals, and dis-
sipated by fungi (*mycosemiotics*). The complexities of zoosemiotics are thus logically consequent on the intermediacy of animals
as transforming agents in this transmission loop. Messages that
decay as a result of fungal action are eventually recyled in plants
and animals; or, as we might say, the molecules are refabricated
into novel strings of signs through the acquisition of further
interpretants. The semiosic cycle of growth, maturity, and dis-
solution goes on and on.

How humans signify and communicate (*anthroposemiotics*) is
the immense and multifarious field of inquiry—a world of our
own intellective construction, imaginatively furnished with objects and events—that normally and routinely preoccupies most
semioticians. This whole world is made up of intricate if only
partially shared systems of signified content, tools with which
each of us learns to establish liaison with our fellows by way of
an ever-shifting mixture of verbal and nonverbal signs.

Messages are a proper subject matter for semiotics (cf. Sebeok
1985:1), as they are for evolutionary biology, providing "the only
connections between life now and life a million or a billion years
ago" (Cairns-Smith 1985:28, and Ch. 2). But, according to some,
they constitute the proper subject matter of all social and behavioral sciences as well. For, as Norbert Wiener argued three
decades ago, "the social system is an organization, like the individual, that is bound together by a system of communication"
(1948:24), and that "society can only be understood through a
study of messages and the communication facilities which belong to it" (1950:9). The social production of meaning entails
"the possibility that sign systems might program social control,"
as Beniger (1986:90) notes in the course of his discussion of semiotics in his remarkable book on the origins and present state of
the Information Society. Explorations of this topic in its multiple
ramifications, that is, of the impact of the semiotic standpoint
on "the control revolution," will no doubt intensify despite, or

perhaps because of, Margaret Mead's caution that it is of the utmost importance that continuing work on semiotics "should take place not in the context of power and manipulation" (in Sebeok et al. 1972:286).

Wiener presciently added to his thesis that "in the future development of these messages and communication facilities, messages between man and machines, between machine and man, and between machine and machine, are destined to play an ever-increasing part" (1950:9). His foresight provides one of the most intriguing opportunities for the semiotician on both the near and distant horizon in the hybrid field called *cybersymbiosis*, but which I prefer to think of as *cybersemiosis*. By this I refer to those arenas of human sign action where either the message source or the message destination is not a life form but an electronically driven robot (a vision fleshed out in Sagan and Margulis 1987; cf. Sebeok 1988c) or a commingled composite of human and manufactured parts. Computer technology and robotics offer engrossing openings for the alert semiotician of today and tomorrow at these exciting frontiers of biotechnology.

I tried at various times to inject catastrophe-theoretical concepts into semiotics (cf. Sebeok 1986a:25f.), following René Thom's germinal ideas, building on Peirce, himself a powerful mathematician—Jastrow characterized Peirce as "deeply mathematical, his thinking has not the trace of scholastic quality" (1916:723)—and Uexküll, among others. Petitot-Cocorda (1985), in Paris, succeeded admirably in reinterpreting Jakobsonian structuralism in these terms, but only a handful of American scholars have followed. Myrdene Anderson (Sebeok 1986a, Ch. 3) and Floyd Merrell (1982:156, n. 10), both at Purdue University, are exceptional in this regard. (See also Johnson 1988, Ch. 37, for an entertaining, far-ranging synthesis.) The reason is, I think, that few of our semioticians are able to handle the requisite mathematical concepts and operations—if anything, less so than those of physics or biology.

A new project, also inspired by Peirce, providing a semiotic analysis of mathematical signs (including particularly of "zero" as a key to the naively naturalistic links between systems of representation and the "reality" they are assumed to stand for), has recently been launched by Brian Rotman (1987, 1988); the effects of his fascinating, and I think undoubtedly productive, constructivist efforts have yet to become plain. The Romanian

114   Thomas A. Sebeok

mathematician and semiotician Solomon Marcus has suggested
to me (in a personal communication, July 1990) that Kurt Gödel,
late of the Princeton Institute for Advanced Study, has made a
fundamental contribution to semiotics by virtue of the fact that
he was the first to prove that there exists a genuine, unavoidable
gap between semantics and syntax, embodied in his basic theo-
rem about incompleteness of the formal system of arithmetics,
showing that there always exist true sentences which cannot be
obtained by the syntactic rules of the system. Marcus is also of
the opinion that Samuel Eilenberg and Saunders MacLane, as
authors of the mathematical theory of categories, have supplemented the basic system of signs of the Cantorian Mathematics
of the nineteenth century (i.e., set theory), formed by elements
and sets; with these two mathematicians, morphisms and func-
tors came to enrich the system of scientific signs as to a higher
level of abstraction, providing a new "language" to assist the
unification of human knowledge. (As a sidelight, I might mention here that Eilenberg was a regular chess partner of John Lotz,
the Columbia University semiotician mentioned earlier in this
monograph.)

The name of Joseph Jastrow came up in this book, in connection with Peirce, a couple of times. No one thinks of Jastrow,
although he was a student of Peirce, as a semiotician. He is
usually mentioned as the first American Ph.D. (1886) in psychology. "Mr. Peirce's courses," he once remarked, "gave me
my first real experience of intellectual muscle. Though I
promptly took to the laboratory of psychology when that was
first established by Stanley Hall"—William James's student, the
founder and promoter of organized psychology as a science and
profession in America—"it was Peirce who gave me my first
training in the handling of a psychological problem" (1916:724)
(which was, in fact, a new way to determine the difference in
limen, that is, the point of just-perceptible difference in discrimi-
nating a sensation, a subject on which he published an early
paper jointly with Peirce).

Jastrow became best known as a popularizer of psychology
and a dedicated skeptic (as well as, incidentally, a sharp and
cogent critic of Freudian theory). It is Jastrow the skeptic who
chiefly interests me in this context. As early as 1888, he published
a popular study (later included in Jastrow 1900) on the tech-

niques of deception, including those employed in stage conjury and the claims of spiritualistic mediums. His interest in such matters "was strongly affected," he recorded, "by the public attention given to the movement inaugurated in 1882 by the Society for Psychical Research" (Jastrow 1930:143). He shrewdly connected this "popular interest" to allied "problems" in abnormal and social psychology, and this aroused his curiosity in the arts of deception on and off stage. He sought the personal acquaintanceship of such leaders in the art of conjury as Alexander Herrman, Harry Kellar, Harry Houdini, and Howard Franklin Thurston (who so enchanted the young Charles Morris—see Sebeok 1981b:84f.). These attractions, enhanced by his concern with the mechanisms underlying hypnotic and trance states, spurred Jastrow's skepticism and led to a number of his subsequent publications in the "province of logic" (read: semiotics), with particular attention to credulity and superstition (ibid. 145).

Jastrow wrote several remarkable books of a skeptical cast. His *Fact and Fable in Psychology* (1900) featured chapters ranging from "The Modern Occult" to "The Psychology of Deception," on hypnotism and spiritualism, and "A Study of Involuntary Movements." In his *Wish and Wisdom* (1935) he had an excellent chapter on animal "geniuses," notably recounting the tale of the notorious Clever Hans ("a simple fact, though a clever stunt," ibid. 205) and the hilarious case of Lola, the dog who kept a diary and rapped alphabetic messages with her paw onto her trainer's palm. These were two among other illustrations of "how a simple humanizing error in observation under a prepossession can compromise rationality, as wish diverges from wisdom" (ibid. 213)—as, unfortunately, it still does, although now tending to star apes and diverse species of marine mammals (cf., e.g., Sebeok and Umiker-Sebeok 1981; Sebeok 1986c).

These days, the indispensable and unending efforts of "skeptics"—a vocation, actually, of exceptionally dedicated scientists, philosophers, conjurers, and others—are being carried forward on a systematic, institutionalized basis by the (Buffalo-based) Committee for the Scientific Investigation of Claims of the Paranormal, which now maintains an international network of such people, and which publishes an outstanding journal, the *Skeptical Inquirer* (currently in its thirteenth volume). Its pages are filled with up-to-date articles precisely of the type pioneered by Jastrow.

Inspection of these articles and related "skeptical" books and publications reveals a pervasive resemblance to certain fundamental semiotic (including antisemiotic) writings. Too, deconstruction, a readerly philological conceit and practice that takes semiotic failure for granted, is but "a moment in the history of skepticism," as Donoghue (1989:39) has rightly noted in his revealing article "The Strange Case of Paul de Man" (on de Man's critique of semiotics, see further MacCannell 1985:139–42).

None of this should occasion surprise for those acquainted with the *Treatise* (1739) of the acute Scottish skeptical philosopher David Hume. It was Hume who transformed the notion of "sign" into the notion of "cause" (Book I, Parts IV and VII, and in the first *Enquiry* [1748], Section XII). Interestingly enough, Alexander Bryan Johnson's thought was clearly linked to Hume's nominalistic skepticism, while he was at the same time savagely critical of his illustrious predecessor, as well as of Locke, accusing both of failing utterly to understand the nature of language. Yet also, as I noted early in this book, the congruence of Johnson—who had declared: "I am the first philosopher who has gone deeper than language" (Todd and Blackwood 1969:xvii)—with Wittgenstein, the quintessential modern Pyrrhonian skeptic, or, for that matter, with the second-century Pyrrhonist Sextus Empiricus, the astute critic of Stoic theories of knowledge and of signs, is both surprising and quite remarkable (Stough 1969, Ch. 5, discusses Sextus Empiricus on signs and the relation thereof to empiricism and skepticism).

At the outset of his introductory handbook to skeptical thought, the *Outlines of Pyrrhonism*, Sextus had written:

> Those who investigate any subject are likely either to make a discovery or to deny the possibility of discovery and agree that nothing can be apprehended or else to persist in their investigations. That, no doubt, is why of those who undertake philosophical investigations some say that they have discovered the truth, others deny the possibility of apprehending it, and others are still pursuing their investigations. Those who are properly called dogmatists . . . think they have discovered the truth; [others] have said that the truth cannot be apprehended; and the skeptics persist in their investigations.

The ancient skeptics opposed themselves to dogmatists—those who subscribed to dogmas, or rigid doctrines. In the major tradition of contemporary semiotics, there are many skeptics who suspend judgment over the substantial range of questions addressed and whose goal is to perpetually persist in their quest. American semioticians tend to be skeptics—in the moderate sense, like Hume, of suspending the claim to have knowledge, not, at least not often, in the radical sense of suspending belief. There remain, to be sure, plenty of dogmatists—for instance, the Paris School semioticians, engaged in a pursuit they habitually refer to as "le projet sémiotique," and their epigones in the Western Hemisphere—but here they constitute but a sporadic rear guard, hacking away in a minor tradition.

Hume's influence on Peirce (and, via him and James, on Jastrow), on the one hand, and on the contemporary "skeptical" movement, on the other, can hardly be overestimated. As Martin Gardner recently pointed out (1989:261), "American philosophy has for half a century been tramping to the beat of British skepticism. . . . Hume has had far more effect on American philosophy . . . than have the German metaphysicians." Suffice it to point here to Miller's splendid demonstrations (1979, 1986) of the way Hume went about reducing causal relations (see further Beauchamp and Rosenberg 1981) to what his predecessors had understood to be natural indicative signs. In sum, the consanguinity of these grand, and after Hume indeed twinned, movements of our day—semiotics and skepticism—needs further careful exploration and documentation.

May I, in conclusion, gratify a hobby of mine, which I see as deeply implicated no less in semiotics than in the modern skeptical attitude? Maritain (1956:61), no vulgar skeptic, once wrote that "magic makes use of signs." Performing magic is an activity which can boast of the finest connoisseurs of conjury in our noble profession, including, in our day, Morris's student Martin Gardner. The youthful Charles Morris himself, in 1911, declared that he wished to adopt conjury as his career, a craft in honor of which he produced, even as late as 1966, a quasi-religious poem portraying such stage acts as "the pantomimes, the gestures, the replicas . . . mimes of the Great Magician" (Sebeok 1981a).

A detailed analysis of magic acts, for instance as exposed in Dariel Fitzroy, or "Fitzkee's," trilogy *Showmanship for Magicians,*

The Trick Brain, and *Magic by Misdirection*, reveals that the principles on which magical illusions are constructed are, on far
deeper levels than is commonly allowed, identical with those of
pure semiotics. Whether or not Morris was explicitly aware of
these, he and others have surely grasped them intuitively. In
the Renaissance, the man of science was still the magus; while
over the centuries the professions of semiotician and illusionist
necessarily followed diverging pathways, the academic personality remains forever the double-ganger of the entertainer.

It was therefore delightful to have been present when Naomi
Baron delivered her presidential address to the Semiotic Society
of America in October 1987 in Pensacola. She set forth (Baron
1988) the first serious comprehension, as far as I know, of this
by no means trivial area of prospective research. Baron's further
formation in her paper, which was titled "When Seeing's Not
Believing: Language, Magic, and AI" (1988), of a vinculum with
linguistics at one end and work in artificial intelligence at the
other, is but a hint of the promises inherent in this line of inquiry.

As Jaron Lanier remarked, "We really have to create a world
of illusion in order to deal with the physical world, because we
don't have omnipresent sensory capacity. . . . People really
want to believe in reality" (Wright 1987:9). In the last paragraph
of my "Vital Signs" (see Appendix below), I already dared call
attention to this central—and now I would add perennial—
preoccupation of semiotics with "an illimitable array of concordant illusions."

I here repeat that semiotics' overriding mission is and will be
"to mediate between reality and illusion," to penetrate to the
illusion behind reality—these being complementary universes
of signs—to decompose it, demystify it, and, in back of that,
unveil yet another reality, of an intenser texture still. For, as
Philodemus (1978:6.1–14), reporting Stoic arguments against Epicurean semiotics, queried as early as the first century B.C., "why
will the apparent any more be a sign of the non-apparent than
vice versa? Besides," he added, "if indiscernibility obtains we
will no longer have one thing apparent and the other non-evi-
dent."

APPENDIX

Vital Signs

When a physician sets out to evaluate a somatic system, he relies on established procedures drawn from accumulated biomedical knowledge—his personal long-term memory store, supplemented, when necessary, by a literature search—which leads to the formulation of hypotheses that become progressively narrowed with increasing specificity. "Abduction," said Peirce, "makes its start from facts, without, at the outset, having any particular theory in view, though it is motivated by the feeling that a theory is needed to explain the surprising facts. . . . The mode of suggestion by which, in abduction, the facts suggest the hypothesis is by *resemblance*—the resemblance of the facts to the consequences of the hypothesis" (1935–66:7.128; see further Sebeok and Umiker-Sebeok, in Eco and Sebeok 1983:18–19, and passim). The generation of clinical hypotheses is based on cues (Elstein et al. 1978:279–80), or the use of indicators of disease (Fabrega 1980:125), or, more exactly, a Gestalt-yielding composite of reported (subjective) symptoms and observed (objective) signs (see Ch. 4)—in a word, diagnosis. Faced at the start with an ill-defined problem, the physician progresses toward a solution by selective cue acquisition, according to a plan—delineated by Hippocrates and Galen—that facilitates and will perhaps result in the identification of a certain state of affairs in terms of a set of coherent defining characteristics. Since this abductive operation, which is a facet of memory organization and retrieval, is but poorly understood, it is hardly surprising that even experienced physicians will differ in style and substance as to their inferential ability and so sometimes construct dramatically dissimilar prognostic models.

When a patient initially encounters a licensed physician (or surrogate medical technician functioning under his authority or direction), a so-called general survey ensues. This rapid scan of the subject's apparent state of health, summed up from an array of verbal and nonverbal signs that are transmitted mainly via the auditory, optical, tactile, and olfactory channels, is followed by a compulsory registration of three or four factors which together are called *vital signs* (or merely, as a nominalized attribute, *vitals*): the pulse rate, respiration, and blood pressure,

Presidential address to the Semiotic Society of America, delivered to the Ninth Annual Meeting, held in Bloomington, Indiana, October 12, 1984. The pronominal vocables *he* and *she* are freely interconvertible. This address was also published in the *American Journal of Semiotics*, Vol. 3 (1985), pp. 1–27.

with temperature frequently being added. The accurate recording of these values provides indispensable, integrated data for the abductive sequence and continual heuristic evaluation supervening. (For the assessment of vital signs, particularly suited tools have even been designed and are wontedly kept handy: the stethoscope, the sphygmomanometer, and the thermometer; Barber and Dillman 1981, Ch. 9.)

In Peirce's pragmatism, what I am is what I do, and what I do is tantamount to what I signify. This is clearly the implication of his famous dictum "man is an external sign," or, as he amplified, "my language is the sum total of myself" (5.314; cf. Sebeok 1988a:61–73). Transmuted into Peirce's nomenclature, a vital sign—namely, its recorded value— must be indexical, "by virtue of being really affected" by the object denoted, and because it is actually modified by the object in some respects (2.248). "The value of an index is that it assures us of positive fact" (4.448). Or, as Thom (1983:267) later put it, with a Gallic touch, "the index is always an actant which is, or has been, in contact with its object, if it is not actually part of it." Finally, as Jakobson (1971:347) noted (interchanging *symptom* with *sign*), "the acceleration of pulse as a probable symptom of fever is, in Peirce's view, an index, and in such cases his semiotic actually merges with the medical inquiry into the symptoms of diseases."

A human body is thus an inextricably complex text that has been encoded and determined by the combined action of nature and nurture (or that minuscule segment of nature some anthropologists grandly compartmentalize as culture). This text may at once be utilized and referred to. It perdures through life by unremittingly giving off streams of signs, among them, imperatively, the vitals. Any elucidating interpretation of a consecution of such signs constitutes a message referring to a code; it is therefore a duplex overlapping structure, which, as Jakobson (1971:65–70), pointed out, is cast in the autonymous mode. Merleau-Ponty (1964:65–70), in a brilliant disquisition on signs (which deserves to be better known than it seems to be), elevated the level of discourse by telling us to see the term *body* as designating

> a system of systems devoted to the inspection of a world and capable of leaping over distances, piercing into the perceptual future, and outlining hollows and reliefs, distances and deviations—a meaning—in the inconceivable flatness of being. . . . Already in its pointing gestures [viz., indexical signs] the body not only flows over into a world whose schema it bears in itself but possesses this world at a distance rather than being possessed by it. . . . the primary operation which first constitutes signs as signs, makes that which is expressed dwell in them through the eloquence of their arrangement and configuration alone, implants a meaning in that which did not have one, and thus—far from exhausting itself in the instant at which it occurs—inaugurates an order and founds an institution or a tradition. (p. 67)

The fall of 1984 marked my forty-first year at Indiana University, and nearly the span of my entire career in scholarship as well. Over these four decades and more, I have delivered countless lectures and seminars on a variety of academic topics, which since the early 1960s have tended to cumulate with an upsurge in semiotics rather than, as formerly, in linguistics as such or elsewhere at its periphery. Accordingly, I feel that I have earned the *apanage*—which, having "bread" at its etymological core, is a natural accompaniment to any banquet such as ours, and which surely harks back at least to a Socratic feast held in Athens in the year 416 B.C., where the conversation centered on the vital signs of life and love, and is therefore still remembered—of the president of an American learned society to preempt this perhaps only remaining opportunity to indulge in personal reminiscences, comment on the institutionalization of our common cardinal concerns, and then prognosticate about the direction in which we may be headed. It remains to be seen whether your response to me will be the same as that of Phaedrus the Myrrhinusian, at the symposium in the House of Agathon, to Eryximachus the physician: "I always do what you advise, and especially what you prescribe as a physician . . . and the rest of the company, if they are wise, will do the same."

An abiding responsibility of a physician is to validate his professional credentials—you find appropriately reassuring documentation to this effect hanging on the walls of most consulting rooms. Props such as certificates help set the stage, define the situation, or, in Bouissac's (1976a:190) happy phrase, provide "the semiotic key" to the interaction to follow. Highlights of my intellectual genealogy might help convince my captive audience that I am experienced and, conceivably, an "authority." The keying should elicit your collective reaction not to my message as such but to the message as encoded in terms of your traditions, including expectations and attitudes you yourself have brought with you to this dinner. The role of the receiver (listener or reader), in what nowadays might be dubbed a cognitive framework, was foreseen by Peirce and substantially fleshed out afresh by Eco (1979, especially Ch. 7).

My first fumbling outreach toward the theory of signs, and of their influence upon human life and thought in numberless unexpected ways, dates from 1936, the year that I encountered the fourth edition of *The Meaning of Meaning*, that flawed patchwork of a masterpiece of which Charles Morris (1971:337) was to pronounce a decade afterwards that the semiotic of Ogden and Richards continued the development of the British empiricist line of analysis of signification "in terms of a psychology which progressively became individualistic and sensationalistic." Their work has also been called "as seminal as the *Origin of Species*. . . . Ogden and Richards were concerned to give shape to the pattern of thought, to chart the psychological and the metaphysical, which is like navigating without a compass. Their achievement was to construct a compass. It was imperfect and in many ways crude, but it was a compass" (Anderson, in Florence and Anderson 1977:238). Many Cambridge undergraduates of that period, certainly, devoured and debated this book; as a compass, it served to point me in several directions at once, but, to begin with, toward Ivor Richards himself. This self-declared materialist and neo-Benthamite was, at the time, the most eminent Fellow of Magdalene College, where I was sent up for 1936–37 as an unripe undergraduate, and where I sought out the Guru of Cambridge—I think the epithet was coined by Basil Willey of Pembroke—at the Pepysian Library. Richards's explosive semantic energy—his vitality—and eventual development of new critical devices that he later came to call "speculative instruments" subtly influenced my views of linguistic instability and diversity, and focused my interest on the controls exerted upon meaning by context—the very themes Richards was to dwell on in one of his several wise contributions to the 1958 Conference on Style (Sebeok 1960:241–52), to which I would later invite him. (During the week he was our guest in Bloomington, the two of us regenerated our acquaintanceship of more than twenty years. Following the text of this appendix, I reproduce most of Richards's inherently tantalizing last letter to me, handwritten about fourteen months before his death.)

My critical interests during the intervening decades and after took a radically different turn, as I have summed up elsewhere (Sebeok 1974b). I might enlarge on them here, however, by quoting from an autobiographical fragment by one of the acutest and most accessible teachers of criticism and literary history that I was ever inspired by, the Scotsman David Daiches at the University of Chicago (1971:35–36):

> I liked my Chicago students and made friends with many of them. Some are now distinguished professors, a fact which can cause me embarrassment as well as pride. In 1957 I was lecturing at Indiana University and there met Thomas Sebeok, the linguist, who as a mature graduate student, refugee from Europe, had attended some of my classes at Chicago. He is older than I am, and as he has grown older has acquired an air of venerable wisdom which I have never been able to achieve. Professor Sebeok seized my arm at the party when I appeared and proceeded to introduce me to a number of people with the formula, "I'd like you to meet my old teacher." People turned expecting to meet a wizened old man: I was in fact forty-four at the time. When they saw me, they concluded that this was some esoteric joke of Sebeok's and it proved difficult to explain that he was in a sense telling the truth.

I opt to cite this passage less to round out my portrait of the semiotician as a young man than to supply one more illustration of the devious workings of the Clever Hans effect upon the mind's recall: I was not "a mature graduate student" at the time but a struggling junior, and the actuarial fact is that I was born in 1920, Professor Daiches in 1912!

I gained my first ghostly glimpse of Peirce from a generous summary of his account of signs reprinted in Appendix D of *The Meaning of Meaning*, where it was reproduced "by the kindness of Sir Charles Welby," who, together with his wife, Victoria, seems to have been friendly with the ubiquitous polymath Ogden. I never met this remarkably erudite, eccentric man, but I became responsible, in 1967, for the reprinting of his astonishingly prescient essay *Opposition*, with a newly commissioned introduction by his erstwhile collaborator I. A. Richards. Another figure

I first encountered through the pages of *The Meaning of Meaning* was Bronislaw Malinowski, lately come back, exhausted, from the Trobriand Islands. "After our first four hours of discussing Theory of Signs and the fundamentals of Reference" with Ogden, Richards reported (Florence and Anderson 1977:104) that Malinowski suddenly announced that he had to rest. "Had Ogden a sofa available: and some high quality pornography? He needed to quieten his mind"—an affection for which I have a lot of fellow feeling! Nowadays, Malinowski is seldom discussed in a semiotic ambience, although the second volume of his *Coral Gardens and Their Magic* was, in my view, a major effort at a synthesis of verbal and nonverbal encounters; as he wrote in 1935, "please remember that the integral role of gesture in speech is quite as important to the understanding of an utterance as the one or two significant movements or indications [read 'indexical signs'] which replace an uttered word" (Malinowski 1965:26; cf. Sebeok 1988a:50). Malinowski's kinship with George Herbert Mead, and especially with John Dewey's concept of experience and nature—the distinguishing characteristics of which are to be located in the type of language and communication that humans have developed—is worthy of note, and surely merits further explication beyond the well-known attempts of J. R. Firth, Fortes, and Leach (in R. Firth 1957; cf. Malinowski 1965:59–60, n. 1). Let me just add that I was sufficiently aroused by this rare but seminal work in the early 1960s to borrow Fred Eggan's copy, and to insist that it be reprinted in my (now defunct) series History and Theory of Linguistics.

I have, on occasion, remarked that the real influence of *The Meaning of Meaning* lay less in the text than in the five appendixes and the two supplements (which altogether occupy almost a third of the volume). It was Supplement II, written by a physician, which—as I look back half a century—decisively influenced my perduring perception of semiotics in its multiform relationships to the art of medicine; more broadly, to the life science; and more widely by far, to the science of nature. I shall return to this *idée fixe* presently.

In the late 1930s, at the University of Chicago, Charles Morris began to offer a series of seminars devoted to the theory of signs, which must have been the very first sequence of courses in semiotics, so labeled, in any curriculum anywhere. Martin Gardner participated in the first (Sebeok 1978), I in the second, along with the late Walter Pitts, who, even in his teens (he was about fourteen years old at the time), was a scintillating mathematician and delightful oddball. After each seminar, Pitts and I fell into the habit of going out for coffee to discuss Morris's colloquia, and a stream of oddments. I clearly recall what Pitts once told me: "Semiotics, you see, according to Morris, is, like Gaul, divided into three parts." "Go on," I prompted. "That's all there is to it," he sighed, and soon afterwards he left Chicago (where "I had nothing more to teach the faculty!") for MIT. There, he began to collaborate with Warren S. McCulloch on several epochal papers, which remain to this day of pivotal consequence for general semiotics.

Since so much has recently been published about Morris (see, e.g., Eschbach 1981), including something by me (1987a:267–84), this is not the place to add anything of substance to that already voluminous literature. I often told Morris, a teacher for whom I felt the greatest affection, which, I have reason to believe, he reciprocated—and a man of whom Crito might have truly said, "that of all the men of his time that I have known, he was the wisest, justest, and best," albeit with a twist of Zen, and whom I visited once or more a year, up to his death in 1979, at his lonely Gainesville house—that I had serious reservations about the increasingly behavioristic turn his work had taken between 1938 and 1946. He took my strictures on the issue with equanimity and always in the best of spirits.

At this point, I should confess that although I have collaborated, in sundry ways, with a dozen or so prominent psychologists of my generation—Brown, Carroll, Ekman, Jenkins, Mahl, Miller, Rosenthal, Russell, Osgood (and became, in fact, in 1954, coeditor and coauthor of *Psycholinguistics* with the latter)—I had audited only a single formal course in that subject during all my graduate years, but that with no less a personage than B. F. Skinner. He became a visiting professor at the University of Chicago in the summer of 1940, where he gave an early version of his later-to-become-famous—or infamous—Harvard William James lectures on verbal behavior. Chomsky and Jakobson intensely disliked his eventual book, and I was amused to read of my own reaction, as reported in Skinner's autobiography (1979:249), to the Chicago version:

> I had plenty of material on literature and language, but for the first time I ran into criticism. When I said that a word that is only slowly recalled is pronounced more forcefully the longer the delay, two of my students measured the latency and loudness of responses to a list of questions and found that their subjects did not speak more loudly when it took them longer to answer. I should have specified the contingencies more accurately. It is only in a conversational setting, where a listener is waiting and one must say something, that a longer pause builds up more aversive situations from which one is more strongly moved to escape. An auditor in my course on language was Thomas A. Sebeok, already an accomplished linguist, and I had to watch myself when I strayed into that field, which was not close to my own. Tom arranged for me to speak to the Linguistics Club.

The researches of Rosenthal must be singled out here. His ever-escalating discoveries concerning the Pygmalion effect and its obverse, the Golem effect, have such blood-and-guts implications for each of us that it is bewildering to me why a legion of inquirers fails to labor at this inordinately fecund interface between our field and experimental psychology at its most exciting. By "exciting," I wish here to suggest the palpable, or at least plausible, impingement and spillover from psychology into neuroendocrinology. It is precisely in the dynamism of the brain and the self-organizing properties of neural networks, driven, as they are, by experience throughout life, where the next and perhaps final frontier of semiotic inquest will find its be-all and end-all resolution (Sebeok and Rosenthal 1981:199–205).

In the 1970s, I was overcome by a regrettable terminological exuberance and began to wallow in a tumult of neologisms, among them the cheerfully anticipative coinage *psychosemiotics* (Sebeok 1985:141, 1988a:260), given currency by I. M. Ullman (1975) and others. The truth is that I don't really know what this portentous word means, save that it smacks of contentious reductionism. There is a difference, after all, between *psychosemiotics* and semiotics informed by psychology. This notwithstanding, since the heady years of *Psycholinguistics*, my interest in human psychology has steadily eroded, with, to be sure, notable areas of exception—cf. my work on Bühler (Sebeok 1981b, Ch. 5), Krampen's (1981a) on Piaget, and, of course, the monumental achievements of Bruner and his students in this country, and of Vygotsky and Luria in the Soviet Union, to identify but a few relevant pacesetters. Recent work in animal psychology, especially as concerns the semiotic comportment of certain mammals, has proved so calamitously flawed (Sebeok 1988a, Ch. 5; 1981b, Chs. 7–8) that research in that bailiwick is likely to stay moribund until the advent of a superlative theoretical mind comparable to Jakob von Uexküll's in scope and originality (Sebeok 1988a, Ch. 10; see also *Semiotica* 42:1–87), harnessed to that of an observer of the minutiae of animal behavior comparable to Heini Hediger's in insight and power.

Before leaving Skinner, I do want to affirm that our personal relations have always remained most cordial, especially since he became my affable neighbor during his tenure at Indiana University. Our concerns have diverged until quite recently, when he demonstrated that a pair of pigeons could accurately engage in sustained and natural conversation without human intervention, and that a pigeon can transmit information to another entirely through the use of symbols (Epstein, Lanza, and Skinner 1980). This piece of clever lampoonery decisively abrogates decades of high-priced pretentiousness, while it clearly attests to the uniqueness of language, but it does so, as it were, by an *argumentum a contrario per positionem*. I would also like to echo an observation of Jakobson's (1971:670) about all forms of semiotic communication and communication in general (which are fused in a dialectic, by virtue of their exactly communal *renvoi*): that all the *signantia* and *signata* in their interrelations require first and foremost a purely semiotic analysis and interpretation, and that the "continuous efforts to substitute a psychological treatment" for indispensable semiotic operations are doomed to failure.

I hold this sort of censure to be true *a fortiori* of sophistic and baleful Freudian and pseudo-Freudian junkets into the semiotic domain. Psychoanalysis is dying at its cocaine-dusted roots, so attempts to replant this mystical fabrication in our midst amount to mere desperate diablerie. Incidentally, I have often been asked to comment on the semiotic contributions of Lacan (1966), to which I usually respond by repeating what Robert Frost told Lincoln MacVeagh about Carl Sandburg: "he was the kind of writer who had everything to gain and nothing to lose by being translated into a different language."

In passing, let me also assert—leaving the documentation for a future occasion—that, in a parallel manner, *mutatis mutandis*, the failed marriage of semiotics with a jejune version of Marxism that even Marx himself would surely have disavowed—following a period of furious flirtations that climaxed in East Germany with Klaus (1962) and in Russia with Reznikov (1964), but that are still iterated, here and there, at the periphery of Europe—has ended up a herring that I deem both red *and* dead. (Ponzio [1984] spells out the reasons for this judgment in compelling fashion and puts forth several interesting arguments for a relationship of complementarity between semiotics and Marxism as an open system.)

If you have attended my humble pedigree so far, you will have discerned repeated referrals—as Jakobson (1980:22) preferred to render his French *renvoi*, a word by which he deftly captured and transfixed each and every sign process conforming to the classic formula *aliquid stat pro aliquo*—to our lodestar, C. S. Peirce. Peirce figured, however evanescently, in Ogden and Richards, who influenced Morris, whose acquaintance with Peirce was earnest and far more extensive, although filtered through his idiosyncratic applications of behavioristic attitudes; Morris's "behavioral semiotic" has not much in common with Peirce's— John Dewey allegedly dubbed it "a complete inversion of Peirce" (Morris 1971:444), a judgment with which I happen to concur. However that may be, Morris fancied his position to have been "very close indeed to that of Peirce" (ibid. 446) and set me to reading assiduously whatever fragments of his semeiotic were accessible at Chicago in the late 1930s.

By the early 1940s, I had become ensorcelled by Roman Jakobson (Sebeok 1974b, Foreword; 1988a, Ch. 13), whose indelible effects on my scholarly development became pervasive and overriding, although, I trust, never epigonic. I am thus unique in having undergone formal training by both the philosopher Morris and the linguist Jakobson. The two men were acquainted, of course, but by no means intimate; I dimly remember the three of us dining together in a Manhattan café. They cited one another at practically no time; it would take a separate effort to account for their distressing mutual intellectual and temperamental aloofness.

Jakobson visited Bloomington on several memorable occasions, but the one event I want to single out here is the momentous—yet in some important ways oddly barren—Conference of Anthropologists and Linguists, in July 1952 (written up in Lévi-Strauss et al. 1953; cf. Lévi-Strauss 1985 for delightful recollections of his ten days in Indiana). The results of this conference were summed up in a tripartite report. From the point of view of anthropology, the *rapporteur* was Lévi-Strauss (pp. 1–10), in an intoxicating paper that later (1958:77–110) became a passport to the architectonic apprehension of this world-class contemporary thinker. He also came to conclude in this same book (p. 399) that anthropology not only is closest to humanistic studies but aims to be a "science sémeiologique," because "elle se situe resolument au niveau de la signification," that is, takes *meaning* for its guiding principle. By 1960, he expanded this view: "Nous concevons donc l'anthropologie comme l'occupant de bonne foi de ce domaine de la sémeiologie que la linguistique n'a pas déjà revendique pour sien" (Lévi-Strauss 1973:18). It is difficult to be sure of when or how Lévi-Strauss arrived at this conception about the heart of his science, which I take to be the perpetual search for invariances in society and culture, and that all human relationships are fundamentally to be regarded as a function of Kantian categories (or the like) that all of us use to organize experience. This quintessentially semiotic procedure uncannily resembles Jakob von Uexküll's *Umweltlehre* when extrapolated from nature to culture through the media of chiefly verbal signs. When Lévi-Strauss arrived in Bloomington, he came with an already well worked out model of the properties of mind, as I well know, since I distributed the draft of his paper, then titled "Toward a General Theory of Communication." Yet his local exposure to Jakobson—by then, and especially just that summer, saturated with Peircean ideas—and to the strongly Saussure-impelled Louis Hjelmslev—during that very summer engaged in completing, on this campus, the first English rendition of his 1943 Danish monograph (Hjelmslev 1953)—could hardly have failed to touch him and perhaps caused him to sharpen and even reforge his model in some respects.

Jakobson was our other major *rapporteur*, and he spoke nominally from the point of view of linguistics, but more so from the standpoint of the then-fashionable "theory of communication" (Lévi-Strauss et al. 1953:15–16), a partially fleeting *nom de guerre* for semiotics. At the outset, he observed that language "is an instance of that subclass of *signs* which under the name of *symbols* have been astutely described by [Y. R.] Chao" (p. 12) (who, by the way, was another active participant in our conference). Jakobson then went on to tell us:

> In the impending task of analyzing and comparing the various semiotic systems, we must remember not only the slogan of de Saussure that linguistics is a part of the science of signs, but, first and foremost, the life work of his no whit less eminent contemporary and one of the greatest pioneers of structural linguistic analysis, Charles Sanders Peirce. Peirce not only stated the need of semiotics but drafted, moreover, its basic lines. His fundamental ideas and devices in the theory of symbols, particularly of linguistic symbols, when carefully studied, will be of substantial support for the investigation of language and its relation to the other systems of signs. (Ibid.)

He then emphatically repeated that Peirce "must be regarded as the genuine and bold forerunner of structural linguistics" (p. 20). To appreciate the force of Jakobson's *obiter dicta*, one must attend to the time of their delivery and the composition of his audience. He was not only the "first linguist to become aware of Peirce's relevance to the advancement of linguistic theory" (Shapiro 1983:6; for a listing of other, successively later, reappraisals of Peirce by Jakobson, see Eco 1977:55, n. 3, to which should be added Jakobson 1980:31–38, revised from a 1975 oral presentation) but a seemingly quixotic adventurer into very hostile territory indeed. Intending no condescension, but after rereading again the third part of our report (this compiled by Voegelin and me [Lévi-

Strauss et al. 1953:22–67]), I really doubt if more than perchance a mere
handful out of some forty scholars assembled have ever even heard the
name of Peirce—let alone in the context of linguistics—or had an inkling
of what the word *semiotics* denoted and connoted. At the risk of doing
several distinguished colleagues of mine serious injustice, the only ones
I can be sure of were Yehoshua Bar-Hillel and Rulon Wells, as to the
identity of Peirce, and Chao, Hjelmslev, Lévi-Strauss, John Lotz, and
Alf Sommerfelt, as to the associated *termini technici*. (This is not to say
that topics we would now consider of salient semiotic import, especially
to nonverbal communication studies, were not—if more or less casually—alluded to, by, for instance, Ray L. Birdwhistell [p. 29], Norman
A. McQuown [pp. 57–58], and others.)

On alighting from a Greyhound bus upon his initial arrival in Indiana
back in 1944, Jakobson's first question to me was: "Well, Tom, where
are the Indians?" By 1952, he found out: he was surrounded and be-
sieged by them. This was still during the ignominious epoch he later
characterized (1971:594; cf. Sebeok 1988a:227) as a "stage of relative
particularism, a segregation . . . in the linguistic life of the U.S.A.,"
where the Archimedean battle cry prevailed: *Noli tangere circulos meos!*
The American linguists present were especially inimical to and suspi-
cious of this alien intruder in their Tory know-it-all midst, but he han-
dled them, in his brilliant summation, with his accustomed graceful
elegance. The goings-on have, as he put it, "a polyphonic structure,"
but he pledged to try "to be as objective as I can" (Lévi-Strauss et al.
1953:11). His master stratagem—one he was later frequently to reem-
ploy, with unpredictable outcome—promoting other American autochthonous heroes, such as Whitney, Boas, Sapir, and, even, when
opportune, L. Bloomfield, consisted of deftly turning the tables on his
adversaries, by proving to them that the ideas they deemed outlandish
were, in fact, embedded in the bedrock of their own glorious patrimony,
to which they were lamentably blind and deaf.

Playing the role of a conjurer pulling a rabbit out of a hat, for this
particular audience, was a magisterial ploy, which had the added virtue
of being genuinely heartfelt, although, alas, not readily substantiatable.
Jakobson's intuitions were uncanny, and his prophecies both foreshad-
owed and helped shape things to come. Unfortunately, to surmise that
if the ideas of Saussure and Peirce, "both concordant and rival," could
have been matched in the years following World War I, such a juxta-
position "would perhaps have altered the history of general linguistics
and the beginnings of semiotics" (Jakobson 1980:33), is a scarcely ver-
ifiable "what might have been"—a historical romance.[1]

I remarked earlier that the aftermath of this conference was, in some
respects, curiously sterile. In particular, I was adverting to its con-
founding lack of traceable impact on Hjelmslev. The Great Dane, as
Jakobson insisted on identifying him, spent his entire summer in
Bloomington and, as far as I can recall, took a full and active part in
our meetings when he was not closeted with his American admirer and
temporary collaborator Francis J. Whitfield, laboring on his distinctive
brand of formalized structural linguistics, dubbed "glossematics." It

would be out of place to track the short but Byzantine history of glossematics in all its Western ramifications, but a few of them may be
worthy of mention. First, within Denmark itself, glossematics has virtually ceased to exist. Second, in North America, it occupies today a
minuscular niche; its sole professors are Lamb (1981) and a handful of
his students. In a spirited rear-guard defense of glossematics, Lamb (p.
24) argued that Hjelmslev "shows that the methods and concepts he
develops can be extended to other systems not generally considered to
be languages. . . . The systems of this larger class that has language at
its center he calls 'semiotics.' That is, a semiotic is a quasi language that
can be illuminated by the methods developed in immanent [vs. tran-
scendent] linguistics. And it turns out that every science is a semiotic."
    The sorry fact is that the program so confidently advertised has never
been carried out successfully in any domain of science, all the while
leaving wide open the thorny questions of whether linguistics is a part
of semiotics, semiotics is a part of linguistics, or whether the tête-à-tête
adjacency of this pair of substantives may well be of a different cognitive
order entirely (cf. Sebeok 1988a:63). In the Germanic world, we must
concur with Th. Kotschi's 1977 judgment (adverted to by Jurgen Trabant,
in Krampen et al. 1987, Ch. 4) that glossematics as an important school
of European structuralism, if ever countenanced at all, has sunk into
oblivion. Trabant, who is a specialist in Romance linguistics and phil-
ology, argues that Hjelmslev must be fairly adjudged a founder of general semiotics, and this is indeed how he may have been perceived
among certain Francophones, notably by (the early) Roland Barthes,
and particularly by A. J. Greimas and his adherents, who form the
imposingly self-designated Ecole de Paris (Coquet 1982). Greimas and
Courtés (1979:167), for example, claim that "la théorie du language,
présentée par L. Hjelmslev, peut être considerée comme la première
théorie sémiotique cohérente et achévée: elle a été un facteur décisif
dans la formation de la sémiotique en France." This last pretense leaves
one profoundly perplexed if one considers French semiotics in its entire
rich range. Thus Hjelmslev's name is rarely even mentioned in—and
does not figure at all in the bibliography of—Guiraud's best-selling La
sémiologie (1971), or Deledalle's keen Théorie et pratique du signe (1979).
Moreover, Hjelmslev was subjected to severe criticism by Mounin
(1970:99), who was of the opinion that "au fond la sémiologie en elle-
même ne l'interesse pas." France's most creative figure in modern semiotic theory, Thom, seems wholly unaffected by Hjelmslev, and, as if
all this were not bewildering enough, Lavers (1982:181–82), who takes
it upon herself to trace Greimas's "sources of inspiration," excludes
Hjelmslev but includes Viggo Brøndal, his compatriot and arch adver-
sary. Although I deprecated, two paragraphs back, cogitations of the
"what if" kind, I must admit that it is fun, and can't help speculating
about the course of modern Continental semiotics had Hjelmslev become sensitized to Peirce that hot summer in Bloomington. Perhaps, if
so, the Semiotic Square associated with Greimas (1979:29–33) might
today be called the Semiotic Tricorn!
    Before I bid farewell to glossematics, I should record that Hjelmslev

was an extraordinarily erudite and charming gentleman, as well as a genial guest and host with whom I loved to visit, especially at his home in Charlottenlund. On the other hand, I found it unworkable to dispute the subject with him, since its very formalization presupposed a limitless chain of antecedents and implicated an endless concatenation of consequents. So our social exchanges, *chez nous* or *chez lui*, turned into little more than elegant academic gossip sessions, which, I believe, we both thoroughly enjoyed.

You may think that I have dwelt at inordinate length on a parley that was orchestrated in this small university town in July of 1952, sounding a cacophonous medley of voices, some alas, now, stilled, others seldom raised these days. In part, I was simply carrying out Galen's prescription for anamnesis, the bringing of the past into focus (Sebeok 1984b:220) to build up a case history for etiology's sake. As Benjamin Miller (1978:380) explains, your "doctor or his nurse will ask a great many questions at your first checkup in order to learn every detail of your health background. . . . This means he has to work like a detective searching for all sorts of clues." The probe for the vital signs is only stage alpha in the quest for a prognosis.

You may, moreover, frown on the dropping of names, especially if you are as sympathetic as I am to Bouissac's (1976b:372) Golden Legend prospect of the lip service we tend to pay to the so-called fathers and forefathers of semiotics. But it behooves members of our profession to be mindful that names, that is, singular proper names, constitute a conspicuous subclass of indexical signs (Sebeok 1985:138–40): they are senseful, if imprecise, but they acquire rigidity and take on specificity the more descriptions they are augmented by; the Bacons—Roger and Francis—exemplify this process close to home. Such names function, in Erving Goffman's matchless expression, as "identity pegs" (ibid. 139) on which to hang descriptions, a capacity involving a universal meta-semiotic operation. Besides, "name magic" may be one device by which we mortals fancy to exert control over the universe. And finally, as Peirce (4.568) put the matter in a nutshell—yes, here I go again—"The first time one hears a Proper Name pronounced, it is but a name, predicated, as one usually gathers, of an existent, or at least historically existent, individual object, of which, or of whom, one almost always gathers some additional information. The next time one hears a name, it is by so much the more definite; and almost every time one hears the name, one gains familiarity with the object."

Since 1952, I have participated in an untold number of other deliberations, here, elsewhere in this country, indeed all over the globe. To pick just two of the latter at random, I might mention the 1970 Amsterdam Conference on Interaction Ethology (Sherzer 1971:19–21), which I coorganized with the late Goffman, who sometimes practiced his distinctive brand of semiotics under the phrase featured in the title; and the 1970 Jerusalem exploration of the elusive subject of pragmatics (Staal 1971:29–32), convened by the late Bar Hillel, the leading expert on indexical expressions, during whose eventually fatal illness Max

Black became our master of ceremonies. To enumerate them all—let alone the names of all the participants—would be as entertaining as a recitation of the phone directory, but a passing mention of a few may help trace the long path we have traversed on the way to this dinner. Although I am sure that our guest of honor, Professor Leach, won't remember this at all, there really did take place, in August of 1960, a meeting, in Paris, which Lévi-Strauss and I coorganized. It was titled "Analyse structurale et sémantique des mythes et de la littérature orale." Leach spoke often and with his usual witty eloquence. A slender but fascinating written resumé has been preserved (Leroi-Gourhan et al. 1964:643–47)—fascinating, because the partakers included the cream of English anthropology. I learned only about six months after my return, in a tactful but *desolée* letter from my dear friend Geneviève Calame-Griaule, that the local low-tech operator of the recording device had installed the wire backwards. I regret not only the lost words of the likes of Firth, Forge, Fortes, Leach, Pocock, and all the rest, but that I thereby forfeited my only chance to have coedited a volume jointly with Lévi-Strauss.

Two conferences, both of them held in this building, have to be alluded to in even the most minimal list for their inseminating effects on the flowering of semiotics. The earlier was the already mentioned 1958 Conference on Style (Sebeok 1960), where Jakobson spoke on "Linguistics and Poetics" (pp. 350–77), which, he later confided to me, became his single most often cited paper, and hence the most influential among a multitude. The other one was a congregation, in May 1962, of sixty scholars of various persuasions, ruled over and harmonized by the indomitable Margaret Mead. "As we build a science of semiotics," she fatidically insisted (ibid. 279),

> it will be necessary to assimilate . . . discrepant sequences of research experience. Some are hundreds of years old, some are extremely recent. Some result from the vicissitudes of systems of prestige, or methods of instrumentation, or local cultural hierarchies among the sensory modalities. . . . Some result from accidents of professional interests or the availability of research funds at a particular period. . . . Still others are the result of fashion in research.

In 1960–61, I spent the first twelve of what was later to amount to about twenty-six months of my life at the Center for Advanced Study in the Behavioral Sciences at Stanford. This was a vintage year there for linguists, who included Jakobson, and for anthropologists, who included Leach, and perhaps a dozen or so others in both fields combined. For my personal unfolding, however, those months were a watershed for quite a different reason. In my undergraduate years, I received sound basic training in biology, particularly in genetics, which led me to agonize, in the 1940s, about my choice of a career. World War II propelled me to clutch the verbal code rather than the molecular code, and that retained me for two busy decades. At Stanford, however, my yearning for nature became overwhelming, and, rather naively, I tried to catch up with a twenty-year stockpile of facts and trends in the life science. Soon realizing that my ambition was a pipe dream, I decided to, as it were, specialize on a single facet, and chose ethology in general and animal communication studies in particular; in those days the two labels, and comparative psychology besides, shared much the same referent. My preoccupation during that priceless period of freedom resulted in a book (Sebeok 1972), a conference report (Sebeok and Ramsay 1969), two cumbrous collections of papers (1968, 1977a), coresponsibility with my wife, Jean Umiker-Sebeok, for a freshly launched series of volumes on animal communication, and my resting forever saddled with the word *zoosemiotics* and its equally obnoxious spinoffs. Eventually, it also landed us at the storm center of a foolish controversy (Sebeok and Umiker-Sebeok 1980) about whether animals have language, to which the one-word answer is: No!

Eventually, after years of reflection, I concluded that semiosis is *the* criterial attribute of life, an axiom that I continued to build on throughout my "semiotic trilogy" (which in the meantime has fanned out into a tetralogy), and in a number of shorter publications. I have presented hundreds of pages of arguments for this obsession of mine, which, however, fits comfortably within a neo-semiotic tradition perspicuously maintained by Peirce, and is currently fostered, in a highly original fashion, by René Thom. Its most distinctive and explicit contributor was Jakob von Uexküll, that demiurgic but largely misunderstood creative genius of biology, whose best work dates from the first half of this century. Steeped as he was in the teachings of Kant, Uexküll's technical writings were enshrouded in a sometimes unduly opaque philosophical wrapping. One revealing paragraph neatly condensed his conception of reality (or as he termed it, *Natur*), which I quote here both for its own sake and because it accurately stands for an opinion I still share: "true reality," Uexküll observed in his elder son Thure's recent edition (1982:3), which "lies beyond or behind the nature that physicists, chemists, and microbiologists conceive of in their scientific systems, reveals itself through signs. These signs are therefore the only true reality, and the rules and laws to which the signs and sign-processes are subject are the only real laws of nature. 'As the activity of our mind is the only piece of nature directly known to us, its laws are the only ones that have the right to be called laws of Nature.' " Peirce wrote the same thing to Lady Welby (Hardwick 1977:141): "It is perfectly true that we can never attain a knowledge of things as they are. We can only know their human aspect. But that is all the universe is for us." And, in the footsteps of Uexküll, the great French geneticist François Jacob (1982:56) put the matter most generally and, withal, most picturesquely:

> No matter how an organism investigates its environment, the perception it gets must necessarily reflect so-called "reality" and, more specifically, those aspects of reality which are directly related to its own behavior. If the image that a bird gets of the insects it needs to feed its progeny does not reflect at least some aspects of reality, then there are no more progeny. If the representation that a monkey builds of the branch it wants to leap

to has nothing to do with reality, then there is no more monkey. And if this did not apply to ourselves, we would not be here to discuss this point. Perceiving certain aspects of reality is a biological necessity; certain aspects only, for obviously our perception of the external world is massively filtered. Our sensory equipment allows us to see a tiger entering our room, but not the cloud of particles which, according to physicists, constitutes the reality of a tiger. The external world, the "reality" of which we all have intuitive knowledge, thus appears as a creation of the nervous system. It is, in a way, a possible world, a model allowing the organism to handle the bulk of incoming information and make it useful for its everyday life. One is thus led to define some kind of "biological reality" as the particular representation of the external world that the brain of a given species is able to build. The quality of such biological reality evolves with the nervous system in general and the brain in particular.

The principle that signs are the only true reality is generalized in Peirce's famous challenge that all this universe is perfused with signs, if it is not composed exclusively of signs (cf. Sebeok 1977c:v), and carried further by Thom (1983:264–76) when he depicted the dynamic of semiosis as "the very image of life," adding that the "voice of reality is in the significance of the symbol."

It appears from Leach's spirited Patten Lecture of October 23, 1984, that our respective positions on this constitutive issue are largely consonant. Leach stated: "I see no reason at all to believe that more than a very small fragment of reality out there could ever be registered by a human brain," and that "elements of real world structure can somehow be perceived . . . as patterns of interpretable signs" (Leach 1984). Certainly, this standpoint, which I have tried to succinctly instantiate, is akin to but by no means identical with either problematic idealism, often attributed to Descartes, or the dogmatic idealism ("immaterialism") Kant erroneously imputed to Berkeley.

To spell out my present opinion on the relations of semiotics to the idealist movement would require a monograph, such as the case of the giant rat of Sumatra, a story for which, as Sherlock Holmes announced, the world is not yet prepared. Let me just tell you that I reckon this problematic to lie in the innermost heart of the contemporary semiotic enterprise. In its essence, the enigma is equivalent to the multifaceted system of "ancient questions about the nature of the mental and its relations to the bodily" (Bunge 1980:xiii), or what is often discussed under the ticket of "mind and brain," in its many monistic and dualistic permutations (e.g., Eccles 1982:239–45). I have previously (Sebeok 1981b:13) declared that my personal bias inclines me toward that variant of the dualist-interactionist theory, maintained by J. Z. Young, which involves a principle of double coding and control. I define "mind" as a system of signs which is roughly tantamount to Uexküll's *Umwelt*, and "brain" as a system of signs displayed, for example, as a physical network, or structure, of neurons. The question to be investigated is how mental manifestation of the information in the mind is transcoded into our central nervous system, and vice versa. The solution must come from neuroendocrinology, and, once the solution is apparent, once the information engineering specifications are blocked out, much of what we call semiotics today, including notably linguistics, will become superfluous.

Take this, if you will, as my prognosis, in which you can place as much confidence as you are willing to consign to your physician. In the meantime, you can take comfort from the most lyrical stance on the subject so far, articulated by that glorious group of modern philosophers The Beatles, from whose song "Strawberry Fields Forever" I would have liked to borrow—copyright laws permitting—ten apt lines about the nature of reality. The simplicity of their sentiment bears out Peirce's (1984:263–64) generalization about philosophy in Britain, which I should like to quote, but with the liberty to substitute three other words for "Berkeley is": "From very early times, it has been the chief intellectual characteristic of the English to wish to effect everything by the plainest and directest means, without unnecessary contrivance. . . . The Beatles are an admirable illustration of this national character, as well as that strange union of nominalism with Platonism."

Theoretic biology is a hot field, with important concerns of its own, tossed about in a *Sturm und Drang* at its own frontiers. What six of us (Anderson et al. 1984) have lately attempted to do was to construct a provisional framework compacting what appeared to us a number of new developments in the life science, using bricks and mortar made up of semiotic elements as our tools. We offer this paper (prepublished by courtesy of the Toronto Semiotic Circle in 1984) as a target for critical discussion from which, we very much hope, some sort of reasonable consensus will emerge. Our article will appear cheek by jowl with a pivotal guest editorial, by Jean-Claude Gardin, Paul Bouissac, and Kenneth E. Foote (1984), concisely presenting ten interrelated theses which every practitioner of semiotics must make it his or her business to assimilate or take issue with, but which none can afford to ignore.

The domain of semiosis most assuredly extends over all terrestrial biological systems, bounded at their lowest limit by molecular mechanisms, and at their upper limit by a hypothetical entity baptized, about 1979, *Gaia* (cf. Seielstad 1983, Ch. 8; Anderson et al. 1984). There is a growing conviction, held by an increasing number of scientists in a surprisingly diverse array of disciplines, that life and its environment evolved together as a single tightly coupled system. James E. Lovelock, a gas chromatographer, Lynn Margulis, a biologist, Lewis Thomas, a research physician, and others, including myself, have embraced this notion, perhaps gauchely named after the Greek goddess of the earth. Gaia, if it exists, is the largest living organism we know of, with devices for sensing the surrounding environment, undergoing internal metabolic changes and adapting to them, and regulating the entire megamachinery solely by way of precise and subtle message exchanges. This is a system informed, through and through, by sign action; therefore, we are responsible to be heedful, or at least mindful, of it, whether it is in a state of equilibrium—which is, fortunately, most of the time— or under threat of gross perturbation. This is so because we—I mean

not just members of this profession but all members of the species—
are an articulately conscious cog (very likely the only one) occupying
this huge space vehicle.

The province of semiosis, I repeat, envelops life in all its manifestations: the diminutive Lilliputian islands of the molecular geneticists and
virologists; Gulliver's middle-sized world, the theater most of us are
familiar with, and in which the action—the sign action, that is—unrolls
from instant to instant; and the Brobdingnag demesne, hanging there
in space, as a gigantic closed ecosystem named Gaia. But is this the
end of the story? Does it make any sense to say that semiosis tempers
more than this grand biogeochemical system in which are inalienably
bound all the conjugated components of a unique set of planetary processes?

Since I gave a talk in West Germany in the fall of 1981, in the context
of Peirce's cosmology, concerning the quasi-fallacy (as I insist it is) that
reality exists outside us—touching, along the way, on sundry deep
conundrums about von Neumann's chain, on the pair of paradoxes of
Schrödinger's cat and Wigner's friend, and above all on Professor Wheeler's mind-blowing conception of the participatory universe (Gardner
1983, Ch. 19)—my nagging doubts continued to both multiply and
magnify. Possibilities for aligning physics and semiotics are slowly beginning to swim into focus, and by this I mean to forecast that the
means of entry to the universe will be found in the classic adage *Nosce
teipsum*. The key is concealed within us.[2]

For me, this coming together was traversed mainly via two paths.
The first of these was called the anthropic principle, by Robert Dicke,
in 1961; it has since then been greatly extended by Brandon Carter and
has now limpidly been elucidated by Davies (1980, Ch. 8). The point
about the anthropic principle that interested me was that it offered a
rational explanation for the fact that we happen to be alive at just the
era when the age of the universe is equal to about 15 billion years, or
1.5×10^{10}, an enormous number which is dwarfed when one considers
that gravity is weaker than electromagnetism by a factor of 5×10^{39},
or, to put it another way, that this principle provided an alternative to
coincidence. There are only two interpretations possible of quantum
theory as a framework for understanding the world as it is: either chance
or choice. There exists a vast array of universes, but, as far as we know,
only one of these is inhabited by creatures endowed with the semiosic
capacity, on which hinge all knowledge of existence and cosmology,
and much besides. A preordained ecosystem, a world tailor-made for
its denizens, inevitably has to be a universe perfused with signs. Con-
sequently, I am strongly drawn to Wheeler's suggestion that the fundamental physical constants, the nuclear and cosmological parameters,
and others, are constrained by the unbudging requirement that life
evolve, and that these constants are altered by our consciousness of
them. In brief, life modifies the universe to meet its needs, and accom-
plishes this by means of sign action. (Incidentally, Bense [1984] came
to the identical conclusion that the anthropic principle is a semiotic

principle, although I am at a loss to follow his dense yet exiguous argumentation.)

The second path became patent to me in July 1984 during an exciting in-flight conversation with a wonderfully imaginative and endlessly knowledgeable medical engineer, F. Eugene Yates, concerning the leap from kinetics to kinematics—the study of motion exclusive of the influences of mass and force. His exposition is available for all to read in a pathbreaking paper (Yates and Kugler 1984), which, in my estimation, will herald for us yet another spectacular vista to hurry in pursuit of.

In medicine, the word *syndrome* refers, collectively, to a rule-governed configuration of signs which are assumed to have the same cause. The cardinal point about the indexical signs I have been discussing is that each and every one of them points in the same direction. The body semiotic disembogues scores of encouraging vital signs which not only fit snugly with the basic sciences of nature but are appreciated by leading mathematicians and scientists of both inanimate and animate creation once they grasp what semiotics is truly about. Ten years ago (Sebeok 1974b:211), I characterized semiotics as a mode of extending mankind's perception of the world, and depicted its subject matter as "the exchange of any messages whatever and of the systems of signs which underlie them." I now have impressive progress to report: the central preoccupation of semiotics is an illimitable array of concordant illusions; its main mission is to mediate between reality and illusion—to reveal the substratal illusion underlying reality and to search for the reality that may, after all, lurk behind that illusion. This abductive assignment becomes, henceforth, the privilege of future generations to pursue, insofar as young people can be induced to heed the advice of their elected medicine men.[3]

Magdalene College,   17 Feb 78
Cambridge,
UK .

Dear Professor Sebeok,

I am pained to say that—after all your most courteous and patient correspondence and your sending the Peirce-Welby Correspondence Book: *Semiotics [sic] and Significs*, I find I am having to be to you a total disappointment. I have done more than a little exploring into the book, but somehow the topics treated, the assumptions made and the tones taken by *both* parties have become so remote from my present thinking that anything I could write would be, I know, imperceptive and unfair.

Originally, it was C. K. Ogden who was interested both in Welby and in Peirce, and I had hoped that I would be able to revive the curiosity with which he infected me in 1920. But, alas, NO. (I will be 85 in a few days time now and doubtless *that* is the real explanation of my inability.)

You would have had this apology far earlier but *influenza* has been playing its part—happily well over now. I will gladly send the book back but hold it for the moment in case there is someone this side of the Atlantic to whom you would wish it to go. With real regrets,

> Sincerely,
>
> I. A. Richards

P.S. The Editorial Introduction (Charles S. Hardwick [1977]) is strangely ill-informed. E.g., p. xxxi, he seems to know nothing to the point about F. P. Ramsey (who virtually translated Wittgenstein's Tractatus and was immensely indebted to C. K. Ogden from the time when Ramsey, as a Winchester Schoolboy, used to review the toughest things (Major Douglas & Keynes etc., etc. for Ogden's *Cambridge Magazine*) . . .

NOTES

1. An attempt at such a reconstruction constituted the thrust of my presidential address to the Linguistic Society of America, delivered in San Francisco on December 30, 1975, under the title "The Pertinence of Peirce to Linguistics." The reason I never published this piece was that so much of it was necessarily speculative. When the monumental Peirce Edition Project (Vol. I, 1982; Vol. II, 1984) is brought to an end, perhaps some future historian of twentieth-century linguistics and semiotics ought to try again. The earnest endeavor of Shapiro (1983:ix) to "found a Peircean linguistics" has so far been met by a resounding silence.

2. "The Role of the Observer" was the title I gave to this invited lecture, delivered October 7, 1981, in Hamburg, to the third Semiotisches Kolloquium of the Deutsche Gesellschaft für Semiotik. My paper remains unpublished, *mea culpa*, because the confluence of new theories of physics—known as "unified theories"—and the newest ideas in cosmology is an ongoing process about the outcome of which an outsider such as I can at this juncture surmise little of semiotic pertinence. The fact that the universe is evolving increases semioticians' chances for a useful contribution eventually, but not at a time when, to paraphrase a recent reflection by John A. Wheeler, increasing knowledge of detail is bringing an increasing ignorance of plan. The justification for the last sentence footnoted here was superbly stated by Heisenberg (1955:29): "The old division of the world into objective processes in space and time and the mind in which these processes are mirrored—in other words, the Cartesian difference between *res cogitans* and *res extensa*—is no longer a suitable starting point for our understanding of modern science. Science, we find, is now focused on the network of relationships between man and nature, on the framework

which makes us as living beings dependent parts of nature, and which we as human beings have simultaneously made the object of our thoughts and actions. Science no longer confronts nature as an objective observer, but sees itself as an actor in this interplay between man and nature. . . . In other words, method and object can no longer be separated. *The scientific world-view has ceased to be a scientific view in the true sense of the word."*

3. Like any other academic pursuit, semiotics is made up of an inner form, or intellective construct, expressed in an outer form, which takes on many traditional guises. The famous Saussurean comparison of language to a sheet of paper comes to mind: you can't take a pair of scissors and cut the outer form without at the same time cutting the inner form. One can well adapt Saussure's point (1972:157) that semiotics operates "sur le terrain limitrophe," in other words, that it is not comprehensible apart from its social context, which has a compelling historical dimension as well. Vital signs of this kind, which were not even adverted to above, include organizations, such as the International Association for Semiotic Studies and its quinquennial congresses; many local societies, with annual, biennial, or occasional meetings, the largest of these being the Semiotic Society of America, conceived at the first North American Semiotics Colloquium, held at the University of South Florida in 1975 (Sebeok 1977a), and realized, a brief fourteen months later, at the Georgia Institute of Technology; and the immensely successful sequence of International Institutes for Semiotic and Structural Studies held, or scheduled to be held, at the University of Toronto, Vanderbilt University, Indiana University, and Northwestern University during the summer, and in India and probably Latin America during the winter, to say nothing of the summer sessions of the Centro Internazionale di Semiotica e di Linguistica, convened every July for the past fifteen years. Corresponding to such sodalities, there are numerous book and monograph series, journals, and news outlets to accommodate all tastes. Last but not least, there are curricular configurations of diverse cast, some emphasizing teaching, some research, and some both. While a complete report would fairly note those that have died, those that seem moribund, the morbidity rate is reassuringly small. The health inventory of semiotics has never been more pleasing than in the mid-1980s.

REFERENCES

A Genealogy of Semiotics in the United States

Abbreviations

AiS = Advances in Semiotics. Series edited by Thomas A. Sebeok, published by Indiana University Press (Bloomington).
AtS = Approaches to Semiotics. Series edited by Thomas A. Sebeok, published by Mouton (The Hague) or Mouton de Gruyter (Berlin).
EDS = Encyclopedic Dictionary of Semiotics, ed. Thomas A. Sebeok, AtS 73 (1986).
PiCS = Problems in Contemporary Semiotics. Series coedited by Thomas A. Sebeok and Jean Umiker-Sebeok, published by Plenum Press (New York).
SiS = Studies in Semiotics. Series edited by Thomas A. Sebeok for Indiana University Publications.
WEB, followed by a designation of the year and page numbers = *The Semiotic Web*, coedited by Thomas A. Sebeok and Jean Umiker-Sebeok, published by Mouton de Gruyter (Berlin) (1987, 1988, 1989, 1990). Also in AtS.
Ackerknecht, Erwin H. 1953. *Rudolf Virchow: Doctor, Statesman, Anthropologist*. Madison: University of Wisconsin Press.
Anderson, Myrdene, John Deely, Martin Krampen, Joseph Ransdell, Thomas A. Sebeok, and Thure von Uexküll. 1984. A Semiotic Perspective on the Sciences: Steps toward a New Paradigm. *Semiotica* 52:7–47.
Anderson, Myrdene, and Floyd Merrell, eds. 1991. *On Semiotic Modeling*. AtS.
Andrews, Edna. 1990. A Dialogue on the Sign: Can Peirce and Jakobson Be Reconciled? *Semiotica* 82:1–13.
Apel, Karl-Otto. 1959. Sprache und Wahrheit in der gegenwärtigen Situation der Philosophie. *Philosophische Rundschau* 7:161–84.
Apel, Karl-Otto. 1973. Charles Morris und das Problem einer pragmatisch integrierten Semiotik. In: *Zeichen, Sprache und Verhalten*, pp. 9–66. Düsseldorf: Schwann.
Arbib, Michael, and Mary Hesse. 1986. *The Construction of Reality*. Cambridge: Cambridge University Press.
Armstrong, Nancy. 1986. Semiotics and Ideology. WEB 1987:309–21.
Ascher, Marcia, and Robert Ascher. 1981. *Code of the Quipu: A Study in*

Media, Mathematics, and Culture. Ann Arbor: University of Michigan Press.

Babcock, Barbara A., and John J. MacAloon. 1987. Victor W. Turner (1920–1983). *Semiotica* 65:1–27.

Baer, Eugen. 1983. Freud and the Trope of Enigma. In: *Semiotics Unfolding*, ed. Tasso Borbé, 1:11–20. AtS 68.

Baer, Eugen. 1988. *Medical Semiotics*. Lanham: University Press of America.

Baer, Eugen. 1989. Semiotics and Medicine. WEB 1988:215–69.

Bailey, Richard W. 1978. William Dwight Whitney and the Origins of Semiotics. In: *The Sign: Semiotics around the World*, ed. R. W. Bailey, L. Matejka, and P. Steiner, pp. 68–80. Ann Arbor: Michigan Slavic Publications.

Bailey, Richard W., and Seymour Chatman. 1974. Literary Semiotics in North America. *Versus* 8/9:227–44.

Baran, Henryk. 1976. *Semiotics and Structuralism: Readings from the Soviet Union*. White Plains: International Arts and Sciences Press.

Barber, Janet M., and Peter A. Dillman. 1981. *Emergency Patient Care for the EMT-A*. Reston, Va.: Reston Publishing.

Baron, Naomi S. 1979. Linguistics and Semiotics: Two Disciplines in Search of a Subject. *Semiotica* 26:289–310.

Baron, Naomi S. 1988. When Seeing's Not Believing: Language, Magic, and AI. *American Journal of Semiotics* 5:321–39.

Barrow, John D., and Joseph Silk. 1983. *The Left Hand of Creation: The Origin and Evolution of the Expanding Universe*. New York: Basic Books.

Barthes, Roland. 1968. *Elements of Semiology*. New York: Hill and Wang.

Barthes, Roland. 1988. *The Semiotic Challenge*. New York: Hill and Wang.

Baudrillard, Jean. 1988. *America*. New York: Verso.

Bauman, Richard. 1982. Conceptions of Folklore in the Development of Literary Semiotics. *Semiotica* 39:1–20.

Bär [= Baer], Eugen. 1975. *Semiotic Approaches to Psychotherapy*. SiS 1.

Beauchamp, Tom L., and Alexander Rosenberg. 1981. *Hume and the Problem of Causation*. New York: Oxford University Press.

Beckner, Morton. 1959. *The Biological Way of Thought*. New York: Columbia University Press.

Beniger, James R. 1986. *The Control Revolution: Technological and Economic Origins of the Information Society*. Cambridge: Harvard University Press.

Bense, Max. 1984. The So-Called "Anthropic Principle" as a Semiotic Principle in Empirical Theory Formation. *American Journal of Semiotics* 2:93–97.

Berger, Arthur Asa. 1987. Semiotics and Popular Culture. WEB 1986:355–66.

Bertalanffy, Ludwig von. 1968. *General System Theory: Foundations, Development, Applications*. New York: George Braziller.

Berthoff, Ann E. 1988. Sapir and the Two Tasks of Language. *Semiotica* 71:1–47.

Birdwhistell, Ray L. 1970. *Kinesics and Context: Essays on Body Motion Communication*. Philadelphia: University of Pennsylvania Press.

Blanchard, Marc Eli. 1983. In the World of the Seven Cubit Spear: The Semiotic Status of the Object in Ancient Greek Art and Literature. *Semiotica* 43:205–44.

Blanck, Peter David, Robert Rosenthal, and LaDoris Hazzard Cordell. 1985. The Appearance of Justice: Judges' Verbal and Nonverbal Behavior in Criminal Jury Trials. *Stanford Law Review* 38:89–164 (November).

Blois, Marsden S. 1984. *Information and Medicine: The Nature of Medical Descriptions*. Berkeley: University of California Press.

Blumenberg, Hans. 1986. *Die Lesbarkeit der Welt*. Frankfurt am Main: Suhrkamp.

Blumer, Herbert. 1969. *Symbolic Interaction: Perspective and Method*. Englewood Cliffs: Prentice-Hall.

Bouissac, Paul. 1976a. *Circus and Culture: A Semiotic Approach*. AiS.

Bouissac, Paul. 1976b. The "Golden Legend" of Semiotics. *Semiotica* 17:371–84.

Bower, Gordon H., and Daniel G. Morrow. 1990. Mental Models in Narrative Comprehension. *Science* 247:44–48.

Bowyer, J. Barton. 1980. *Cheating: Deception in War & Magic, Games & Sports, Sex & Religion, Business & Con Games, Politics & Espionage, Art & Science*. New York: St. Martin's Press.

Brent, Joseph Lancaster III. 1960. A Study of the Life of Charles Sanders Peirce. Ph.D. diss., University of California at Los Angeles.

Brent, Joseph. 1991. *The Wasp in the Bottle: The Life of Charles Sanders Peirce*. AiS.

Broms, Henri, and Rebecca Kaufmann, eds. 1988. *Semiotics of Culture*. Helsinki: Arator.

Broughton, Panthea Reid. 1979. *The Art of Walker Percy*. Baton Rouge: Louisiana State University Press.

Bruss, Neal H. In press. *Freud's Semiotics: The Psychoanalytic Theory of Interpretation*. AiS.

Buchanan, Scott. 1937–38. The New Program at Saint John's College. *The 1937–38 Catalogue of Saint John's College*, Appendix II, *Embers of the World*.

Buczyńska-Garewicz, Hanna. 1987. Semiotics in Poland. WEB 1988:267–90.

Bunge, Mario. 1980. *The Mind-Body Problem: A Psychobiological Approach*. Oxford: Pergamon.

Burke, Kenneth. 1966. *Language as Symbolic Action*. Berkeley: University of California Press.

Cairns-Smith, A. G. 1985. *Seven Clues to the Origin of Life: A Scientific Detective Story*. Cambridge: Cambridge University Press.

Calderwood, James L. 1989. *The Properties of Othello*. Amherst: University of Massachusetts Press.

Calvet, Louis-Jean, and Albert Valdman. 1989. The Semiotics of Pierre Guiraud. WEB 1988:53–69.

Calvino, Italo. 1985. Le livre de la nature chez Galileo. In: *Aims and Prospects of Semiotics: Essays in Honor of Algirdas Julien Greimas*, ed. Herman Parret and Hans-George Ruprecht, pp. 683–88. Amsterdam: John Benjamins.

Careri, Giorgio. 1984. *Order and Disorder in Matter*. Menlo Park: Benjamin/Cummings Publishing Co.

Carlson, Marvin. 1988a. Semiotics of Theater. WEB 1987:323–53.

Carlson, Marvin. 1988b. The Old Vic: A Semiotic Analysis. *Semiotica* 71:187–212.

Carlson, Marvin. 1989. *Places of Performance: The Semiotics of Theatre Architecture*. Ithaca: Cornell University Press.

Carlson, Marvin. 1990. *Theatre Semiotics: Signs of Life*. AiS.

Carnap, Rudolf. 1942. *Introduction to Semantics*. Cambridge: Harvard University Press.

Carr, B. J., and M. J. Reese. 1979. The Anthropic Principle and the Structure of the Physical World. *Nature* 278:605–12.

Carroll, John M. 1980. *Toward a Structural Psychology of Cinema*. AtS 55.

Casalis, Matthieu. 1975. The Discourse of *Penthouse* Rhetoric and Ideology. *Semiotica* 15:355–91.

Casalis, Matthieu. 1983. The Semiotics of the Visible in Japanese Rock Gardens. *Semiotica* 44:349–62.

Cassirer, Ernst. 1923. *Philosophie der Symbolischen Formen: I. Die Sprache*. Berlin: Bruno Cassirer.

Cassirer, Ernst. 1944. *An Essay on Man: An Introduction to a Philosophy of Human Culture*. New Haven: Yale University Press.

Cassirer, Ernst. 1945. Structuralism in Modern Linguistics. *Word* 1:99–120.

Cassirer, Ernst. 1946. *Language and Myth*. New York: Harper and Brothers.

Cassirer, Ernst. 1953–57. *Philosophy of Symbolic Forms*. 3 vols. New Haven: Yale University Press.

Chaitin, Gilbert. 1988. Lacan and Semiosis. WEB 1989:37–63.

Chao, Yuen Ren. 1968. *Language and Symbolic Systems*. Cambridge: Cambridge University Press.

Chomsky, Noam. 1979. Human Language and Other Semiotic Systems. *Semiotica* 25:31–44.

Chomsky, Noam. 1980. *Rules and Representations*. New York: Columbia University Press.

Clarke, D. S., Jr. 1987. *Principles of Semiotic*. London: Routledge and Kegan Paul.

Clarke, D. S., Jr. 1990. *Sources of Semiotic: Readings with Commentary from Antiquity to the Present*. Carbondale: Southern Illinois University Press.

Coles, Robert. 1978. *Walker Percy: An American Search*. Boston: Little, Brown.

Conkin, Paul K. 1976. *Puritans and Pragmatists: Eight Eminent American Thinkers*. Bloomington: Indiana University Press.

Coquet, Jean-Claude. 1982. *Sémiotique—l'Ecole de Paris*. Paris: Hachette.

Corti, Maria. 1978. *An Introduction to Literary Semiotics*. AiS.

Craik, K. J. W. 1967. *The Nature of Explanation*. 2nd ed. Cambridge: Cambridge University Press.

Crumrine, Ross N., and Marjorie Halpin, eds. 1983. *The Power of the Symbol: Masks and Masquerade in the Americas*. Vancouver: University of British Columbia Press.

Crystal, David. 1974. Paralinguistics. In: *Current Trends in Linguistics*, ed. Thomas A. Sebeok, Vol. 12, pp. 265–95. The Hague: Mouton.

Crystal, David. 1980. *A First Dictionary of Linguistics and Phonetics*. London: André Deutsch.

Culler, Jonathan. 1981. Semiotics of Tourism. *American Journal of Semiotics* 1:127–40.

Culler, Jonathan. 1983. *Barthes*. London: Fontana.

Culler, Jonathan. 1986. *Ferdinand de Saussure*. Ithaca: Cornell University Press.

Cunningham, Donald J. 1987. Semiotics and Education—Strands in the Web. WEB 1986:367–78.

Daddesio, Thomas C. 1989. Review of Arbib and Hesse (1989). *American Journal of Semiotics* 6:312–24.

Daiches, David. 1971. *A Third World*. Sussex: Sussex University Press.

Dauben, Joseph W. 1982. Peirce's Place in Mathematics. *Historia Mathematica* 9:311–25.

Davies, Paul. 1980. *Other Worlds*. New York: Simon and Schuster.

Davis, Martha. 1972. *Understanding Body Movement: An Annotated Bibliography*. AiS.

Davis, Martha, and Janet Skupien. 1982. *Body Movement and Nonverbal Communication: An Annotated Bibliography, 1971–80*. AiS.

Deely, John. 1956. Semiotic in the Thought of Jacques Maritain. *Recherches Sémiotiques/Semiotic Inquiry* 6:112–42.

Deely, John. 1988. The Semiotic of John Poinsot: Yesterday and Tomorrow. *Semiotica* 69:31–127.

Deely, John. 1990. *Basics of Semiotics*. AiS.

Deely, John, Brooke Williams, and Felicia E. Kruse. 1986. *Frontiers in Semiotics*. AiS.

De George, Richard T., ed. 1981. *Semiotic Themes*. Lawrence: University of Kansas Humanistic Studies, No. 53.

Deledalle, Gérard. 1979. *Théorie et pratique du signe*. Paris: Payot.

Demers, Richard A. 1988. Linguistics and Animal Communication. In: *Linguistics: The Cambridge Survey*, ed. Frederick J. Newmeyer, 3:314–35. Cambridge: Cambridge University Press.

Donnelly, Eleanor. 1987. Semiotics and Nursing. WEB 1986:379–87.

Donoghue, Denis. 1989. The Strange Case of Paul de Man. *New York Review of Books* 36:11:32–39.

Douglas, Mary. 1982. The Future of Semiotics. *Semiotica* 38:197–203.

Drew, Paul, and Anthony Wootton, eds. 1988. *Erving Goffman: Exploring the Interaction Order*. Boston: Northeastern University Press.

Ducrot, Oswald, and Tzvetan Todorov. 1979 [1972]. *Encyclopedic Dictionary of the Sciences of Language*. Baltimore: Johns Hopkins University Press.

144   References

Duncan, Hugh Dalziel. 1968. *Symbols in Society*. New York: Oxford University Press.
Eccles, John, ed. 1982. *Mind and Brain: The Many-Faceted Problems*. Washington: Paragon House.
Eco, Umberto. 1977. The Influence of Roman Jakobson on the Development of Semiotics. In: Daniel Armstrong and C. H. van Schooneveld, *Roman Jakobson: Echoes of His Scholarship*, pp. 39–58. Lisse: Peter de Ridder Press.
Eco, Umberto. 1979. *The Role of the Reader: Explorations in the Semiotics of Texts*. AiS.
Eco, Umberto. 1983. Proposals for a History of Semiotics. In: *Semiotics Unfolding*, ed. Tasso Borbé. AtS 68:1:75–89.
Eco, Umberto. 1984. *Semiotics and the Philosophy of Language*. AiS.
Eco, Umberto. 1987. The Influence of Roman Jakobson on the Development of Semiotics. In: *Classics of Semiotics*, ed. Martin Krampen, Klaus Oehler, Roland Posner, Thomas A. Sebeok, and Thure von Uexküll, pp. 109–27. PiCS.
Eco, Umberto. Forthcoming. History and Historiography of Semiotics. In: *Semiotik: Ein Handbuch zu den zeichentheoretischen Grundlagen von Natur und Kultur*, ed. Roland Posner, Klaus Robering, and Thomas A. Sebeok. Berlin: Walter de Gruyter.
Eco, Umberto, Marco Santambrogio, and Patrizia Violi, eds. 1988. *Meaning and Mental Representations*. AiS.
Eco, Umberto, and Thomas A. Sebeok, eds. 1983. *The Sign of Three: Dupin, Holmes, Peirce*. AiS.
Edelman, Gerald M. 1988. *Topobiology: An Introduction to Molecular Embryology*. New York: Basic Books.
Efron, David. 1972 [1941]. *Gesture, Race and Culture*. AtS 9.
Efron, David. 1979. Semiotics and Telepathy. In: *A Semiotic Landscape*, ed. Seymour Chatman, Umberto Eco, and Jean-Marie Klinkenberg. AtS 29:1102–1108.
Eggers, Walter, and Sigrid Mayer. 1988. *Ernst Cassirer: An Annotated Bibliography*. New York: Garland.
Eisenberg, J. F., and Wilton Dillon, eds. 1971. *Man and Beast: Comparative Social Behavior*. Washington, D.C.: Smithsonian Institution Press.
Ekman, Paul. 1985. *Telling Lies: Clues to Deceit in the Marketplace, Politics, and Marriage*. New York: W. W. Norton.
Ekman, Paul. 1987. A Life's Pursuit. WEB 1986:3–45.
Ekman, Paul, and Wallace C. Friesen. 1969. The Repertoire of Nonverbal Behavior: Categories, Origins, Usage, and Coding. *Semiotica* 1:49–98.
Elstein, Arthur S., et al. 1978. *Medical Problem Solving: An Analysis of Clinical Reasoning*. Cambridge: Harvard University Press.
Engler, Rudolf. 1968. *Lexique de la terminologie Saussurienne*. Utrecht: Spectrum.
Epstein, Robert, Robert P. Lanza, and B. F. Skinner. 1980. Symbolic Communication between Two Pigeons (*Columbia livia domestica*). *Science* 207:543–45.

References 145

Eschbach, Achim, ed. 1981. *Zeichen über Zeichen über Zeichen.* Tübingen: Gunter Narr.
Esposito, Joseph L. 1980. *Evolutionary Metaphysics: The Development of Peirce's Theory of Categories.* Athens: Ohio University Press.
Evans, Jonathan, and André Helbo, eds. 1986. *Semiotics and International Scholarship: Towards a Language of Theory.* Dordrecht: Martinus Nijhoff.
Fabrega, Horacio, Jr. 1980 [1974]. *Disease and Social Behavior: An Interdisciplinary Perspective.* Cambridge: MIT Press.
Fann, K. T. 1970. *Peirce's Theory of Abduction.* The Hague: Martinus Nijhoff.
Fann, K. T. 1990. The Semiotics of A. B. Johnson. WEB 1989:31–59.
Feehan, Michael. 1989. Kenneth Burke's Contribution to a Theory of Language. *Semiotica* 76:245–66.
Finlay-Pelinski, Marike. 1982. Semiotics or History. *Semiotica* 40:229–66.
Fiordo, Richard. 1978. Kenneth Burke's Semiotic. *Semiotica* 23:53–75.
Firth, Raymond. 1957. *Man and Culture.* London: Routledge and Kegan Paul.
Fisch, Max H. 1986. *Peirce, Semeiotic, and Pragmatism,* ed. Kenneth Laine Ketner and Christian J. W. Kloesel. Bloomington: Indiana University Press.
Fiske, John, and John Hartley. 1978. *Reading Television.* London: Methuen.
Florence, P. Sargant, and J. R. L. Anderson. 1977. *C. K. Ogden: A Collective Memoir.* London: Elek Pemberton.
Flynn, Pierce Julius. 1991. *The Ethnomethodological Method: A Sociosemiotic Approach.* AtS.
Foote, Kenneth E. 1985. Space, Territory, and Landscape: The Borderlands of Geography and Semiotics. *Recherches Sémiotiques/Semiotic Inquiry* 5:158–75.
Foote, Kenneth E. 1988. Object as Memory: The Material Foundations of Human Semiosis. *Semiotica* 69:243–68.
Fox, Sidney. 1988. *The Emergence of Life: Darwinian Evolution from the Inside.* New York: Basic Books.
French, A. P., and P. J. Kennedy, eds. 1985. *Niels Bohr: A Centenary Volume.* Cambridge: Harvard University Press.
Frutiger, Adrian. 1989. *Signs and Symbols: Their Design and Meaning.* New York: Van Nostrand Reinhold.
Galan, F. W. 1985. *Historic Structures: The Prague School Project, 1928–1946.* Austin: University of Texas Press.
Galileo Galilei. 1957. The Assayer [Il saggiatore]. In: *Discoveries and Opinions of Galileo,* trans. Stillman Drake, pp. 217–80. New York: Doubleday.
Gardin, Jean-Claude. 1988. Semiotics and Archaeology. WEB 1987:377–87.
Gardin, Jean-Claude, Paul Bouissac, and Kenneth E. Foote. 1984. A Program for Semiotics. *Semiotica* 53:1–5.
Gardner, Martin. 1983. *Order and Surprise.* Buffalo: Prometheus Books.

146   References

Gardner, Martin. 1989. *Gardner's Whys and Wherefores*. Chicago: University of Chicago Press.
Glassie, Henry. 1973. Structure and Function: Folklore and the Artifact. *Semiotica* 7:313–51.
Glynn, Prudence. 1982. *Skin to Skin: Eroticism in Dress*. New York: Oxford University Press.
Godzich, Wlad. 1978. The Construction of Meaning. *New Literary History* 9:389–97.
Goffman, Erving. 1961. *Encounters*. Indianapolis: Bobbs-Merrill.
Goffman, Erving. 1963. *Stigma: Notes on the Management of Spoiled Identity*. Englewood Cliffs: Prentice-Hall.
Goffman, Erving. 1979. Footing. *Semiotica* 25:1–29.
Golliher, Jeffrey Mark. 1987. The Meaning of Bodily Artifacts: Variation in Domain Structure, Communicative Functions, and Social Context. *Semiotica* 65:107–27.
Gombrich, Ernst H. 1981. Image and Code: Scope and Limits of Conventionalism in Pictorial Representation. In: *Image and Code*, ed. Wendy Steiner, pp. 11–42. Ann Arbor: Michigan Studies in the Humanities.
Goodman, Nelson. 1968. *Languages of Art: An Approach to a Theory of Symbols*. Indianapolis: Bobbs-Merrill.
Goodman, Nelson. 1978. *Ways of Worldmaking*. Indianapolis: Hackett.
Gottdiener, Mark, and Alexandros Ph. Lagopoulos, eds. 1986. *The City and the Sign: An Introduction to Urban Semiotics*. New York: Columbia University Press.
Gottschall, Edward M. 1989. *Typographic Communications Today*. Cambridge: MIT Press.
Grace, George W. 1987. *The Linguistic Construction of Reality*. London: Croom Helm.
Grace, George W. 1989. The Meaning of Meaning. *Semiotica* 73:351–62.
Gregory, Bruce. 1988. *Inventing Reality: Physics as Language*. New York: Wiley.
Greimas, Algirdas Julien, and Joseph Courtés. 1979. *Sémiotique: dictionnaire raisonné de la théorie du langage*. Paris: Classiques Hachette.
Greimas, Algirdas Julien, and Joseph Courtés. 1982. *Semiotics and Language: An Analytical Dictionary*. AiS.
Grinker, Roy R., Jr., ed. 1956. *Toward a Unified Theory of Human Behavior*. New York: Basic Books.
Grünbaum, Adolf. 1984. *The Foundations of Psychoanalysis: A Philosophical Critique*. Berkeley: University of California Press.
Guiraud, Pierre. 1971. *La sémiologie*. Paris: Presses Universitaires de France.
Guiraud, Pierre. 1975. *Semiology*. Boston: Routledge and Kegan Paul.
Haidu, Peter. 1982. Semiotics and History. *Semiotica* 40:187–228.
Hall, Edward T. 1968. Proxemics. *Current Anthropology* 9:83–108.
Hall, Peter M., and Dee Ann Spencer Hall. 1983. The Handshake Interaction. *Semiotica* 45:249–64.
Hamburg, Carl H. 1949. Cassirer's Conception of Philosophy. In: *The*

Philosophy of Ernst Cassirer, ed. Paul Arthur Schilpp, pp. 73–119. Evanston: Library of Living Philosophers.

Hanna, Judith Lynne. 1986. Dance. EDS.

Hardwick, Charles S. 1977. *Semiotic and Significs: The Correspondence between Charles S. Peirce and Victoria Lady Welby*. Bloomington: Indiana University Press.

Harland, Richard. 1987. *Superstructuralism: The Philosophy of Structuralism and Post-Structuralism*. London: Methuen.

Hartshorne, Charles. 1973. *Born to Sing: An Interpretation and World Survey of Bird Song*. Bloomington: Indiana University Press.

Hasenmueller, Christine. 1984. Images and Codes: Implications of the Exegesis of Illusionism for Semiotics. *Semiotica* 50:335–57.

Heath, Robert L. 1986. *Realism and Relativism: A Perspective on Kenneth Burke*. Macon: Mercer University Press.

Hediger, Heini. 1980. *Tiere Verstehen*. Munich: Kindler.

Heisenberg, Werner. 1955. *The Physicist's Conception of Nature*. New York: Harcourt, Brace.

Hendricks, William O. 1989. Circling the Square: On Greimas's Semiotics. *Semiotica* 75:95–122.

Henle, Paul, ed. 1958. *Language, Thought, and Culture*. Ann Arbor: University of Michigan Press.

Herzfeld, Michael. 1986. Signs in the Field: Semiotic Perspectives on Ethnography. *Semiotica* 46:99–106.

Herzfeld, Michael. 1987. *Anthropology through the Looking-Glass: Critical Ethnography in the Margins of Europe*. Cambridge: Cambridge University Press.

Hjelmslev, Louis. 1953. *Prolegomena to a Theory of Language: International Journal of American Linguistics*. Memoir 7. Baltimore: Waverly Press.

Holenstein, Elmar. 1982. On the Cognitive Underpinnings of Language. *Semiotica* 41:107–34.

Holenstein, Elmar. 1986. Vom Ursprung der Sprache. *Neue Rundschau* 97:213:190–207.

Honko, Lauri. 1990. Recommendation on the Safeguarding of Traditional Culture and Folklore Adopted by Unesco. *Nordic Institute of Folklore Newsletter* 1:3–7.

Hudson, Deal W., and Matthew J. Mancini, eds. 1987. *Understanding Maritain: Philosopher and Friend*. Macon: Mercer University Press.

Hume, David. 1739–40. *A Treatise of Human Nature*. London: J. Noon.

Hume, David. 1748. *Enquiry concerning Human Understanding*. London: A. Millar.

Hunt, Earl. 1989. Cognitive Science: Definition, Status, and Questions. *Annual Review of Psychology* 40:603–29.

Husserl, Edmund. 1913. *Ideen zu einer reinen Phänomenologie und phänomenologischen Philosophie*, Vol. I. Halle: Martin Niemeyer.

Hymes, Dell. 1968. Essays on Life, Literature, and Method. *Language* 44:664–69.

Hymes, Dell. 1978. Comments. *New Literary History* 9:399–411.

148   References

Innis, Robert E. 1985. *Semiotics: An Introductory Anthology*. AiS.
Jacob, François. 1982. *The Possible and the Actual*. Seattle: University of Washington Press.
Jakobson, Roman. 1960. Linguistics and Poetics. In: *Style in Language*, ed. Thomas A. Sebeok, pp. 350–77. New York: Wiley.
Jakobson, Roman. 1971. *Selected Writings II: Word and Language*. The Hague: Mouton.
Jakobson, Roman. 1972. Motor Signs for "Yes" and "No." *Language in Society* 1:91–96.
Jakobson, Roman. 1973. *Main Trends in the Science of Language*. New York: Harper and Row.
Jakobson, Roman. 1978. Interview with Roman Jakobson: Poetics. *Philosophy Today* (Spring): 65–72.
Jakobson, Roman. 1980. *The Framework of Language*. Ann Arbor: Michigan Studies in the Humanities.
Jakobson, Roman. 1981. *Selected Writings III: Poetry of Grammar and Grammar of Poetry*. The Hague: Mouton.
Jakobson, Roman, and Krystyna Pomorska. 1983. *Dialogues*. Cambridge: MIT Press.
Jastrow, Joseph. 1900. *Fact and Fable in Psychology*. Boston: Houghton, Mifflin.
Jastrow, Joseph. 1916. Charles S. Peirce as a Teacher. *Journal of Philosophy* 13:723–26.
Jastrow, Joseph. 1930. Joseph Jastrow [Autobiography]. In: *A History of Psychology in Autobiography*, ed. Carl Murchison, 1:135–62. Worcester: Clark University Press.
Jastrow, Joseph. 1935. *Wish and Wisdom: Episodes in the Vagaries of Belief*. New York: D. Appleton-Century.
Jerne, Niels K. 1985. The Generative Grammar of the Immune System. *Science* 229:1057–59.
Jervis, Robert. 1970. *The Logic of Images in International Relations*. Princeton: Princeton University Press.
Jervis, Robert. 1987. *The Symbolic Nature of Nuclear Politics*. Urbana: University of Illinois Department of Political Science.
Johnson, Alexander Bryan. 1947 [1836]. *A Treatise on Language*, ed. David Rynin. Berkeley: University of California Press.
Johnson, George. 1990. New Mind, No Clothes. *The Sciences* (July/August): 45–49.
Johnson, Mark. 1987. *The Body in Mind: The Bodily Basis of Meaning, Imagination, and Reason*. Chicago: University of Chicago Press.
Johnson, Michael L. 1988. *Mind, Language, Machine: Artificial Intelligence in the Poststructuralist Age*. New York: St. Martin's Press.
Johnson-Laird, P. N. 1988. *The Computer and the Mind: An Introduction to Cognitive Science*. Cambridge: Harvard University Press.
Jones, Edwin. 1989. *Reading the Book of Nature: A Phenomenological Study of Creative Expression in Science and Painting*. Athens: Ohio University Press.
Jorna, René J. 1991. An Analysis of Approaches to Mental Representation(s). *Semiotica*.

Joseph, Nathan. 1986. *Uniforms and Nonuniforms: Communication through Clothing.* New York: Greenwood.

Jules-Rosette, Bennetta. 1984. *The Messages of Tourist Art: An African Semiotic System in Comparative Perspective.* AiS.

Kahn, David. 1967. *The Codebreakers: The Story of Secret Writing.* New York: Macmillan.

Kahn, David. 1986. Cryptology. EDS.

Kantor, Jacob R. 1936. *An Objective Psychology of Grammar.* Science Series 1. Bloomington: Indiana University Publications.

Kaplan, Abraham. 1943. Content Analysis and the Theory of Signs. *Philosophy of Science* 10:230–47.

Karp, Ivan. 1986. Anthropology. EDS.

Kendon, Adam. 1986. Nonverbal Communication. EDS 609–22.

Kergosien, Y. L. 1985. Sémiotique de la nature. In: *Actes du IVe Séminaire de l'Ecole de Biologie Théorique,* ed. G. Benchetrit and J. Demongeot, pp. 11–26. Paris: Centre National de la Recherche Scientifique.

Kevelson, Roberta. 1986. Semiotics in the United States. In: *The Semiotic Sphere,* ed. Thomas A. Sebeok and Jean Umiker-Sebeok, pp. 519–54. PiCS.

Kevelson, Roberta. 1988. *The Law as a System of Signs.* PiCS.

Klaus, Georg. 1962. *Semiotik und Erkenntnistheorie.* Munich: Wilhelm Fink.

Klima, Edward, Ursula Bellugi, et al. 1979. *The Signs of Language.* Cambridge: Harvard University Press.

Kobernick, Mark. 1989. *Semiotics of the Drama and the Style of Eugene O'Neill.* Amsterdam: Benjamins.

Krampen, Martin. 1981a. The Developmental Semiotics of Jean Piaget (1896–1980). *Semiotica* 34:193–218.

Krampen, Martin. 1981b. Phytosemiotics. *Semiotica* 36:187–209.

Krampen, Martin. 1983. Icons of the Road. *Semiotica* 43:1–204.

Krampen, Martin. 1986a. Notational System. EDS.

Krampen, Martin. 1986b. Phytosemiotics. EDS.

Krampen, Martin, Klaus Oehler, Roland Posner, Thomas A. Sebeok, and Thure von Uexküll, eds. 1987. *Classics of Semiotics.* PiCS.

Krois, John Michael. 1987. *Cassirer: Symbolic Forms and History.* New Haven: Yale University Press.

Lacan, Jacques. 1966. *Écrits.* Paris: Seuil.

Lakoff, George. 1987. *Women, Fire, and Dangerous Things: What Categories Reveal about the Mind.* Chicago: University of Chicago Press.

Lakoff, George, and Mark Johnson. 1980. *Metaphors We Live By.* Chicago: University of Chicago Press.

Lamb, Sydney M. 1981. On the Gains of Linguistics. In: *The Seventh LACUS Forum 1980,* pp. 17–27. Columbia, S.C.: Hornbeam Press.

Lamb, Sydney M., et al. 1982. *Whitehead and Lamb: A New Network of Connection.* Claremont: Claremont Graduate School.

Lamb, Sydney M. 1984. On the Aims of Linguistics. In: *New Directions in Linguistics and Semiotics,* ed. James E. Copeland, pp. 1–11. Houston: Rice University Studies.

Landowski, Eric. 1988. Towards a Semiotic and Narrative Approach to Law. *International Journal for the Semiotics of Law* 1:79–105.

Langacker, Ronald W. 1987. *Foundations of Cognitive Grammar*, Vol. 1: *Theoretical Prerequisites*. Stanford: Stanford University Press.

Langer, Susanne K. 1942. *Philosophy in a New Key: A Study in the Symbolism of Reason, Rite, and Art*. New York: Penguin.

Langer, Susanne K. 1962. *Philosophical Sketches*. Baltimore: Johns Hopkins University Press.

Larsen, Svend Erik. 1989. Greimas or Grimace? *Semiotica* 75:123–30.

Lavers, Annette. 1982. *Roland Barthes: Structuralism and After*. London: Methuen.

Leach, Edmund. 1984. Semiotics, Ethology, and the Limits of Human Understanding. Patten Foundation Lecture I, Indiana University, Bloomington, October 9.

Lee, Benjamin, and Greg Urban, eds. 1989. *Semiotics, Self, and Society*. AtS 84.

Lehrer, Adrienne. 1978. We Drank Wine, We Talked, and a Good Time Was Had by All. *Semiotica* 23:243–78.

Leroi-Gourhan, André, Pierre Champion, and Monique de Fontanes, eds. 1964. *VIᵉ Congrès International des Sciences Anthropologiques et Ethnologiques* 2. Paris: Musée de l'Homme.

Levelt, Willem J. M. 1989. *Speaking: From Intention to Articulation*. Cambridge: MIT Press.

Lévi-Strauss, Claude. 1958. *Anthropologie structurale*. Paris: Plon.

Lévi-Strauss, Claude. 1966. *The Savage Mind*. Chicago: University of Chicago Press.

Lévi-Strauss, Claude. 1973. *Anthropologie structurale deux*. Paris: Plon.

Lévi-Strauss, Claude. 1985. Avant-propos. In: *Iconicity: Essays on the Nature of Culture*, ed. Paul Bouissac, Michael Herzfeld, and Roland Posner. Tübingen: Stauffenburg.

Lévi-Strauss, Claude, Roman Jakobson, C. F. Voegelin, and Thomas A. Sebeok. 1953. *Results of the Conference of Anthropologists and Linguists: International Journal of American Linguistics*. Memoir 8. Baltimore: Waverly Press.

Lieberman, Philip. 1988. Voice in the Wilderness: How Humans Acquired the Power of Speech. *Sciences* 28:4:23–29.

Lipset, David. 1980. *Gregory Bateson: The Legacy of a Scientist*. Englewood Cliffs: Prentice-Hall.

Loveday, Leo, and Satomi Chiba. 1985. Partaking with the Divine and Symbolizing the Societal: The Semiotics of Japanese Food and Drink. *Semiotica* 56:115–31.

Lowe, Victor. 1985, 1990. *Alfred North Whitehead: The Man and His Work*, I (1861–1910), II (1910–1947). Baltimore: Johns Hopkins University Press.

Lucid, Daniel P. 1988 [1977]. *Soviet Semiotics: An Anthology*. Baltimore: Johns Hopkins University Press.

Lumsden, Charles J. 1986. The Gene and the Sign: Giving Structure to Postmodernity. *Semiotica* 62:191–206.

Lumsden, Charles J., and Edward O. Wilson. 1981. *Genes, Mind, and*

Culture: The Coevolutionary Process. Cambridge: Harvard University Press.

Lurie, Alison. 1981. *The Language of Clothes.* New York: Random House.

MacCannell, Dean. 1976a. *The Tourist: A New Theory of the Leisure Class.* New York: Schocken.

MacCannell, Dean. 1976b. The Past and Future of "Symbolic Interactionism." *Semiotica* 16:99–114.

MacCannell, Dean. 1983. Erving Goffman. *Semiotica* 45:1–33.

MacCannell, Dean. 1986. Semiotics and Sociology. *Semiotica* 61:193–200.

MacCannell, Dean, and Juliet Flower MacCannell. 1982. *The Time of the Sign: A Semiotic Interpretation of Modern Culture.* AiS.

MacCannell, Juliet Flower. 1985. Paul de Man. *Semiotica* 55:129–66.

Magli, Patrizia. 1986. De Iorio, Andrea (1769–1851). EDS.

Mahl, George F. 1987. *Explorations in Nonverbal and Vocal Behavior.* Hillsdale: Erlbaum.

Maletic, Vera. 1987. *Body—Space—Expression: The Development of Rudolf Laban's Movement and Dance Concepts.* AtS 75.

Malinowski, Bronislaw. 1965 [1935]. *The Language of Magic and Gardening.* Bloomington: Indiana University Press.

Mallery, Garrick. 1972 [1881]. *Sign Language among North American Indians Compared with That among Other Peoples and Deaf-Mutes.* AtS 14.

Marcus, Steven. 1974. Introduction to *The Continental Op,* by Dashiell Hammett. Pp. ix-xxix. New York: Random House.

Margulis, Lynn, and Dorion Sagan. 1986a. *Microcosmos: Four Billion Years of Evolution from Our Microbial Ancestors.* New York: Summit.

Margulis, Lynn, and Dorion Sagan. 1986b. Strange Fruit on the Tree of Life. *Sciences* 26:3:38–45.

Maritain, Jacques. 1956. Language and the Magic Sign. *Explorations* 6:58–64.

Maritain, Jacques. 1957. Language and the Theory of Sign. In: *Language: An Enquiry into Its Meaning,* ed. Ruth Nanda Anshen, pp. 86–101. New York: Harper and Brothers.

Marrone, Gianfranco, ed. 1986. *Dove va la semiotica? Quaderni del Circolo Semiologico Siciliano* 24.

Mars, Gerald. 1982. *Cheats at Work: An Anthropology of Workplace Crime.* Boston: Allen and Unwin.

Martin, Richard M. 1978. *Semiotics and Linguistic Structure: A Primer of Philosophic Logic.* Albany: State University of New York Press.

McCulloch, Warren S. 1965. *Embodiments of Mind.* Cambridge: MIT Press.

McDowell, John H. 1986. Folkloristics. EDS.

McLuhan, Marshall. 1946. Footprints in the Sands of Time. *Sewanee Review,* October, pp. 617–34.

McNeill, David. 1979. *The Conceptual Basis of Language.* Hillsdale: Lawrence Erlbaum.

Mead, George H. 1934. *Mind, Self, and Society: From the Standpoint of a Social Behaviorist,* ed. Charles W. Morris. Chicago: University of Chicago Press.

Mechling, Jay. 1987. Dress Right, Dress: The Boy Scout Uniform as a Folk Costume. *Semiotica* 64:319–33.

Merleau-Ponty, Maurice. 1964 [1960]. *Signs.* Evanston: Northwestern University Press.

Merrell, Floyd. 1982. *Semiotic Foundations: Steps toward an Epistemology of Written Texts.* AiS.

Merrell, Floyd. 1987. Of Position Papers, Paradigms, and Paradoxes. *Semiotica* 65:191–223.

Merrell, Floyd. 1991a. *Sign, Textuality, World.* AiS.

Merrell, Floyd. 1991b. *Signs Becoming Signs: Our Perfusive, Pervasive Universe.* AiS.

Merrell, Floyd. 1991c. *Self-Excited Signs.* AiS.

Mertz, Elizabeth, and Richard J. Parmentier. 1985. *Semiotic Mediation: Sociocultural and Psychological Perspectives.* Orlando: Academic Press.

Metz, Christian. 1974. *Language and Cinema.* AtS 26.

Meyer, Leonard B. 1967. *Music, the Arts, and Ideas: Patterns and Predictions in Twentieth-Century Culture.* Chicago: University of Chicago Press.

Mick, David G. 1986. Consumer Research and Semiotics: Exploring the Morphology of Signs, Symbols, and Significance. *Journal of Consumer Research* 13:196–213.

Mick, David G. 1988. Schema-Theoretics and Semiotics: Toward More Holistic, Programmatic Research on Marketing Communication. *Semiotica* 70:1–26.

Miller, Benjamin F. 1978. *The Complete Medical Guide.* New York: Simon and Schuster.

Miller, Eugene F. 1979. Hume's Reduction of Cause to Sign. *New Scholasticism* 53:42–75.

Miller, Eugene F. 1986. David Hume. EDS.

Millikan, Ruth Garrett. 1984. *Language, Thought, and Other Biological Categories: New Foundations for Realism.* Cambridge: MIT Press.

Mininni, Giuseppe. 1982. *Psicosemiotica.* Bari: Adriatica.

Minsky, Marvin. 1986. *The Society of Mind.* New York: Simon and Schuster.

Mitchell, Robert W., and Nicholas S. Thompson, eds. 1986. *Deception: Perspectives on Human and Nonhuman Deceit.* Albany: State University of New York Press.

Monod, Jacques. 1971. *Chance and Necessity: An Essay on the Natural Philosophy of Modern Biology.* New York: Knopf.

Moore, Charles W., William J. Mitchell, and William Turnbull, Jr. 1989. *The Poetics of Gardens.* Cambridge: MIT Press.

Morris, Charles. 1946. *Signs, Language and Behavior.* New York: Prentice-Hall.

Morris, Charles. 1964. *Signification and Significance: A Study of the Relations of Signs and Values.* Cambridge: MIT Press.

Morris, Charles. 1970. *The Pragmatic Movement in American Philosophy.* New York: George Braziller.

Morris, Charles. 1971. *Writings on the General Theory of Signs.* AtS 16.

Morris, Desmond. 1977. *Manwatching: A Field Guide to Human Behaviour.* London: Jonathan Cape.

Morris, Desmond. 1981. *The Soccer Tribe.* London: Jonathan Cape.

Mounin, Georges. 1970. *Introduction à la sémiologie.* Paris: Minuit.

Mounin, Georges. 1985. *Semiotic Praxis: Studies in Pertinence and in the Means of Expression and Communication.* PiCS.

Nagel, Ernest. 1982. Charles Peirce's Place in Philosophy. *Historia Mathematica* 9:302–10.

Nesher, Dan. 1990. Understanding Sign Semiosis as Cognition and as Self-Conscious Process: A Reconstruction of Some Basic Conceptions in Peirce's Semiotics. *Semiotica* 79:1–49.

Neurath, Otto, Rudolf Carnap, and Charles Morris, eds. 1955. *International Encyclopedia of Unified Science,* Vols. I (Nos. 1–5) and II (Nos. 6–10). Chicago: University of Chicago Press.

Nida, Eugene A. 1975. *Componential Analysis of Meaning: An Introduction to Semantic Structures.* AtS 57.

Nöth, Winfried. 1989. *Handbook of Semiotics.* AiS.

Nowakowska, Maria. 1986. *Cognitive Sciences: Basic Problems, New Perspectives, and Implications for Artificial Intelligence.* Orlando: Academic Press.

Nye, David E. 1983. *The Invented Self: An Anti-biography, from Documents of Thomas A. Edison.* Odense: Odense University Press.

O'Donnell, Patrick, and Robert Con Davis. 1989. *Intertextuality and Contemporary American Fiction.* Baltimore: Johns Hopkins University Press.

Ogden, C. K. 1967 [1932]. *Opposition.* Bloomington: Indiana University Press.

Ogilvie, John, ed. 1883. *The Imperial Dictionary of the English Language,* Vol. IV. New York: Century Co.

Ouellet, Pierre, ed. 1989. *Semiotics, Cognition, and Artificial Intelligence,* Special Issue, *Semiotica* 77–1/3:1–362.

Pagnini, Marcello. 1987. *The Pragmatics of Literature.* AiS.

Parmentier, Richard J. 1989. Disciplining Semiotics. *Semiotics* 74:109–20.

Parret, Herman. 1984. Peirce and Hjelmslev: The Two Semiotics. *Language Sciences* 6:217–27.

Parry, Albert. 1933. *Tattoo: Secrets of a Strange Art.* New York: Simon and Schuster.

Paulson, William R. 1988. *The Noise of Culture: Literary Texts in a World of Information.* Ithaca: Cornell University Press.

Paz, Octavio. 1990. The Power of Ancient Mexican Art. *The New York Review of Books,* December 6, pp. 18–21.

Peck, H. Daniel. 1977. *A World by Itself: The Pastoral Moment in Cooper's Fiction.* New Haven: Yale University Press.

Peckham, Morse. 1979. *Explanation and Power: The Control of Human Behavior.* Minneapolis: University of Minnesota Press.

Peirce, Charles S. 1935–66. *Collected Papers of Charles Sanders Peirce,* ed. Charles Hartshorne, Paul Weiss, and A. W. Burks. Cambridge: Harvard University Press. [References are to volumes and paragraphs (not pages).]

Peirce, Charles S. 1982. *Writings of Charles S. Peirce: A Chronological Edition*. Vol. 1, 1857–66. Bloomington: Indiana University Press.
Peirce, Charles S. 1984. *Writings of Charles S. Peirce: A Chronological Edition*. Vol. 2, 1867–71. Bloomington: Indiana University Press.
Pelc, Jerzy. 1981. Theoretical Foundations of Semiotics. *American Journal of Semiotics* 1:15–45.
Percy, Walker. 1981. *The Message in the Bottle: How Queer Man Is, How Queer Language Is, and What One Has to Do with the Other*. New York: Farrar, Straus and Giroux.
Petitot-Cocorda, Jean. 1985. *Les catastrophes de la parole: de Roman Jakobson à René Thom*. Paris: Maloine.
Pharies, David A. 1985. *Charles S. Peirce and the Linguistic Sign*. Amsterdam: Benjamins.
Philodemus. 1978. *On Methods of Inference*, ed. Phillip Howard De Lacy and Estelle Allen De Lacy. Naples: Bibliopolis.
Pike, Kenneth L. 1967. *Language in Relation to a Unified Theory of the Structure of Human Behavior*. The Hague: Mouton.
Poinsot, John. 1985. *Tractatus de Signis: The Semiotic of John Poinsot*, ed. John N. Deely. Berkeley: University of California Press.
Polan, Dana. 1989. Cine-semiotics. WEB 1988:333–52.
Polanyi, Livia. 1985. *Telling the American Story: A Structural and Cultural Analysis of Conversational Storytelling*. Norwood: Ablex.
Pollan, Michael. 1989. Why Mow? *New York Times Magazine*, May 28.
Ponzio, Augusto. 1984. Notes on Semiotics and Marxism. *Recherches Sémiotiques/Semiotic Inquiry* 4:293–302.
Ponzio, Augusto. 1989. Semiotics and Marxism. WEB 1988:387–416.
Popper, Karl. 1972. *Objective Knowledge: An Evolutionary Approach*. Oxford: Clarendon Press.
Posner, Roland, et al., eds. 1984. Und in alle Ewigkeit: Kommunikation über 10,000 Jahre. *Zeitschrift für Semiotik* 6:195–330.
Poteat, Patricia Lewis. 1985. *Walker Percy and the Old Modern Age: Reflections on Language, Argument, and the Telling of Stories*. Baton Rouge: Louisiana State University Press.
Preziosi, Donald. 1986. Architecture. EDS.
Preziosi, Donald. 1989. *Rethinking Art History: Meditations on a Coy Science*. New Haven: Yale University Press.
Price-Williams, Douglass, and Sharon Sabsay. 1979. Communicative Competence among Severely Retarded Persons. *Semiotica* 26:35–63.
Proni, Giampaolo. 1988. Umberto Eco: An Intellectual Biography. WEB 1987:3–22
Prosser, C. Ladd. 1985. Modes of Communication. In: *Comparative Neurobiology*, ed. Melvin J. Cohen and Felix Sturmwasser. New York: John Wiley.
Rancour-Laferriere, Daniel. 1985. *Signs of the Flesh: An Essay on the Evolution of Hominid Sexuality*. AtS 71.
Ransdell, Joseph. 1980. Semiotic and Linguistics. In: *The Signifying Animal: The Grammar of Language and Experience*, ed. Irmengard Rauch and Gerald F. Carr, pp. 135–85. AiS.

Ransdell, Joseph. 1986. Peirce. EDS.
Ransdell, Joseph. 1991. *Charles S. Peirce: The Grammar of Representation.*
    AiS.
Rauch, Frederick A. 1840. *Psychology; or A View of the Human Soul: In-
    cluding Anthropology.* New York: M. W. Dodd.
Rauch, Irmengard. 1978. The State of the Semiotics Curriculum. *Semiotic
    Scene* 2:151–55.
Rauch, Irmengard. 1986. The Semiotic Circle of California. WEB
    1987:625–26.
Rauch, Irmengard. 1987. Peirce: "With No Pretension of Being a Lin-
    guist." *Semiotica* 65:29–43.
Rauch, Irmengard, and Gerald F. Carr. 1980. *The Signifying Animal: The
    Grammar of Language and Experience.* AiS.
Read, Allen Walker. 1973. Approaches to Lexicography and Semantics.
    In: *Current Trends in Linguistics,* ed. Thomas A. Sebeok, Vol. 10,
    pp. 145–205. The Hague: Mouton.
Rey, Alain. 1984. What Does Semiotics Come From? *Semiotica* 52:79–93.
Riffaterre, Michael. 1978. *Semiotics of Poetry.* AiS.
Riggins, Steven, ed. 1990. *Beyond Goffman.* AtS 96.
Rjeznikov, L. O. 1964. *Gnoseologičeskie voprosy semiotiki.* Leningrad: Uni-
    versity.
Roback, A. A. 1952. *History of American Psychology.* New York: Library
    Publishers.
Roberts, Don D. 1973. *The Existential Graphs of Charles S. Peirce.* AtS 27.
Rossi-Landi, Ferruccio. 1953. *Charles Morris.* Rome: Fratelli Bocca.
Roth, Jesse, and Derek LeRoith. 1987. Chemical Cross Talk. *Sciences*
    27:3:51–54.
Rotman, Brian. 1987. *Signifying Nothing: The Semiotics of Zero.* New York:
    St. Martin's Press.
Rotman, Brian. 1988. Towards a Semiotics of Mathematics. *Semiotica*
    72:1–35.
Royce, Anya Peterson. 1987. Limits of Innovation in Dance and Mime.
    Semiotica 65:269–84.
Rudy, Stephen. 1986. Semiotics in the U.S.S.R. In: *The Semiotic Sphere,*
    ed. Thomas A. Sebeok and Jean Umiker-Sebeok, pp. 555–82.
    PiCS.
Ruesch, Jurgen, 1961. *Therapeutic Communication.* New York: W. W. Nor-
    ton.
Ruesch, Jurgen, 1972. *Semiotic Approaches to Human Relations.* AtS 25.
Ruesch, Jurgen. 1975. *Knowledge in Action: Communication, Social Opera-
    tions, and Management.* New York: Jason Aronson.
Ruesch, Jurgen, and Gregory Bateson. 1951. *Communication: The Social
    Matrix of Psychiatry.* New York: W. W. Norton.
Ruesch, Jurgen, and Weldon Kees. 1956. *Nonverbal Communication: Notes
    on the Visual Perception of Human Relations.* Berkeley: University
    of California Press.
Russell, Bertrand. 1940. *An Inquiry into Meaning and Truth.* London:
    Allen and Unwin.
Russell, Bertrand. 1959. *Wisdom of the West.* London: Macdonald.

Russo, John Paul. 1989. *I. A. Richards: His Life and Work.* Baltimore: Johns
    Hopkins University Press.
Rynin, David. 1967. Johnson, Alexander Bryan. In: *The Encyclopedia of
    Philosophy,* ed. Paul Edwards, 4:286–90. New York: Macmillan
    and The Free Press.
Sagan, Dorion, and Lynn Margulis. 1987. Gaia and the Evolution of
    Machines. *Whole Earth Review* 55 (Summer): 15–21.
Sanders, Clinton R. 1988. Marks of Mischief: Becoming and Being Tat-
    tooed. *Journal of Contemporary Ethnography* 16:395–432.
Sanders, Clinton R. 1989. *Customizing the Body: The Art and Culture of
    Tattooing.* Philadelphia: Temple University Press.
Saussure, Ferdinand de. 1972. *Cours de linguistique générale,* ed. Tullio
    de Mauro. Paris: Payot.
Savan, David. 1987–88. *An Introduction to C. S. Peirce's Full System of
    Semeiotic.* Monograph Series of the Toronto Semiotic Circle, No.
    1.
Schaffner, Bertram, ed. 1955–59. *Group Processes.* New York: Josiah
    Macy, Jr., Foundation.
Schapiro, Meyer. 1970. On Some Problems in the Semiotics of Visual
    Art: Field and Vehicle in Image-Signs. In: *Sign. Language. Culture,*
    pp. 487–502. The Hague: Mouton.
Scheflen, Albert E. 1967. Psychoanalytic Terms and Some Problems of
    Semiotics. *Social Science Information* 6:4:113–21.
Scheflen, Albert E. 1972. *Body Language and the Social Order: Communi-
    cation as Behavioral Control.* Englewood Cliffs: Prentice-Hall.
Scheflen, Albert E. 1974. *How Behavior Means: Exploring the Contexts of
    Speech and Meaning—Kinesics, Posture, Interaction, Setting, and
    Culture.* Garden City: Doubleday.
Schelling, Thomas C. 1984. *Choice and Consequence: Perspectives of an Er-
    rant Economist.* Cambridge: Harvard University Press.
Schilpp, Paul Arthur, ed. 1949. *The Philosophy of Ernst Cassirer.* Evanston:
    Library of Living Philosophers.
Schleifer, Ronald. 1987. *A. J. Greimas and the Nature of Meaning: Lin-
    guistics, Semiotics and Discourse Theory.* Lincoln: University of Ne-
    braska Press.
Scholes, Robert. 1982. *Semiotics and Interpretation.* New Haven: Yale Uni-
    versity Press.
Sebeok, Thomas A. 1967. Discussion of Communication Processes. In:
    Social Communication among Primates, ed. Stuart A. Altmann, pp.
    363–69. Chicago: University of Chicago Press.
Sebeok, Thomas A. 1972. *Perspectives in Zoosemiotics.* The Hague: Mou-
    ton.
Sebeok, Thomas A. 1974a. *Structure and Texture.* The Hague: Mouton.
Sebeok, Thomas A. 1974b. Semiotics: A Survey of the State of the Art.
    In: *Current Trends in Linguistics,* ed. Thomas A. Sebeok, 12:1:211–
    64. The Hague: Mouton.
Sebeok, Thomas A. 1978. Note on Martin Gardner and Charles Morris.
    Semiotica 23:1–4.
Sebeok, Thomas A. 1981a. The Image of Charles Morris. In: *Zeichen über*

Zeichen über Zeichen, ed. Achim Eschbach, pp. 267–84. Tübingen: Gunter Narr Verlag.

Sebeok, Thomas A. 1981b. *The Play of Musement*. AiS.

Sebeok, Thomas A. 1984a. *Communication Measures to Bridge Ten Millennia*. Technical Report prepared for the Office of Nuclear Waste Isolation. Columbus: Battelle Memorial Institute.

Sebeok, Thomas A. 1984b. Symptom. In: *New Directions in Linguistics and Semiotics*, ed. James E. Copeland, pp. 211–30. Houston: Rice University Press.

Sebeok, Thomas A. 1985. *Contributions to the Doctrine of Signs*. Lanham: University Press of America.

Sebeok, Thomas A. 1986a. *I Think I Am a Verb*. PiCS.

Sebeok, Thomas A. 1986b. A Signifying Man. *New York Times Book Review*, March 30, pp. 14–15.

Sebeok, Thomas A. 1986c. Clever Hans Redivivus. *Skeptical Inquirer* 10:314–18.

Sebeok, Thomas A. 1987a. Linguistics and Semiotics. In: *Developments in Linguistics and Semiotics, Language Teaching, and Learning Communication across Cultures*, ed. Simon P. X. Battestini, pp. 1–18. Washington, D.C.: Georgetown University Press.

Sebeok, Thomas A. 1987b. Toward a Natural History of Language. *Semiotica* 65:343–58.

Sebeok, Thomas A. 1987c. The Mouton d'Or Award. WEB 1986:720–21.

Sebeok, Thomas A. 1987d. *In hoc signo vinces*: Sign Design. In: *Language Topics: Essays in Honour of Michael Halliday*, ed. Ross Steele and Terry Threadgold, p. 231. Amsterdam: Benjamins.

Sebeok, Thomas A. 1988a. *The Sign & Its Masters*. Lanham: University Press of America.

Sebeok, Thomas A. 1988b. "Animal" in Biological and Semiotic Perspective. In: *What Is an Animal?*, ed. Tim Ingold, pp. 63–76. London: Unwin Hyman.

Sebeok, Thomas A. 1988c. Semiosis and Semiotics: What Lies in Their Future? *International Semiotic Spectrum* 10:2.

Sebeok, Thomas A. 1988d. In What Sense Is Language a "Primary Modeling System"? In: *Semiotics of Culture*, ed. H. Broms and R. Kaufmann, pp. 67–80. Helsinki: Arator.

Sebeok, Thomas A. 1988e. *Conferencias Sobre Semiotica en Buenos Aires*, ed. José Luis Caivano. Universidad de Buenos Aires.

Sebeok, Thomas A. 1989. The Semiotic Self Revisited. In: *Sign, Self, and Society*, ed. Benjamin Lee and Greg Urban. AtS 84:v–xiv.

Sebeok, Thomas A. 1990a. *A Sign Is Just a Sign*. AiS.

Sebeok, Thomas A. 1990b. The Evolution of Semiosis. In: *Semiotik: Ein Handbuch zu den zeichentheoretischen Grundlagen von Natur und Kultur*, ed. Roland Posner, Klaus Robering, and Thomas A. Sebeok. Berlin: Walter de Gruyter.

Sebeok, Thomas A. 1990c. *American Signatures: Semiotic Inquiry and Method*. Norman: University of Oklahoma Press.

Sebeok, Thomas A. 1990d. Die Büchseder Pandora in der Obhuteiner

158   References

Atompriesterschaft. In: *Warnungen an die ferne Zukunft: Atommüll
    als Kommunikationsproblem*, ed. Roland Posner, pp. 141–68. Ber-
    lin: Raben Verlag.
Sebeok, Thomas A. 1990e. *Essays in Zoosemiotics*. Toronto: Toronto Semi-
    otic Circle, Monograph Series #5.
Sebeok, Thomas A. 1991a. Indexicality. *American Journal of Semiotics* 7:7–
    28.
Sebeok, Thomas A. 1991b. From Vico to Cassirer to Langer. AtS.
Sebeok, Thomas A., comp. 1986. On the Goals of Semiotics. *Semiotica*
    61:369–88.
Sebeok, Thomas A., ed. 1960. *Style in Language*. New York: John Wiley
    and Sons.
Sebeok, Thomas A., ed. 1968. *Animal Communication: Techniques of
    Study and Results of Research*. Bloomington: Indiana University
    Press.
Sebeok, Thomas A., ed. 1974. *Current Trends in Linguistics* 12:211–64.
Sebeok, Thomas A., ed. 1977a. *A Perfusion of Signs*. AiS.
Sebeok, Thomas A., ed. 1977b. *How Animals Communicate*. Bloomington:
    Indiana University Press.
Sebeok, Thomas A., S. M. Lamb, and J. O. Regan. 1988. *Semiotics in
    Education: A Dialogue—Issues in Communication* 10. Claremont:
    Claremont Graduate School.
Sebeok, Thomas A., and Jean Umiker-Sebeok. 1980. *"You Know My
    Method"*: A Juxtaposition of Charles S. Peirce and Sherlock Holmes.
    Bloomington: Gaslight Publications.
Sebeok, Thomas A. and Jean Umiker-Sebeok. 1981. Clever Hans and
    Smart Simians: The Self-Fulfilling Prophecy and Kindred Meth-
    odological Pitfalls. *Anthropos* 76:89–165.
Sebeok, Thomas A., Alfred S. Hayes, and Mary Catherine Bateson, eds.
    1972 [1964]. *Approaches to Semiotics: Transactions of the Indiana Uni-
    versity Conference on Paralinguistics and Kinesics*. The Hague: Mou-
    ton.
Sebeok, Thomas A. and Alexandra Ramsay, eds. 1969. *Approaches to
    Animal Communication*. AtS 1.
Sebeok, Thomas A., and Robert Rosenthal, eds. 1981. *The Clever Hans
    Phenomenon: Communication with Horses, Whales, Apes, and People*.
    New York: New York Academy of Sciences.
Sebeok, Thomas A., and Jean Umiker-Sebeok, eds. 1980. *Speaking of
    Apes: A Critical Anthology of Two-Way Communication with Man*.
    New York: Plenum.
Sebeok, Thomas A., and Jean Umiker-Sebeok, eds. 1986. *The Semiotic
    Sphere*. PiCS.
Sebeok, Thomas A., and Jean Umiker-Sebeok, eds. 1988. *The Semiotic
    Web*. AtS 78.
Seeley, Thomas D., and Roger A. Levien. 1987. A Colony of Mind. *The
    Sciences* 27(4):39–42.
Segre, Cesare. 1988. *Introduction to the Analysis of the Literary Text*. AiS.
Seielstad, George A. 1983. *Cosmic Ecology: The View from the Outside In*.
    Berkeley: University of California Press.

Seligmann, Claus. 1982. What Is a Door? Notes Toward a Semiotic Guide to Design. *Semiotica* 38:55–76.

Shands, Harley C. 1960. *Thinking and Psychotherapy: An Inquiry into the Process of Communication.* Cambridge: Harvard University Press.

Shands, Harley C. 1968. Outline of a General Theory of Communication. *Social Science Information* 7:4:55–94.

Shannon, Claude E., and Warren Weaver. 1949. *The Mathematical Theory of Communication.* Urbana: University of Illinois Press.

Shapiro, Marianne. 1981. Preliminaries to a Semiotics of Ballet. In: *The Sign in Music and Literature,* ed. Wendy Steiner, pp. 216–27. Austin: University of Texas Press.

Shapiro, Michael. 1983. *The Sense of Grammar: Language as Semeiotic.* Bloomington: Indiana University Press.

Shaumyan, Sebastian. 1987. *A Semiotic Theory of Language.* AiS.

Sherzer, Dina, and Joel Sherzer. 1987. *Humor and Comedy in Puppetry: Celebration in Popular Culture.* Bowling Green: Bowling Green State University Popular Press.

Sherzer, Joel. 1971. Conference on Interaction Ethology. *Language Sciences* 14:19–21.

Short, T. L. 1982. Life among the Legisigns. *Transactions of the Charles S. Peirce Society* 18:285–310.

Short, T. L. 1988. The Growth of Symbols. *Cruzeiro Semiotico,* January, pp. 81–87.

Silverman, Kaja. 1983. *The Subject of Semiotics.* New York: Oxford University Press.

Singer, Milton. 1984a. *Man's Glassy Essence: Explorations in Semiotic Anthropology.* AiS.

Singer, Milton. 1984b. A Neglected Source of Structuralism: Radcliffe-Brown, Russell, and Whitehead. *Semiotica* 48:11–96.

Skinner, B. F. 1977. Why I Am Not a Cognitive Psychologist. *Behaviorism* 5:1–10.

Skinner, B. F. 1979. *The Shaping of a Behaviorist.* New York: Knopf.

Snow, C. P. 1959. *The Two Cultures and the Scientific Revolution.* New York: Cambridge University Press.

Solomon, Jack. 1988. *The Signs of Our Time: Semiotics—The Hidden Messages of Environments, Objects, and Cultural Images.* Los Angeles: Jeremy P. Tarcher.

Sonea, Sorin. 1988. The Global Organism. *Sciences* 28:4:38–45.

Sonea, Sorin. 1990. Bacterial (Prokaryotic) Communication. *WEB* 1989:639–62.

Staal, J. F. 1971. What Was Left of Pragmatics in Jerusalem. *Language Sciences* 14:29–32.

Stafford, Philip B. 1989. Toward a Semiotics of Old Age. *WEB* 1988:271–300.

Staiano, Kathryn Vance. 1986. *Interpreting Signs of Illness: A Case Study in Medical Semiotics.* AtS 72.

Stallo, Johann Bernhard. 1960 [1881, 1884]. *The Concepts and Theories of Modern Physics,* ed. Percy W. Bridgman. Cambridge: Harvard University Press.

160   References

Steiner, Wendy. 1978. Modern American Semiotics (1930–1978). In: *The Sign: Semiotics around the World*, ed. R. W. Bailey, L. Matejka, and P. Steiner, pp. 99–118. Ann Arbor: Michigan Slavic Publications.
Stevenson, Charles S. 1958. Symbolism in the Nonrepresentative Arts. In: *Language, Thought, and Culture*, ed. P. Henle, Ch. 8, pp. 196–225. Ann Arbor: University of Michigan Press.
Stoeltje, Beverly J., and Richard Bauman. 1988. The Semiotics of Folkloric Performance. WEB 1987:585–99.
Stokoe, William C., Jr. 1972. *Semiotics and Human Sign Languages*. AtS 21.
Stough, Charlotte L. 1969. *Greek Skepticism: A Study in Epistemology*. Berkeley: University of California Press.
Structure of Language and Its Mathematical Aspects. 1961. *Proceedings of Symposia in Applied Mathematics* XII. Providence: American Mathematical Society.
Tannen, Deborah. 1984. *Conversational Style: Analyzing Talk among Friends*. Norwood: Ablex.
Thom, René. 1983. *Mathematical Models of Morphogenesis*. Chichester: Ellis Horwood.
Thom, René. 1990. *Semio Physics: A Sketch*. Redwood City: Addison-Wesley.
Thomas, Donald W. 1976. Semiotics: A Macroscope for Education. *Proceedings of the Semiotic Society of America* 1:185–91. Atlanta: Georgia Institute of Technology.
Thompson, Bradbury. 1988. *The Art of Graphic Design*. New Haven: Yale University Press.
Tiefenbrun, Susan W. 1986. Legal Semiotics. *Cardozo Arts and Entertainment Law Journal* 5:91–156.
Tobin, Yishai, ed. 1988. *The Prague School and Its Legacy*. Amsterdam: Benjamins.
Todd, Charles L., and Russell T. Blackwood, eds. 1969. *Language and Value: Centennial Conference on the Life and Works of Alexander Bryan Johnson*. New York: Greenwood.
Todorov, Tzvetan. 1969. *Grammaire du Décaméron*. AtS 3.
Todorov, Tzvetan. 1984. *The Conquest of America: The Question of the Other*. New York: Harper and Row.
Tomas, David. 1982. The Ritual of Photography. *Semiotica* 40:1–25.
Tomas, David. 1983. A Mechanism for Meaning: A Ritual and the Photographic Process. *Semiotica* 46:1–39.
Tomas, David. 1988. Toward an Anthropology of Sight: Ritual Performance and the Photographic Process. *Semiotica* 68:245–70.
Tomas, David. 1990. Photography and Semiotics. WEB 1989:663–88.
Tomkins, Gordon M. 1975. The Metabolic Code. *Science* 189:760–63.
Trevarthen, Colwyn. 1987. The Structure of Motives. *International Semiotic Spectrum* 8:1–2.
Trevarthen, Colwyn. 1990. Signs before Speech. WEB 1989:689–755.
Tufte, Edward R. 1983. *The Visual Display of Quantitative Information*. Cheshire, Conn.: Graphics Press.

Tufte, Edward R. 1990. *Envisioning Information*. Cheshire, Conn.: Graphics Press.

Tursman, Richard. 1987. *Peirce's Theory of Scientific Discovery: A System of Logic Conceived as Semiotic*. Bloomington: Indiana University Press.

Uexküll, Jakob von. 1982. The Theory of Meaning. *Semiotica* 42:1–87.

Uexküll, Thure von. 1986. Medicine and Semiotics. *Semiotica* 61:201–17.

Uexküll, Thure von. 1987. Semiotics and the Problem of the Observer. In: *Semiotics 1982*, ed. John Deely and Jonathan Evans, pp. 1–25. Lanham: University Press of America.

Uexküll, Thure von. 1989. Jakob von Uexküll's Umwelt-Theory. WEB 1988:129–58.

Uexküll, Thure von. 1991a. Biosemiotik. In: *Semiotik: Ein Handbuch zu den zeichentheoretischen Grundlagen der Natur und Kultur*, ed. Roland Posner, Klaus Robering, and Thomas A. Sebeok. Berlin: Walter de Gruyter.

Uexküll, Thure von. 1991b. Endosemiose. In: *Semiotik: Ein Handbuch zu den zeichentheoretischen Grundlagen der Natur und Kultur*, ed. Roland Posner, Klaus Robering, and Thomas A. Sebeok. Berlin: Walter de Gruyter.

Ullman, I. M. 1975. *Psycholinguistik und Psychosemiotik*. Göttingen: Vanderhoeck und Ruprecht.

Umiker-Sebeok, Jean. 1977. Semiotics of Culture: Great Britain and North America. *Annual Review of Anthropology* 6:121–35.

Umiker-Sebeok, Jean, ed. 1987. *Marketing and Semiotics: New Directions in the Study of Signs for Sale*. AtS 77.

Umiker-Sebeok, Jean, and Thomas A. Sebeok, eds. 1976. *Speech Surrogates: Drum and Whistle Systems*. 2 vols. AtS 23.

Umiker-Sebeok, D. Jean, and Thomas A. Sebeok, eds. 1978. *Aboriginal Sign Languages of the Americas and Australia*. 2 vols. PiCS.

Umiker-Sebeok, Jean, and Thomas A. Sebeok, eds. 1987. *Monastic Sign Languages*. AtS 76.

Urban, Wilbur Marshall. 1939. *Language and Reality: The Philosophy of Language and the Principles of Symbolism*. New York: Macmillan.

Valesio, Paolo. 1980. *Novantiqua: Rhetorics as a Contemporary Theory*. AiS.

Vaughn, Genevieve. 1980. Communication and Exchange. *Semiotica* 29:113–43.

Verene, Donald Phillip. 1986. Ernst Cassirer. EDS.

Vester, Heinz-Günter. 1989. Erving Goffman's Sociology as a Semiotics of Postmodern Culture. *Semiotica* 76:191–203.

Von Foerster, Heinz, et al., eds. 1950–55. *Cybernetics: Circular Causal, and Feedback Mechanisms in Biological and Social Systems*. New York: Josiah Macy, Jr., Foundation.

Walker, Stephen. 1983. *Animal Thought*. Boston: Routledge and Kegan Paul.

Walther, Elisabeth. 1989. *Charles Sanders Peirce: Leben und Werk*. Baden-Baden: Agis-Verlag.

Watt, W. C. 1975. What Is the Proper Characterization of the Alphabet? Part 1: Desiderata. *Visible Language* 9:293–327.

Watt, W. C. 1980. What Is the Proper Characterization of the Alphabet? Part 2: Composition. *Ars Semeiotica* 3:3–46.

Watt, W. C. 1981. What Is the Proper Characterization of the Alphabet? Part 3: Appearance. *Ars Semeiotica* 4:269–313.

Watt, W. C. 1988. What Is the Proper Characterization of the Alphabet? Part 4: Union. *Semiotica* 70:199–241.

Weinreich, Uriel. 1980. *On Semantics*. Philadelphia: University of Pennsylvania Press.

Weizsäcker, Carl Friedrich von. 1971. *Die Einheit der Natur*. Munich: Hanser.

Wellbery, David E. 1984. *Lessing's Laocoon: Semiotics and Aesthetics in the Age of Reason*. Cambridge: Cambridge University Press.

Wellek, René. 1986. *A History of Modern Criticism, 1750–1950*, Vol. 6. New Haven: Yale University Press.

Wells, Rulon. 1967. Distinctively Human Semiotic. *Social Science Information* 6:6:103–24.

West, Candace. 1984. *Routine Complications: Troubles with Talk between Doctors and Patients*. Bloomington: Indiana University Press.

Wheeler, John Archibald. 1984. Bits, Quanta, Meaning. In: *Problems in Theoretical Physics*, ed. A. Giovanni et al., pp. 121–41. Salerno: University of Salerno Press.

Whitehead, Alfred North. 1919. *An Enquiry concerning the Principles of Natural Knowledge*. Cambridge: University Press.

Whitehead, Alfred North. 1927. *Symbolism: Its Meaning and Effect*. New York: Capricorn Books.

Whitfield, I. C. 1984. *Neurocommunications: An Introduction*. New York: John Wiley.

Whitney, William Dwight. 1867. *Language and the Study of Language: Twelve Lectures on the Principles of Linguistic Science*. New York: Charles Scribner's Sons.

Whitney, William Dwight, ed. 1891. *The Century Dictionary and Cyclopedia*. Part 19. New York: Century Co.

Wiener, Norbert. 1948. *Cybernetics or Control and Communication in the Animal and the Machine*. Cambridge: MIT Press.

Wiener, Norbert. 1950. *The Human Use of Human Beings: Cybernetics and Society*. Boston: Houghton Mifflin.

Wilbur, Ronnie Bring. 1979. *American Sign Language and Sign Languages*. Baltimore: University Park Press.

Wildbur, Peter. 1989. *Information Graphics: A Survey of Typographic, Diagrammatic and Cartographic Communication*. New York: Van Nostrand Reinhold.

Wilkins, John. 1984 [1641]. *Mercury: Or the Secret and Swift Messenger*. Amsterdam: Benjamins.

Williams, Allan. 1986. Cinema. EDS.

Williams, Brooke. 1985. What Has History to Do with Semiotic? *Semiotica* 54:267–333.

Winner, Irene Portis. 1987. Research in Semiotics of Culture. WEB 1986:601–36.

Wollheim, Richard. 1987. *Painting as an Art*. Princeton: Princeton University Press.

Wright, Robert. 1987. Virtual Reality. *Sciences* 67:6:8–10.

Wright, Robert. 1988. *Three Scientists and Their Gods: Looking for Meaning in an Age of Information*. New York: Times Books.

Wright, Robert. 1989. Charles S. Peirce Meets Douglas Hofstadter: Pragmatism and the Language of Modern Science. *Semiotica* 73:191–98.

Wylie, Laurence, and Rick Stafford. 1977. *Beaux Gestes: A Guide to French Body Talk*. New York: E. P. Dutton.

Yates, F. Eugene. 1984. Signs, Singularities, and Significance: A Physical Model for Semiotics. *Semiotica* 53:49–77.

Yates, F. Eugene. 1985. Semiotics as Bridge between Information (Biology) and Dynamics (Physics). *Recherches Sémiotiques/Semiotic Inquiry* 5:347–60.

Yates, F. Eugene. Forthcoming [1989]. Bridges between Different Cultures of Knowledge. Lecture to the Semiotic Circle of California, January 20, 1989.

Yates, F. Eugene. 1991a. Microsemiosis. In: *Semiotik: Ein Handbuch zu den zeichentheoretischen Grundlagen von Natur und Kultur*, ed. Roland Posner, Klaus Robering, and Thomas A. Sebeok. Berlin: Walter de Gruyter.

Yates, F. Eugene. 1991b. Pharmacosemiotics: Where Is the Message in the Drug? In press.

Yates, F. Eugene, and Peter N. Kugler. 1984. Signs, Singularities and Significance: A Physical Model for Semiotics. *Semiotica* 52:49–77.

Zellweger, Shea. 1982. Sign-Creation and Man-Sign Engineering. *Semiotica* 38:17–54.

Zellweger, Shea. 1990. Before Peirce and Icon/Index/Symbol. *Semiotic Scene* n.s. 2:1:3.

INDEX OF NAMES

Lifespan, where ascertainable, is supplied in brackets for native American or U.S. resident semioticians, and, for historical or other orientation, for some relevant others whose contributions are discussed or at least mentioned in this book.

Proust, Marcel [1871–1922], 34
Purcell, Henry [1659–1695], 59
Pygmalion (mythical character), 124

Quine, Willard Van Orman [b. 1908], 94

Radcliffe-Brown, A. R. [1881–1955], 51, 159
Ramsay, Alexandra, 22, 111, 132, 158
Ramsey, F. P., 137
Rancour-Laferriere, Daniel [b. 1943], 87, 154
Rapoport, Anatol [b. 1911], 70
Rauch, Frederick A. [1806–1841], 8–11, 18, 155
Rauch, Irmengard [b. 1933], 7, 23, 24, 25, 61, 96, 154, 155
Read, Allen Walker [b. 1906], 11, 23, 27, 98, 155
Redfield, Robert [1897–1958], 51
Reese, M. J., 142
Regan, John O. [b. 1931], 24, 158
Reid, Thomas [1710–1796], 88
Restak, Richard M. [b. 1942], 47
Réthoré, Joëlle, 65
Revzin, Isaak, 93
Revzina, Olga G., 93
Rey, Alain [b. 1928], 2, 12, 20–21, 64, 90, 155
Rey-Debove, Josette [b. 1929], 90
Reznikov, L. O., 85, 126, 154
Richards, I. A. [1893–1979], 35, 67, 72, 89, 121–123, 126, 136–37, 156
Riffaterre, Michael [b. 1924], 31, 155
Riggins, Steven, 22, 155
Rjeznikov. See Reznikov
Roback, A. A., 8, 10, 155
Robering, Klaus, 144, 157, 161, 163
Roberts, Don D. [b. 1932], 33, 155
Rosenberg, Alexander, 117, 140
Rosencrantz (fictional character), 6
Rosenthal, Robert [b. 1933], 32, 124, 141, 158
Rossi-Landi, Ferruccio [1921–198?], 74, 155
Roth, Jesse, 108, 112, 155
Rotman, Brian [b. 1938], 113, 155
Rousseau, Jean-Jacques [1712–1778], 38
Royce, Anya Peterson [b. 1940], 80, 155
Royce, Josiah [1855–1916], 7, 88
Rudy, Stephen [b. 1949], 93, 155

Ruesch, Jurgen [b. 1909], 20, 21, 22, 28, 45, 70–71, 86, 155
Rukeyser, Muriel [1913–1980], 49
Ruprecht, Hans-George, 142
Russell, Bertrand [1872–1970], 51, 60, 63, 89, 124, 155, 159
Russo, John Paul, 67, 89, 156
Rynin, David, 12, 13, 148, 156

Sabsay, Sharon [b. 1946], 33, 154
Safire, William, 61
Sagan, Dorion, 108, 113, 151, 156
Sandburg, Carl, 125
Sanders, Clinton R., 81, 156
Santambrogio, Marco, 3, 4, 144
Saussure, Ferdinand de, 23, 62, 84, 88, 90, 127, 128, 138, 143, 156
Savan, David [b. 1916], 7, 15–16, 64, 156
Schaff, Adam, 85
Schaffner, Bertram, 72, 156
Schapiro, Meyer [b. 1904], 81, 127, 137, 156
Scheflen, Albert E. [1920–1980], 20, 47, 86, 156
Schelling, Thomas C. [b. 1921], 54, 156
Schiller, Ferdinand C. S. [1864–1937], 65
Schiller, Johann Christoph Friedrich von [1759–1805], 9
Schilpp, Paul Arthur, 38, 147, 156
Schleifer, Ronald [b. 1948], 89, 156
Scholes, Robert [b. 1929], 31, 156
Schooneveld, C. H. van, 144
Schrödinger, Erwin, 135
Schütz, Alfred [1899–1959], 88
Ščur, G. S., 73
Sebeok, Thomas A. [b. 1920], 11, 13, 14, 15, 16, 17, 18, 20, 21, 22, 23, 24, 25, 26, 27, 29, 30, 32, 33, 34, 35, 36, 42, 43, 44, 45, 46–47, 49, 53, 57, 58, 60, 62, 63, 64, 70, 76, 79, 80, 83, 84, 85–86, 88, 91, 93, 94, 95, 96, 98, 99, 100, 102, 104, 106, 108, 109, 110, 111, 112, 113, 115, 117, 119, 120, 122, 123, 124, 125, 126, 127, 128, 129, 130, 131, 132, 133, 134, 136, 138, 139, 143, 144, 148, 149, 150, 155, 156–58, 161, 163, 164
Seeley, Thomas D., 111
Segre, Cesare [b. 1928], 92, 158
Seielstad, George A., 134, 158
Seligmann, Claus [b. 1927], 84, 159

172   *Index*

THOMAS A. SEBEOK is Distinguished Professor of Linguistics and Semiotics and Professor of Anthropology and of Folklore at Indiana University. His many publications include the semiotic tetralogy *Contributions to the Doctrine of Signs, The Sign & Its Masters, The Play of Musement,* and *I Think I Am a Verb.*